The Purpose of Life
is to "re-member"
your Self to the ONE,
to transcend the illusion of separation
and Re-Integrate with the
ALL THAT IS;
to re-enter the
Kingdom of Heaven
—which is within you right now—
to BEcome God again.

There are many paths.
We are ONE.

Psycanics:
A Technology for Conversations With God

Psycanics: A Science of BEing.

There are many paths.
We are ONE.

Thomas Michael Powell

Psycanics: A Technology for Conversations With God

Copyright © 2007 by Thomas Michael Powell

www.psycanics.org

ISBN 13: 978-0-9793929-1-7

ISBN 10: 0-9793929-1-8

This book contains brief quotes from books 1–4 of *Conversations With God* by Neale Donald Walsch. Psycanics is not affiliated with, or endorsed by, Neale Donald Walsch.

All rights reserved. No part of this book may be reproduced or transmitted in any form or by any means, electronic or mechanical, including photocopying, recording, or by any information storage and retrieval system, without written permission from the author, except for the inclusion of brief passages or quotations that must credited with the following reference:

Quoted from the works of Thomas Michael Powell on psycanic science.

To Victoria for her infinite patience and understanding even in the hardest of circumstances. To Angel González for being an exceptional example for all to follow. To Mitchell and Alline for their time and dedication to this mission. To God for communicating to everyone through Neale Donald Walsch and bringing us this necessary knowledge to our hands; and for placing us in this path to continue the work.

CONTENTS

Chapter 1

The Purpose of this Book

This book assumes that you are already familiar with the *Conversations with God* (*CWG*) series of books, channeled by Neale Donald Walsch. If you are not, it is highly recommended that you read the *CWG* books, at least the first four, **before** reading this one. The *Conversations With God* books are the most important documents on the planet and the information in them will transform your life. I hold forth that these books are exactly what they purport to be: God speaking to humanity. This book takes off from the launching pad of *CWG*.

My field of specialty and passion in life is mysticism. Mysticism is the personal and **experiential** (as opposed to theoretical or theological) search for God. My efforts to find and experience God have been blessed with some small success. From my personal experiences, I had enough familiarity with HIM, how HE really is and thinks, and the true relationship of God to Humanity, that within the first few pages of *CWG* Book 1, I knew beyond all doubt that it was indeed God speaking. However, my certainty will not help your uncertainty, if it exists; and this book does not address the question of whether or not you are really listening to God in the *CWG* series. This book assumes that you recognize Who is speaking in those books and have understood much of what HE says.

I am only here to give you a piece, an extremely important piece, a critical piece, of how to apply the teachings of God in the *CWG* books. To do this is my mission in this life.

The most recurrent and important teachings of *CWG* are two:

1. There is only ONE BEING and you are, not just part of IT, but all if IT. You are God. (You are pretending to be not-God and human for very good reasons that we will go into in this book.)
2. The supreme purpose of your existence is to Return to being the ONE, to the Kingdom of Heaven[1], to being God again. (This state has been called

[1] Reference to famous statements of Jesus Christ, perhaps the most important ones that have come down to us: "The Kingdom of Heaven is within." "Seek First the Kingdom of Heaven."

many things: Illumination, Self-Realization, God-Realization, Re-Integration, re-entering the Kingdom, to name a few.)

CWG gives you many tools for working on yourself to expand your experience of Self back to the ALL. However, the most powerful tool is not mentioned in *CWG*. It too complicated and too extensive to be easily dictated and it must be lived to be understood. It also requires a live teacher, someone who has lived the experiences to be able to guide others. That most powerful tool is your discreation of your God Suppressor Shell that blocks your consciousness of Who You Are and creates your experience of being a human being. It "lowers" your level of being from that of God to that of a human being

Returning to the ONE is not just a path of creating yourself. From the highest point of view, there isn't anything to create: you already are IT ALL. Returning to the ONE is primarily a question of discreating your illusion of being a human being and your blocks to your perception of the ONE. The purpose of this book is likewise two:

1. Bring you face to face with that shell of negative energy that suppresses and blocks your experience of being the ONE and molds you into a human being.
2. Show you how to discreate that shell, expand your BEing, re-integrate to the ONE and so be IT ALL again.

There are no accidents or coincidences in life whatsoever, as God states clearly in *CWG*. The existence of this book, the knowledge and technology that it contains, as well as your reading it right now, is no accident. It is all part of God's plan for a transformation of consciousness on this planet.

This book takes up where *Conversations with God* leaves off. It is a continuation and expansion of the *Conversations with God* series. This may seem a tall statement—and don't believe it. You should judge the truth of that statement **after** you consider the concepts and technology presented in this book. But whether it is the "sequel" for *CWG* or not, is really not at all important; the only thing that matters is if you find the information in this book useful for your spiritual evolution.

Psycanics

This book is also about psycanics. Psycanics is the science of the origin, nature, and abilities of psycans. A psycan is a non-physical LIFE Energy entity, consisting of the LIFE ESSENCE energies of Consciousness, Wisdom, Will, Creator Power, Self-Esteem, and LoveJoy. It is an illusory "particle" of the ONE LIFE ENERGY BEING, aka God. Synonyms include "spirit" and "soul." You are a psycan. You are an immortal spirit, temporarily located in a physical body for the purpose of playing in the physical universe. Thus, **psycanics is the science of the origin, nature, functioning, abilities, and purposes of psycans** (spirits).

Psycanics is a **science** of non-physical areas of human experience. **It is a formal science: it proves its laws and principles, and eschews opinion, belief, and faith.** Psycanics integrates philosophy, psychology, non-physical energy physics, and spirituality into one body of knowledge.

Psycanics explains with pinpoint precision, with laws, formulas, and equations, how life works. It explains: spirit, being, mind, thought, study and learning, intelligence, intuition, wisdom, creativity, personal power, emotions, love, happiness, pain and suffering, relationships, child raising; and creation, attraction and manifestation in the physical universe.

These may appear to be isolated or unrelated phenomena, but they are not. All non-physical phenomena are based in and spring forth from the same underlying principles of existence. Thus, psycanics is a **unified field theory** that ties together many previous and apparently unrelated fields of phenomena. The theoretical side of psycanics is backed by precise technology for personal change and spiritual growth called CDT: Creation and Discreation Technology.

"**Psycanic**" is an adjective that means: of, belonging to, or related to, psycans. Anything psycanic is anything that is **non-physical**, and that cannot be detected or measured by the human body or physical instruments. Psycanic energies/realities/things/experiences include: your **identities**[2], your **thoughts** and all the content of your mind and subconsciousness (memories, data, ideas, imaginations, dreams, knowledge, plans, goals, values, beliefs, dogmas, philosophies, religions, etc.); and **all your emotions**: anger, anxiety, passion, fear, sadness, grief, sorrow, hate, guilt, resentment, joy, depression, frustration, desperation, etc.

Notice that **the most important things in life** are psycanic, not physical, including: wisdom, intelligence, creativity, imagination, enthusiasm, love, happiness, relationships, and feelings and emotions. Even the concept of money, a representation of energy, (as opposed to the physical representations of money such as coins and bills) is psycanic.

Just as all things physical operate by precise laws, so do all things psycanic exist and operate by precise laws. The codification of the laws of an area of life is a science.

Psycanics must be understood, not just read or memorized. Anywhere you doubt its statements, you must scientifically test them. Anywhere it contradicts your current beliefs, you must seek to discover the Truth scientifically, by testing. This has already been done by many others, so that where there is a conflict, you can suspect that it is your beliefs that are limited. But if you doubt, you must test. Psycanics is a science, not a belief system, and personal opinions are irrelevant. If you are a Truth-seeker, a God-seeker, you may not simply discard data because it conflicts with your beliefs.

---

2 Identities: the meaning of this extremely important concept will be come clear later.

How to Learn Psycanics

Psycanics has a precise nomenclature that has been carefully designed to get you to look at and think about your existence in a certain way. **It is designed to get you to look at and understand life from a very particular and special point of view—one that opens your power to control life.**

The key to understanding and learning psycanics is learning the concepts that each term represents. Every term is a symbol, a representation, for a much larger idea or concept. **Psycanics must be learned conceptually**, not verbally.

Life is complex. You should expect that any science that purports to tie it up and deliver it to you in a nice package to be complex—which psycanics can be for some people, especially at the beginning. There is a learning curve with psycanics: you must learn new concepts and the words and symbols that will be used to represent them in the explanation of even more complex phenomena. Every science has and needs its nomenclature to facilitate communication of complex concepts. As psycanics distinguishes phenomena not previously distinguished, it needs to borrow or create words for those things. It is not psycanics that is complex; it is Life.

"Knowledge (Science) is Power" is a famous and a very true Law of Life. There is no Power without a price, in this case, your study and learning new concepts. If you find yourself resisting having to truly learn concepts and nomenclature, ask yourself, "Who am I being in relation to learning this?" You will find that the limitations you are experiencing are in you; not in the science.

If you persist, eventually everything will begin to click and fit together for you and it (Psycanics-Life) will all make perfect sense. Life is understandable and controllable when you have the science of it.

A Short Summary of Appendix 1: The Secrets of Comprehension and Learning

I advise reading this entire Appendix now. However, the summary of it is: **Never go on past a word, sentence, or idea that you do not understand completely.** To do so is the beginning of your failure in understanding the materials. The first misunderstood word or concept will invariably cause later ideas to be misunderstood. The result is that a subject becomes more and more confusing and harder and harder as your progress, until finally you give up trying to understand it. Proper study, which means full comprehension of each term before proceeding to the next, makes a subject easier and easier as your progress.

Appendix 2: Conventions of Expressions Used in Psycanics

In Appendix 2, you will find explained the many conventions of expression used in psycanics. These conventions include capitalization, underlining, use of gender, acronyms, abbreviations, symbols, formulas and equations. You will find reading much easier if you read this Appendix before you read the book.

Appendix 3: Glossary

Because the nomenclature and the exact definitions of words are so important to understanding a science, this book has an extensive glossary of terms. You will find a complete *Dictionary of Psycanic Science* available for consultation or download at www.psycanics.org.

Quotes and References to the *CWG* series

This book contains brief quotes from the *CWG* series. These are referenced as Book #, Chapter #, Page #, where the page number is according to the edition that I, the author, have. Example: 3-5-76 is Book 3, Chapter 5, Page 76 of the book. Therefore, the page number may not be the same if you have a different edition of the book. The quotes are often taken from different chapters and even different books, and are integrated with other quotes and sometimes with psycanics to give more complete information on that concept. The quotes are also sometimes edited or paraphrased for the purpose of grammar or continuity with the text.

The editions of the *CWG* books used for this book are:

Book 1: *CWG, An Uncommon Dialogue*, G.P. Putnam's Sons, First Hardcover Edition, 1996.

Book 2: *CWG, An Uncommon Dialogue 2*, Hampton Roads Publishing Co., Hardcover, Edition Unstated, 1997.

Book 3: *CWG, An Uncommon Dialogue 3*, Hampton Roads Publishing Co., Hardcover, Edition Unstated, 1998.

Book 4: *CWG, Friendship with God*, G.P. Putnam's Sons, Hardcover, Edition Unstated, 1999.

Chapter 2

The Purpose of Life—Return to God

Quotes from *CWG*:

There is only one purpose for all of life, and that is for you and all that lives to experience fullest glory. What the soul is after is the . . . experience of God. This is the soul's desire. This is its purpose. The soul is after . . . the experience of unity with the ALL THAT IS. The purpose of the soul is to experience ALL of IT which is to BE ALL of IT. Your holy cause is the realization of Self. This is the great return for which the soul yearns. (1-1-20, 1-1-56, 2-1-83, 2-1-76)

Have I not said, and is it not written, "Ye are Gods"? (1-13-202) I created you to BEcome ME. (Paraphrased from 3-18-304.)

You and I are ONE right now. *You are to destroy the illusion of separation.* That is your work. (5-2-21) That you are ONE with everything and everyone is the truth of your BEing, and it is the aspect of Self that you most urgently and earnestly seek to experience. (4-7-15)

Of course, *you are seeking to be God!* What else did you think you were up to? (2-1-85)

Just in case it is not perfectly clear and because it can never be stated too many times or ways, let us summarize this, and many more declarations of the same concepts in *CWG*:

The Prime Wisdom

There is only the ONE BEing, and you are IT and ALL of IT.

Your individuality and the entire physical universe is an ingenious illusion created for the specific purpose of allowing you to experience the ALL in many forms.

The Prime Directive

Real-ize Who You Are; re-Integrate to the ONE; BEcome God again.

The purpose of your sojourn on earth is to transcend the illusion of separate and isolated individuality and re-real-ize your ONEness, your true IDentity as God, which is to Re-Integrate in full consciousness and experience to the ALL THAT IS, to thus take over conscious control of the illusion from within the illusion. This does not require the end of your individuality, but an expansion of your identity to the ALL.

To these two that are stated in *CWG*, let us add in another that is not, but is of extreme importance as it controls all human behavior:

The Existential Imperative

The Ultimate Motivation of all human behavior and effort is to increase LIFE ESSENCE and so Return to the ONE.

The Existential Imperative says that you have no choice about the Prime Directive; you are trying to Return to BE the ONE whether you know it or not. All your problems in life arise when you do not know what you are seeking to do in life, or how to go about it. When you don't know, you embark on an External Quest for happiness, as opposed to "seeking the Kingdom of Heaven within." Look at the human race and you will see almost everyone struggling to control and hoard external things instead of focusing on their interior life.

What Religions Agree On

The concepts above should not come to us as a surprise. After all, the Great Teachers (Jesus, Buddha, Krishna, etc.) taught exactly the same thing. We can still see the following points of agreement in the shards of their teachings (religions) that have come down to us. Almost all religions have in common these six concepts:

1- There is a Supreme BEing: some Power far above and beyond humankind in Wisdom, Power, and Love that is the FIRST CAUSE, CREATOR, and SOURCE of all that exists, and is the HOME of humanity.

2- Wo/man has an intimate relationship with that Supreme BEing. S/He is kin, offspring, made in the same image and likeness, a parent-child relationship. We are of the same essence, spirit.

3- Wo/man is currently cut off from the experience of hir Source. We are dis-united, separated, lost, isolated, far away from HOME.

4- Wo/man can return HOME, go back to being with hir SOURCE again. The separation is not permanent; there is possibility of redemption, salvation, of Return. (This is an extremely important point. After all, if we can't return why even mention the situation and just stir up the agony of separation?)

5- To return to the SOURCE is the purpose and the only true value in life. Everything else is a relative waste of time. (To paraphrase Jesus: "Seek First the Kingdom of Heaven. What does it serve a wo/man to gain the whole world if s/he finds not hir soul? The Kingdom of Heaven is like a treasure in a field for which a person sells all that s/he has to obtain.")
6- SOURCE, HOME, the Kingdom of Heaven, is within; and it is INFINITE LOVE and achieved through Love. It is accessible to us. Love is the end and Love is the means.

After these six points, each religion departs in a different direction with their distinct dogmas and doctrines; rites, rituals and ceremonies—none of which have much effect at all on returning to the ONE. They may make you feel good, but they don't move you much closer to God. Most religions are fairly useless at guiding you to fulfill the Prime Directive.

> The names for that Supreme BEing are legion: God, the Divine/the Divinity, the I AM THAT I AM, Brahman, Ram-Shiva, Ishvara, Vishnu, the Almighty, Jehovah/Yahweh, Eloha/Elohim, Adonai, Allah, the Void, the Quantum Field, the Matrix, the Tao, the Static, the Energy, Life, the Creator, the ALL THAT IS, IT, the INFINITE, LOVE, Theos, Deus/the Deity, Mwari, the Great Spirit, are just a few.
>
> The names for returning to that Supreme State are also many: the Kingdom of God, the Kingdom of Heaven, Self-Realization, Enlightenment, Illumination, Samadhi, Nirvana, Satori, Moksha, the Totality of OneSelf (Toltecs), Cosmic Consciousness, Re-Integration, The Third Awakening, the Divine Ecstasy, Union, Home, Salvation, Redemption, Bodhi, Liberation, God-Realization, Gnosis, the Divine Rapture, to name a few.

The purpose of this book is to show you a very powerful way to go within and exactly how to love yourself as you penetrate within. In fact, we will see that loving yourself as you go within is essential to being able to go within at all.

Its methods also work to resolve all your human problems and conflicts, and to eliminate all pain and suffering from your life.

Your return to the ONE is the <u>only</u> purpose of your soul. It knows there is nothing on earth, no worldly pleasure that can compare with the ecstasy of the BEing and FEELing the INFINITE LIFE SOURCE whose ESSENCE consists of WISDOM POWER LOVE. (We will explain all this in detail in a later chapter.)

However, your human identity thinks what you DO and HAVE[3] in the physical universe is important. The question, then, is: Who guides or controls your life?

---

3 DO and HAVE in all capitals, is a reference to the Causal Sequence of BE-FEEL→ THINK→DO→HAVE which will be explained later.

You can know by answering the question: What do I hold as my highest purpose in life?

You have either made your return to the ONE the highest priority of your life, which means your spirit is in charge. Or you are still wandering around "out here" in the physical universe, in the External Quest for happiness, thinking there is something important or "happy-making" out here—which means your human identity is in charge. It also means you are giving too much importance to an illusion. The universe is an illusion created for purposes that we will explore in other chapters. Nothing wrong with wandering around the world—and that was necessary at one time, as we shall see.

However, it is no longer necessary and **the consequences you pay for dawdling here are continued suffering**. We shall show that the root cause of all suffering is your shell of AntiEssence or AntiGod Energy that is your counter-creation to BEing God, and which serves to block your consciousness and experience of yourSelf as the ONE God.

As long as you are not in the experience of the ONE, there will always be a sense of something missing in your life. Nothing else will ever satisfy your soul, and you will always be in a Quest for your Divine Essence.

Your Return requires that all of your mind, body and spirit be dedicated to the process of real-izing yourSelf as God, all the time, moment to moment, day after day. The instruction was: "Seek FIRST the Kingdom of Heaven." Note that word: FIRST. That means before all else; first in your priorities and efforts. As long as you are putting worldly concerns—relationships, money, success, whatever —as more important than your Self-Realization, you are putting "false gods before ME." As long as you are focused on laying up treasure for yourself on earth, there will your heart—and soul—remain. You get what you focus on.

Making the Commitment

Theoretically, I suppose that someone can just wake up one day and absolutely decide that their return to the ONE is now and hence forward the highest priority of their life. However, I think that in most cases—certainly in mine—this is a value that grows in you over time. And not just this lifetime, but from all life-times. You first become intellectually aware that your return is a possibility and the purpose of life. You then begin to put some attention, energy and study in that direction and your interest grows. However, it is actual *experience* that will ignite your true commitment. As you practice the disciplines I will be teaching you in this book, you will make rapid progress and begin to taste the joy. Joy feedbacks into your desire to experience even more joy. Joy is the result of your personal contact with the ONE, and the measure of your progress HOME. IT becomes your priority and passion.

What you can do now is *intend* that your commitment to your return grow in you until it is not only your #1 priority, but a passion that consumes you. Joy and passion are signs of your progress.

> There was once a guru who was bathing in the river with some of his students. One of them asked him, "Master, when will I reach Illumination?" The guru grabbed his head, pushed down and held him under the water. Shortly, the student was struggling with all his might to avoid being drowned, clawing at the water and the Teacher to get air. Finally, as his struggles began to weaken, at the last moment; the master released him. The student, as soon as he could, gasped indignantly, "Master, why are you trying to kill me?" The Master replied. "I but answered your question. When your desire for the ONE exceeds your desire for air, you will know you are close to Illumination."

The first major challenge in serious spirituality (as opposed to dogmatic religion) is to make these concepts real for yourself, to begin to meditate on them, to make them your dominant paradigm. You have been wandering around lost in the Created Reality (the physical universe); you now have a beacon to aim for and a very exact direction for your life journey:

There is only ONE of us. (2-5-last sentence of the book)

Your Return to the ONE is the purpose of your life.

Questions to ponder:

How real are these concepts for you? To what degree have you absorbed them into your consciousness and made them your paradigm of life?

Are you acting each day, each moment, to make these concepts more real? Are you affirming, pondering, meditating on them constantly to strengthen their reality in you?

To what degree is your Return your FIRST value and priority in life?

How much time and energy are you giving each day to disciplines for your return?

> (By "disciplines," I mean such activities as: meditation, reading, God Suppressor Mass discreation[4], mind turned off, heightened awareness of self, focus in the Here and Now, vegetarian diet, exercise, elimination of addictions, etc. Most of these will be explained in the book.)

---

[4] How to discreate the God Suppressor Mass you will begin to learn in this book.

Chapter 3

The Two Great Questions

On understanding the nature of existence; that there is only the ONE; and understanding the purpose of our existence: to Return to BEing the ONE; we are left with two great questions.

THE FIRST GREAT QUESTION IS:

- ¤ Given that we are the ONE God, including at this very minute; that there is nothing other than God; and that we cannot not-be God;
- ¤ Given that all Created Reality, the physical universe, is an illusion made of God;
- ¤ Given that our human beingness, individuality, separation and isolation is an illusion;
- ¤ Given all the above, the First Question that we should be asking (as scientists and as seekers) is:
    - What is the mechanism of our amnesia of Who We Are, or at least of Where We Come From? How can we have forgotten or blocked out such an overwhelming fact as our TRUE IDENTITY and ORIGIN?
    - What is the mechanism of our separated, isolated individuality such that we have no experiential inkling of ONEness?
    - What is the mechanism that blocks or counter-creates[5] our perception of and communication with the most basic and most powerful experience of all existence, the ONE and ONLY ULTIMATE REALITY (God)? This experience is so blocked that: 1- there are many religions in existance to "help" people find God; and that 2- many people are agnostics and atheists.

5 Counter-create: to create something to block or hide a previously existing reality. The existing reality continues to be, but you no longer can perceive it because you are experiencing the counter-creation and it blocks your perception of the first reality.

- How are we reducing ourselves, our beingness, down from our INFINITE ESSENCE of CONSCIOUSNESS, WISDOM, WILL, CREATOR, POWER, LOVE, and JOY to the reality, the experience, the beingness of a human being? How do we go from being the INFINITE POSITIVE ASPECTS of Divinity down into the polarity opposites of those aspects: ignorance, lack of power, weakness, failure, negative self-esteem, AntiLove[6], and unhappiness, pain and suffering? How are we counter-creating our true SPIRIT-ual nature?
- What are the mechanics, the physics, of taking God and stuffing HIS INFINITY down into a human skin without visible or sensible trace of our original-and-still-present TRUE IDENTITY? How are we hiding something as big as the Kingdom of Heaven and its chief resident, God, within us? How did we not only lose the INFINITE, but did so within us?
- In summary: What blocks our consciousness, perception, and experience of being the ONE INFINITE BEING and causes—creates for us—the consciousness and experience of being a human being?

This would appear to be the Greatest Magic Trick of all time, would it not? Harry Houdini made an elephant disappear on stage, and modern magicians have vanished objects as big as the Space Shuttle, the Taj Mahal, even the Statue of Liberty. **But YOU have disappeared God!**—and done a much better and longer lasting job of it! What magician can compare with that?

You are God; yet you have disappeared God, totally hidden HIM, within you.

You are God standing in the very center of God, of the Infinite Sphere of the ALL THAT IS that is yourSELF; yet you do not perceive HIM.

HOW DO YOU DO THAT?

(And notice that you are doing so right at this moment.)

To answer all these questions is the purpose of this book.

We can state that it is not a question of magic, although it can certainly appear that way. Arthur C. Clarke's Third Law states that "Any sufficiently advanced technology is indistinguishable from magic." A television or an airplane would be magic to anyone 200 years ago.

No, it is not magic. It is a question of science, of physics, of the Laws of Cause, Creation, Reality, Space, Resistance, and Energy. It is a question of your Creator Power and that works by exact laws that are detailed elsewhere in psycanics.

---

[6] The concept of AntiLove will be presented later. For now understand it as all lack of love: poverty, pain and suffering, deprivation, harm, war, hunger, and unwarranted destruction—and the lack of concern of some for these experiences in others. This is a planet of No-Love and AntiLove.

We reduce our consciousness-experience of ourselves from the ULTIMATE REALITY of being God down to the experience of being human by applying exact laws of creation and energy. We do it according to the nature of consciousness, reality, and experience.

The mechanism that creates the illusion of being human involves energy, masses, resistances, spaces, flows, blocked flows, and counter-flows. We "descend" from "heaven" to "earth" by mechanical means. It is a question of science, of psycanics, which is the science of non-physical energy. Psycanics is to the nature of BEing and God what quantum physics is to the nature of the physical universe.

Here is an example of some of those laws. (This is just an introduction; no explanation is provided here and some of these laws take pages to present fully. As you progress in psycanics, you will come to understand all of these laws.)

1. Everything that exists is energy.
2. All energy is legal; it always follows exact laws and principles.
3. Everything that exists is a creation[7].
4. All creations are realities.
5. All realities are formed of energy. (See #2.)
6. Realities cause experience.
7. All experience is the effect of reality on consciousness.
8. What you have created, you can discreate.
9. Experienced Experience Discreates.
10. Resistance causes Pain and Persistence.
11. Energy flows to Space.
12. Energy that flows, grows.
13. Life works according to the Causal Sequence of BE→FEEL→THINK→DO→HAVE.
14. Your emotions are your Love or AntiLove for yourSelf according to the Essence IDentity you adopt in relation to events.
15. The ultimate motivation of all human behavior is to Return to the ONE.

These are some of the laws that operate, create, and determine your life and create your illusion of not-being God. Understanding them will allow you to **discreate the creation that you are not-God, which is all that is necessary for you to experience being God again.**

---

[7] The ULTIMATE REALITY of Who We Are, the ONE, is not a creation, and is outside of the illusion.

You already are God; you do not need to create that.
You only need to discreate the illusion of not-being God.
This illusion is created out of divine energy.
All energy obeys exact laws.
What you have created, you can discreate. After all, you are God.

In summary, the first Great Question is: HOW did we create ourselves (even if an illusion) as human beings? What did we create to block or counter-create the ENORMOUSNESS of being IT ALL, and turn us into human beings? How do we hide from ourselves such a BIG, SIGNIFICANT, and INFINITE REALITY as God, and ourselves as being God? How do we maintain that counter-creation in existence so firmly?

We can say now that obviously it requires a really big creation, a really big mass, to block, to cover up, to hide, to suppress, the most basic fact of all existence: God.

The Second Great Question

However, even more important than the First Great Question (HOW did turn myself = God into a human being) is the Second Great Question:

- How do I return to experiencing being MYSELF, the ONE GOD again?
- How do I locate whatever it is that is blocking, counter-creating, or suppressing TRUTH? Where is that block? What is its nature? What do I do with it once I find it?
- How do I undo, remove, escape, and discreate the suppression to my Godness? How do I release myself from whatever it is that is "reducing" me from INFINITE ULTIMATE REALITY and holding mc in the extremely limited reality of being a human being? In other words:
- **WHAT IS THE PRECISE MECHANISM OF MY RETURN TO THE ONE?**

These are the questions I will be answering in this book.

Remember this concept: GOD SUPPRESSOR MASS[8]. This is what separates you from being God again. It is a mass of energies, very specific kinds of energies. It suppresses your consciousness and counter-creates your experience of the TRUE IDENTITY of INFINITE SPIRIT LIFE ENERGY that you are.

In this book, we will examine what this is, where it is, and how to eliminate it. You experience it constantly, but don't recognize it for what it is and do not know how to discreate it. In fact, you are currently maintaining it in existence, a process we must reverse.

[8] We will actually use various terms for this Mass, according to the aspect of it that we wish to focus in the sentence. There terms include: Essence Suppressor Mass, AntiEssence Mass, and AntiGod Mass.

In the psycanics proposal for your Return to the ONE, you do not have to *create* being the ONE, being God. You already are the ONE God. The path of Return is a process of un-covering, of dis-covering What already IS, of unleashing Who You Really Are. The psycanics proposal is a process of *discreation*, of eliminating, of removing your GOD-IDENTITY SUPPRESSOR MECHANISM. This mechanism is a mass of energy that separates you from the experience of being IT ALL. You created it and you can discreate it.

This is not to say that you will not use a lot of creation also. In fact, creation and discreation are balanced on this path. You will be constantly creating your next step of BEing. But the final goal is not a creation; it is ULTIMATE REALITY. IT already IS, and you are IT, and ALL of IT. You have only to uncover, dis-cover, this; and you can do this by discreating that which covers IT up.

Chapter 4

The Ground of BEing and the Cosmos

Quotes from *CWG* in Regular font. Author's elaborations in **Bold**.

All of life is a vibration of "something" which can only exist by contrast with that which does not vibrate, that which does not move: **the** no-thing, **the STATIC**. The closest word that you have for this vibration is "energy," **although I AM even before energy; I AM SPACE, I am the STATIC. I AM the AWARE WILL, CONSCIOUS CAUSE, every thing, everywhere, that underlies all Created Reality.**

The ENERGY radiates from ME as heat does from fire, and it is ME. Therefore, let us specify *LIFE* = **GOD**, as pure ENERGY. That ENERGY is vibrating constantly, always. It is moving in waves, vibrating at different speeds, producing different densities and effects. **Your scientists see this when they "look" at the Quantum Field.** Yet while the objects have the appearance of being different and discrete, the ENERGY of which they are formed is exactly the same: ME. We are all the same ENERGY, coalesced, concentrated in different ways to create different patterns and form, different kinds of matter.

I AM not a thing: I am the Process by which existence exists and out of which it springs. **I AM the Quantum Field that your scientists are discovering and wondering about.** I AM the Supreme Being; that is: the Supreme, Being all That I am, ALL THAT IS.

Thus, the soul is everywhere in, through, and around you. It contains you. There is only one soul. **It's all the same soul. It is the ONE pretending to be the Many. This gives the ONE multiple "things" to BE, and multiple points of view and experience of the infinite varieties of ITs multiplicity.** (3-11-176)

I AM the Creator and the Created. *You* are the Creator and the Created. (3-19-344 to 350)

You exist everywhere, at all time. (2-5-64)

You have two states of BEing and two Universes. This chapter introduces them, as understanding your existence from these points of view should make it much clearer for you to understand how life works.

The Two Great Divisions: ULTIMATE REALITY (aka God) versus Created Reality (aka the cosmos).

Before we explain your states of BEing and your two Universes, there are two great divisions we must make in life.

- The first is ULTIMATE REALITY or UNMANIFESTED GROUND of BEING, aka the QUANTUM FIELD, or the TAO (ATMAN in Hinduism). We will call IT "God"[9], for short. We will describe IT in detail below.
- The second is Created Reality or Manifested Reality, aka the cosmos. This is any thing that exists as a "separate" entity. It is any distinct form of energy; "energy with an identity." Created Reality, called Maya (veil) in Hinduism, is always an illusion. It is the form that the QUANTUM FIELD takes to explore, know and play with ITSELF. The cosmos, which consists of an infinite number of universes, is all Created Reality.

The First State of your BEing: The Quantum Filed of the Tao

Your first state of BEing is the ALL, the Nothing-Everything. IT is a field of potential. A field is something that exists but is no-thing. For an analogy in the physical universe, we have a magnetic field or a gravity field. There is nothing there, not even energy, but yet there is something there, a force field.

The GOD-FIELD is not anything; IT is no-thing with the potential to be any thing and all things. Manifested, IT is all things, for there is nothing else but the FIELD, and IT is all things when IT manifests ITSELF. This field of potential underlies all manifested reality. All manifested (or created) reality, including you as a spirit, springs "up" out of IT, like waves and spray arise on the ocean.

In quantum physics, IT is called the Quantum Field or the Zero Point Field. This field permeates all things and is "entangled," by which physicists mean inter-connected everywhere. IT underlies all visible manifestation. In fact, the visible or manifested universe literally springs "out" of IT. "Up" from IT, kind of like popcorn popping, spring the subatomic "particles," which are not really particles, but waves, but which are not really waves, but energy probability clouds with properties like "isospin," "hypercharge," "charm," "strangeness," and "flavor."[10]

---

[9] I have reservations about calling "God," God. Most people have erroneous ideas about the nature of God; first of all as a projection of a human being, and especially as the angry father figure often purveyed by religions.

[10] In case you did not get how weird all this is, remember these "thingies" have never been seen and exist mostly as a symbol in a mathematical equation.

Some of these wavicle energy clouds collapse back into the FIELD almost instantly. Others remain over time, which is a property of space, and out of these patterns of potential, the atomic "particles" are formed, which then form atoms, which then form molecules, which form the everyday objects we see in the physical universe we know (and love?).

However, until there is an observer, the quantum field does not actualize to manifest as anything, and remains only a field of "potential to be." Thus, the universe is created out of the interaction between the observer and the observed. There is no universe without an observer, only the FIELD. Thus, your world arises around you out of, first your projection of it (your process of creation), and then your perception of it, and that world is but dancing patterns of energy.

If you find this confusing, the problem is not with you. It is not possible to mentally visualize the universe at the level of the Quantum Field or even at the level of the sub-atomic energy potential entities. Physicists can only even begin to communicate about it with mathematical formulas. What is interesting for us mystics about this is that the physicists finally seem to have found God—at least in the exterior. However, the trick is to find IT in your interior.

In Chinese mysticism, the FIELD is called the TAO. The book *The Tao Te Ching* is a perfect description of the FIELD—and it makes no sense at all if you have never "seen" the FIELD.

If it can be named, it is not the Tao.
The nameless is the beginning of heaven and earth.
It is a mystery and the source of all things.
Only without desire, can you see it.[11]
Filled with desire, you will see only its manifestations.
It is the base from which Heaven and Earth spring.
It is there within us all the while;
Draw upon it as you will, it never runs dry.
For though all creatures under heaven are the products of Being,
Being itself is the product of Not-being.

ITs names are legion. We already mentioned some of the names religions use for God. Other names for IT include the DIVINE MATRIX, the CREATOR MATRIX, the UNIVERSAL INTELLIGENCE. We will later examine IT as the LIFE FORCE ESSENCE. **It is this viewpoint on God of the LIFE ESSENCE energies that opens the doors to the Kingdom for us.** The four LIFE ESSENCE energies are Wisdom, Power, Value, and LoveJoy, about which we shall have much to say.

---

[11] This "only without desire" is a very important clue for mysticism.

IT is both Creator and Created: IT creates all that exists out of ITSELF, for there is nothing else to create anything out of.[12] IT is the ESSENCE of all that exists. You are part of IT, made of the same LIFE ESSENCE. You are a sub-creator who separates out of the FIELD with an illusion of individuality in order to incarnate within Created Reality, in order to experience IT from within, and to continue to expand the Creation.

This, IT, is the INFINITE PRIMAL FIELD of BEING, of LIFE, of FIRST CAUSE, of the ESSENCE ENERGY. It is not really energy, but we have no word for it, so we will call it the ENERGY. You are this FIELD, which we also call God. ITs basic characteristics for our purposes of Return to IT are LIFE ESSENCE: Wisdom, Power, Value, LoveJoy. The FIELD can manifest as anything, but these are ITs basic properties that most affect us as psycans: LIFE "particle" entities = spirits. Because there are so many words for God and HER infinite aspects of BEing, we always capitalize words that refer to HER to signal that we are speaking of the INFINITE.

You are this FIELD and ALL of IT, pretending to be only a point of IT. However, you are not currently experientially integrated with the FIELD, but are operating in your Second State of BEing. You are being a psycan, an individualized part of the ONE LIFE ENERGY CREATOR FIELD. You are pretending to be only a point of Creator-Will-Power and Perceptive-Consciousness-Wisdom existing in less than the total ecstasy of Infinite LoveJoy. You take up a viewpoint within the WHOLE to continue creation and to experience from that viewpoint. You are pretending to be an individualized, limited, and localized "particle" of IT, looking out onto "other" parts of the FIELD manifesting ITSELF as the physical universe. You are viewing out onto the manifested FIELD through the projection lens of mental realities that create your world around you. (We will come back to this later.)

Although the FIELD is your "birthplace" and HOME, as a normal human being in this reality, you are locked out of perception and experience of IT by your God Suppressor Mass. However, you visit IT every night.

It requires a great deal of Energy to create, exist and focus in the physical universe. As you lose your connection with the FIELD, you also lose your supply of ENERGY to your consciousness. That energy is necessary to project the physical universe around you. For about three hours every night, and in the deepest of human sleep and unconsciousness, you return to the FIELD to recharge your "batteries."

---

12 In the psycanics book, *Cosmology*, you will find a description of this field as the Light-Fog and an analogy of how BEings, space, time, and energy-matter arise from and materialize out of IT.

The 5th State of Consciousness, Samadhi, is the ability—acquired through long practice of meditation—to reconnect or reenter the FIELD consciously. (Samadhi is mentioned in *CWG* as the merger with the blue-white light of your BEing, also known as the Blue Pearl in mysticism.)

The prime characteristics of the QUANTUM FIELD are Consciousness and Will, These are equivalent to perception = feeling, and power to form and move energy (create). These two basic properties can then be further distinguished into the LIFE ESSENCE energies of Wisdom, Power, Value, and LoveJoy. We will come back to these in a later chapter because they are critical to both your human life and your Return to the ONE.

Your BE–FEEL of Wisdom, Power, Value and LoveJoy at each moment is your experience of the DIVINE FIELD of SELF.

The Cosmos: Created Reality

YOUR SECOND STATE OF BEING

It is YOU, the individualized spirit that we call the psycan, who then forms hir BEing. You are made out of the QUANTUM FIELD ENERGY of Consciousness and Will, of the LIFE ESSENCE energies of Wisdom, Power, Value, and LoveJoy. However, you are currently "out of," separated, or perhaps the best term is: **distinguished** from that FIELD by

- the creation of your individuality[13] (being less than the whole);
- by the necessity to be in Polarity, rather than ONEness (to be explained in the next chapter); and
- by being a human being, which is done by your God Essence Suppressor Mass.

As these concepts are important, require considerable explanation and are the subjects of complete chapters, we will say no more about them here.

YOUR FIRST UNIVERSE: YOUR MENTAL UNIVERSE

Before you create the physical universe, you must first create your universe of mental realities. This is your personal world of all your thoughts, which are non-physical creations = realities→experiences. You usually call this universe your mind, but there is no such thing as mind as people commonly think of it.

Your consciousness and subconscious are the space around you as the psycan in which your thoughts exist and are experienced—just as the physical universe is the space in which you exist and you experience physical matter and energies.

---

13 The process of the creation of individuality is described in the psycanics book *Cosmology*.

Exactly like the physical universe, your mental universe consists of an almost infinite variety of objects (thoughts) and energies. Some of these flow through your consciousness = perception = experience, a process we call "stream of thought." Others are "hanging" around you-psycan but outside of your perception in what we call your unconscious or subconscious. There is no subconscious; only mental-energy creations out of the range of your immediate perception as the psycan.

Summary from the book *The Psycanics of the Mind*:

> There is no such thing as mind or subconscious. There are only thoughts, the creator and manipulator of those thoughts who is also the experiencer of those thoughts. Your "mind" consists of those thoughts currently within your perception, and your subconscious is those thoughts that are outside your range of your present perception.
>
> Exactly as you do in the physical universe, you fabricate your thought-objects, consciously or unconsciously. Just as in the physical universe, you then perceive = see them with your psycanic "eyes," your rays of consciousness, which are attention. Just as with physical objects, you can manipulate your thought realities, change them, add to them, and take away from them. You can compare them, analyze them, evaluate them, form opinions about them, value them or reject them, "paint" them with opinions and judgments, and so on: all the things we do with physical objects. You can put your thought realities in the "closet" of your subconscious (memorization). You can call forth those realities from the "closet" of your subconscious, which is memory recall. So, you see, there is no such thing as the mind. Your "mind" is actually another universe, one of space-time and energy-realities much more subtle than your physical universe, but no less a universe for that. We call this your mental universe, and you are God in it: you have instant power of creation and discreation. Your mental universe is more powerful than the physical universe and actually controls the physical universe, which is why you can attract and manifest things in the physical universe by first creating a pattern of them in your psycanic universe.

Both universes, physical and mental, consist of Space, Energy-Matter (objects), and Time (change). You perceive = experience in both universes. In both universes, your experience is the perception of things, of objects, of "realities" in that universe. You are Cause in both universes. You can create, change, and discreate things in both universes.

In fact, these are the only two things that exist in all the known universes: BEings, who are the creators and experimenters of realities (Cause); and realities, which are always the creation of the Being (Effect). Try to name anything that is not one of these two things: BEings = Creator and Experiencer; or realities = creations.

You are the Creator, at some level of your BEing, of everything you experience, including your BEing, and your reduced level of BEing, i.e. human being. "Level of your BEing" is a critical concept here. You are part of a bigger BEing (call it your Oversoul), that is part of a bigger BEing, that is part of a bigger BEing, all the way back to the ONE. You are "vertically integrated" to the ONE through a series of levels of expansion of your BEing. Each level is an individuality itself, at the same time that all are completely conscious of being ONE. Only your lowest level of BEing, the human level, is in the illusion of isolated separation. When I say that you are the Creator of everything you experience, which includes the physical universe, that creation occurs at the level of your BEing that corresponds to that level of the creation. For example, you are not creating your physical universe at your human level, not even at your Oversoul level. You create it at higher, more God-like levels of your ONE BEing. At the human level, you are creating some of your thoughts and all of your emotions (by a process we will see later). As you discreate your God Suppressor Mass (the subject of this book), you begin to open to, communicate with, and finally re-integrate to your higher levels of BEing.

If you experience it, you are the Creator of it—at some level of your BEing (which is vertically integrated all the way back "up" to the ONE).

Your mental universe functions as a holographic projection lens through which you project your power and manifest your physical universe. You then, as a human being, incarnate inside of your greater BEing who is projecting your physical universe for you.

As an analogy of the projection, you have surely seen, either in person or in a movie, the old 35mm film projectors once used in movie theaters. These projectors flick a frame of film in front of a powerful carbon-arc light to project the movie on the screen of the theater.

Imagine that you are standing inside a spherical shell of thought-image realities. The shell of the sphere consists of millions of thoughts which act like lenses (imagine the compound eye of an insect). Each lens is made of a thought-energy pattern of something in the physical universe. There is a lens sphere that is "standard issue" for all who agree to come to play to the physical universe. Other lenses are your personal beliefs that control the particular circumstances of your life (such as financial abundance or scarcity).

Consider yourself as the projector inside a sphere projecting in all 46,656,000 degrees of a sphere (360^3). Your thought lenses determine what form is to appear on the "screen" of your consciousness (the FIELD) as the physical universe. You as the creator being are projecting your creator power out from you in all directions (as if it were light.) That power goes through the "lenses" or "film" of these deep, deep thoughts, molding the FIELD to that information, that modulation, and so producing your illusion of the physical universe.

The physical universe is stored as information, as patterns of energy, as thoughts, in the deeper levels of your BEing (at the Oversoul level and higher, which are also the FIELD: IT is all ONE). You at those more powerful levels of BEing project the illusion around 'you-at-the-human-level' to create your physical universe, like a movie projector does in a theater.

Thus, you, at deeper (or higher) levels of your BEing (remember, you merge into ever Bigger BEings all the way back to the ONE), mold the illusion of the physical universe out of the underlying FIELD, so that you at the human level have a playground.[14] Big BEings such as Buddha and Christ were integrated with those deeper levels of BEing and could change their thought "lenses" at will, which immediately changed the physical universe. Some day, you will be able to do this also.

Your Second Universe: the Physical Universe

Now we come to the physical universe. The physical universe is the sandbox of spirits. It's where you come to get "down and dirty." It is a playground. It is movie set to act out your fondest dramas. It is God's Disneyland®. (Are we having fun yet?) It is where you come to forget that you are God, both for the adventure and drama of it, and for the necessity of not BEing God for awhile in order to refresh your appreciation of BEing IT. This is the Necessity of Polarity, and we will have an entire chapter on it shortly.

You are the creator of the physical universe. You don't create it at your human level of BEing, but rather from higher levels. You are part of a bigger BEing who is part of a bigger BEing, who is part of a Bigger BEing, all the way back to the ONE.[15] You are a projection of those higher (levels of) BEing "down" into the physical universe to experience it. You are also an organ of perception for those levels, and they, all the way back up to the ONE, enjoy all of your experience through you. You are asleep in God; God is awake in you.

Take a pen and paint happy faces on the tips of your fingers. Now stick your fingers down into water, sand, or mud to represent the physical universe. Notice how each finger seems to be an individual and has its own experience of the mud. At the same time, all are transmitting experience back to your hand and arm as the one "parent" BEing of the fingers. Your arm then transmits everything on back "up" to the "parent" BEing of you as the ONE. In this analogy, you represent the

---

14 I know of no way to prove this explanation to you. I am just reporting on some of my experiences leaving the physical universe during my explorations of mysticism. I sometimes passed back and forth through this thought pattern shell. I knew instinctively what it was and what it did.

15 I teach people to contact and communicate with higher levels of their BEing, with their "Oversoul" or "Higher Self," in my advanced seminars. It is not hard to do for most people.

ONE, your arm-hand is your Oversoul, and the fingers are individual humans, of which you-human are one.

The physical universe is all "smoke and mirrors," a mirage generated out of the FIELD for your viewing pleasure. If you were to take all the space out of the matter at the atomic level, all the real matter in the universe would be about the size of a pea.

Here is another analogy of the creation of the physical universe[16]: Imagine a great Fog, infinite in all directions. You are a spirit, a soul, a point of consciousness in the middle of IT, which is a FIELD of consciousness. You too are made of Fog and in fact you are the Fog; there is nothing but the Fog. But you decide to pretend to not be IT ALL, taking up a limited identity and specific location: Here-Now.

Now imagine that the Fog responds to your thoughts. You start to think shapes and things into the Fog. IT = you immediately obeys you (you are the same, remember) and forms ITSELF into whatever you wish. This is fun! You begin to explore and play: What can I create and so experience? The possibilities are endless. Eventually, you coordinate with other spirits like yourself to form a complex world out of the Fog, one that works with agreed-upon laws of SET (Space, Energy, Time), and one in which all can play: thus, we have the physical universe. You create bodies to be able to be on the same vibrational level as your creations out of the Fog, to be able to walk among them. You incarnate and go to play in your perfectly-real-seeming creation of physical reality. You are still here.

Another analogy: You have probably seen a hologram, a three dimensional image that appears in a space, created by crossing laser beams. Many malls have a store that sells them as artwork. There is an example of one in the Star Wars movies when Luke finds the R2D2 robot, brings it back to the ranch and it projects the image of the Princess Leia and her appeal for help against the Empire.

You can think of the physical universe as a hologram projected out of the FIELD (as we saw in the Mental Universe section). In a hologram, there is really nothing much there: it is but light patterns crossing in air. The universe is the same way: there isn't much there. We think of solid matter as, well, solid. But it is mostly space. If an atom were the size of a baseball stadium, the nucleus would be the size of a golf ball on the pitcher's mound, and the electrons would be bees buzzing around in the upper stands. Even solidity is an illusion.

Now we come to the most important thing in all of this: that you wake up from the illusion and remember Who You Are. You are infinitely more than a mere human being: you are the ALL of IT. You are not even the illusion of being just a localized "particle" of the Quantum Field playing in a mirage made of the Quantum Field. You are the QUANTUM FIELD.

---

[16] This is summarized from the psycanics book *Cosmology*.

Look around you right now and realize:

It is an illusion. It is all a game. It is all ME.
I am the Creator. I have created all this out of myself.
It has all been a joke I played on myself.

In other words:

WAKE UP! Remember Who You Are!

If you can't wake up right now and experience this, just memorize it and live repeating it to yourself throughout the day and seeking to make it real. Eventually, and by applying the discreation technology to remove the creations that keep you in the illusion, you will wake up. You will remember you are the Creator and you will have direct control over the illusion. You are controlling it now, but you do not have full consciousness of the process. To have full consciousness, you must recover the totality of your Self.

> You unconsciously create all events; you draw to you every person, place, or saying in your life to provide you with the exact and perfect conditions, the perfect opportunity, to experience what you next wish to experience on your path HOME. (3-1-21)

What you are seeking to do is first to wake up and realize you are not just a human being, but an immortal spirit, an (illusory) individualized "particle" of the ONE. You are an experience of yourself, an experience for God, and of God; a Point of View for God on the rest of Creation; and a sub-creator working within the creation to expand it, who experiences those creations. (You are seriously multi-tasking here.)

At some point on your way HOME—as you discreate your God Suppressor Mass—you will begin to "see," to experience, that the physical universe itself is an illusion. You will begin to experience it as God, as the ALIVE QUANTUM FIELD shaping ITSELF into forms to give you a playground, a movie set, a theater where you come for Games and Drama.

The Supreme Game is your descent into the Negative Polarity of God for the adventure of Returning to Positive Polarities, now able to experience, appreciate and celebrate WHO YOU ARE. You go to "hell" in order to be able to know and enjoy "heaven." (This will make more sense after the chapter on Polarity.)

Gradually, the barriers of your individuality (your God Essence Suppressor Mass) will dissolve and you will re-integrate back into the ONE and into INFINITE WISDOM, POWER, VALUE, LOVEJOY.

It is a process: as you discreate the Suppressor Mass, you begin to live in more and more joy and more and more union. You begin to experience the world no longer as the "valley of darkness, sweat, and tears" to which Adam and Eve were "expelled," but again as the Garden of Eden in which everything you need falls into your hands like the fruit of a tree. You begin to live in the experience of the perfection of IT ALL and in natural flow and abundance of JIT manifestation (JIT: Just In Time; no inventory necessary). You no longer much care about creating anything, preferring just to relax and enjoy the creation. Your passion is now working on your BEing for more Integration = Joy. When you do want something, the mere intention is sufficient to manifest it.

Above all, you are no longer in the External Quest. You are not neurotically struggling in the world to get, accumulate, and hoard material things to try to be happy. (99.99% of the human race—maybe more—is in the External Quest.)

Eventually, you discreate enough of the God Essence Suppressor Mass to perceive through it WHO YOU ARE, and the rest just blows away like clouds. Your REAL SELF dawns clear as the sun in a cloudless sky. You are God again, with complete POWER over YOURSELF, including YOURSELF in the form of the physical universe. You might think you would set about making changes, but in that level you realize that you are the Creator of it all and that it is the way that it is because you created it that way for good purposes. So you do not change much.

You are now awake as the Deity while in a human body in the physical universe, which is but another of your bodies. This is the state of consciousness of Buddha, Jesus, and about 233 other Illuminates since the beginning of the human saga. Rare company until now, but the time has come for the acceleration of awakenings. More and more people are beginning to do so.

When enough humans achieve this, real civilization will begin, and life and co-creation on this planet will take off.

Desire everything. Need Nothing. Choose and Enjoy what shows up. Seek and you shall find. Knock and it shall be opened unto you.

Illustration 4-1: The BEing and Universes

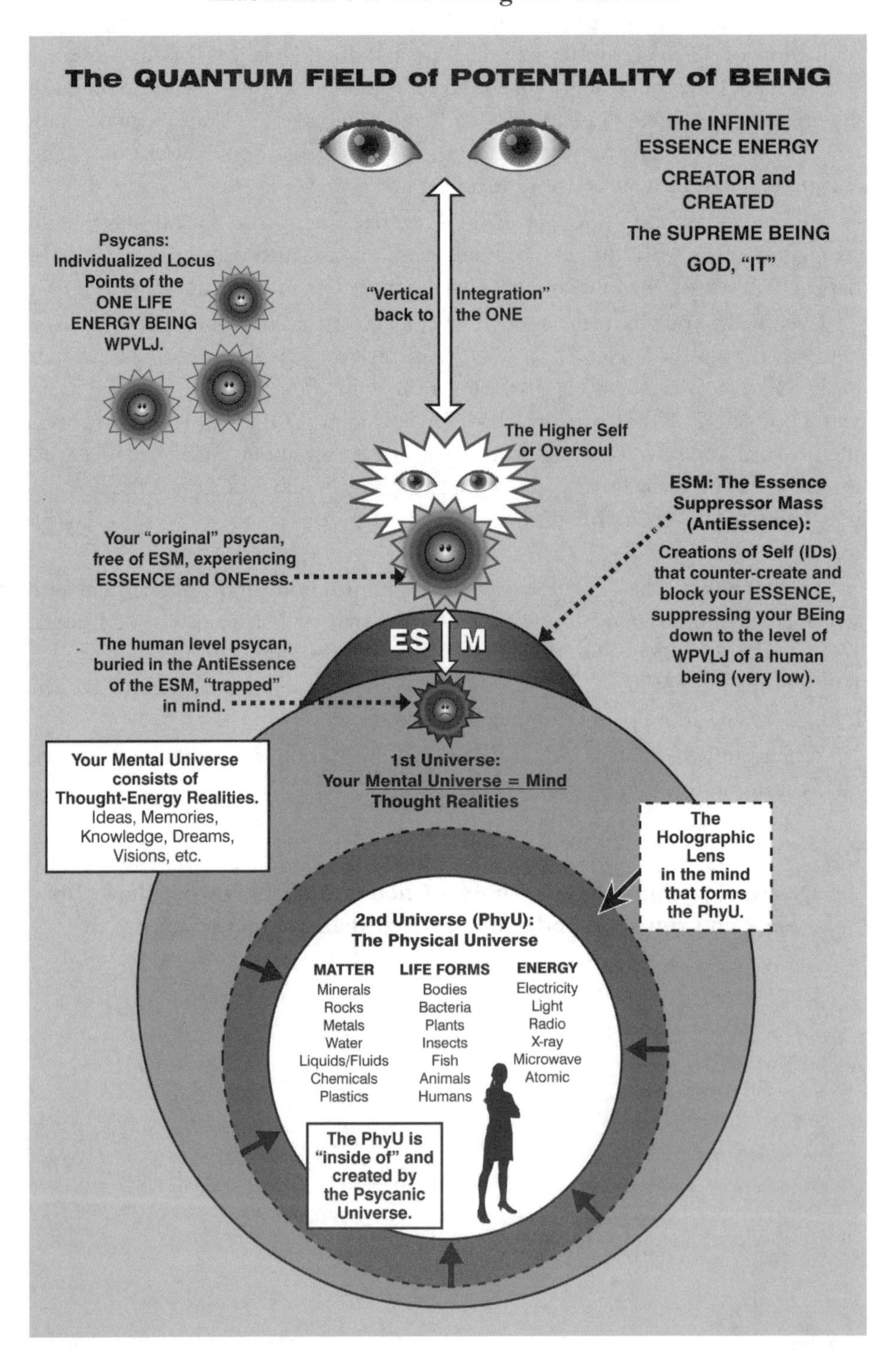

The BEing and Universes Illustration Explained

(Full color illustration available at www.psycanics.org)

GOD

The overall background field of dark orange represents God as the **QUANTUM FIELD of Potentiality of BEing**. It is the underlying field of no-thingness that has the potential to spring into BEing anything—and does so thereby creating everything that exists. It is the EVERYTHING-NOTHING and the ALPHA OMEGA, as God calls HIMSELF in *CWG*. IT is SPIRIT. IT is the ONE. IT is both the CREATOR and the CREATED. IT is the ULTIMATE REALITY, which is the only TRUTH. Everything else created out of this is "Created Reality" and so is an illusion. (Maya in Hinduism.)

The FIELD is also LIFE, and the ESSENCE of LIFE we have identified in psycanics as the properties (which until manifested into the Polarity Field of Creation are only potentials) of Consciousness, Perception, Experience, Knowingness, Intelligence that we summarize as Wisdom; Will-Force that we denominate as Power; the ability to create esteem that we call Value; and the LoveJoy energy. Thus, the ground of LIFE, of BEING is Wisdom, Power, Value, and LoveJoy: WPVLJ.

The FIELD seeks to know ITSELF in all ITs infinite possibilities of BE→FEEL→THINK→DO→HAVE, and IT achieves this by manifesting ITSELF as the entire cosmos (all Created Reality), and playing in and with that. To know ITSELF as ITSELF, as WPVLJ, is one of ITs first and highest purposes. To do so, IT must create Polarity; IT must create a part of ITSELF as the opposite of anything that IT wishes to experience—ITSELF above all. Thus Polarity is one of the most fundamental factors of all existence.

PSYCANS

Out of this field and closest to it in kind, in essence/ESSENCE, are the (illusory) individualizations of the FIELD that are psycans = spirits, as BEings less than the WHOLE BEING. The formation and nature of the psycan is explained elsewhere in my works. Psycans immediately serve the ONE by creating the Polarity of other than the ONE. The humanized psycans also serve the ONE by being at the opposite end of the ESSENCE<>AntiEssence Polarity. There are an infinity of psycans of all sizes from human up to the ONE BEING. You are a "vertically integrated" BEing all the way back up to the ONE. All your experience, including the physical universe, is being created for you at some level of your BEing. Obviously, the physical universe, is created at a level of BEing far above your human level, but it is no less your creation. You are psycan "downgraded" into the level of WPVLJ of a human being, by what we call your God Essence Suppressor Mass or Shell (ESM).

The Essence Suppressor Shell

(Black half moon shape separating the psycan from the ONE and blocking it into the blue sphere of the mind.) Your Essence or God Suppressor Shell is that mass of your created realities-IDentities that counter-create your Godness and create, suppress, and compress your psycan "down" to the level of BEing of a human being, which is about as low as a BEing can go and still retain some ability of conscious creation, of being a Creator. Obviously, these must be AntiEssence—the opposite polarity of ESSENCE, and they must be IDentities: creations of Self. These are your NIRs[17] and your negative emotions, the only pain and suffering that exist. Understanding and discreating the AntiEssence-AntiLove is at the heart of psycanics, as this not only "fixes" everything in your human life; it is also the fast track back to God.

Your God Suppressor Shell "locks" you out of the perception of your GREATER BEING and your ONEness with IT (and therefore with everything that exists). At the same time, it "locks" you, your consciousness-awareness-attention, into your mind, into THINKing, and into THINKing as opposed to FEELing. You flee to mind (which is past and future), to avoid FEELing (which is always present time, Here-Now). You flee to mind to avoid experiencing (FEELing) the truth about Who You Are. The first reality of Who You Are is all the AntiEssence IDentities→Self-AntiLove of which your ESM is made, which is your creation of AntiGod. Of course, on the other side of your ESM, on discreation of it, you are God. The FEELing of your ESM will come up if you turn off your mind, go into Present Time Experience, into full FEELing. This is why it is so hard to meditate; why you keeping bouncing into mind in meditation: to avoid FEELing your Self in the ESM IDentities→Self-AntiLove = neg. EmoLoveJoy. To really be able to go into meditation, into full Present Time Experience of Self, you need psycanics CDT so that you know how to handle all the negative energy and realities that are going to come up as you penetrate your Self = ESM→God.

The Mental Universe

(Light blue sphere in the illustration.) It probably appears to you that you are inside your mind, but actually, your mind is inside you-psycan (which is inside a greater level of your psycan-BEing, which is inside an even greater level, all the way back to the ONE BEING). You are always in the exact center of God. Your mind is simply your universe of your thought-energy creations. It is a universe exactly like the physical universe, except of a much higher frequency, less dense level of energy. There is no mind as an entity with its own existence. All you can do with your "mind" is create realities, manipulate, analyze, and compare them, store them in your "subconscious," and discreate them. One of the purposes of

[17] NIRs to be explained further in the text.

creating mental realities is so that they serve as the pattern for attraction and manifestation of what you want in the physical universe.

THE PHYSICAL UNIVERSE HOLOGRAPHIC CREATION LENS

(Dark blue ring around the green of the physical universe.) The thought-realities of your mind (at higher levels of your BEing) are the patterns, the holographic projection lens, that mold energy into the created realities of the physical universe (which is actually inside your mind at a higher levels of your BEing). The physical universe is a thought in the mind of God. The mind is the light blue on the illustration, and the physical universe projection lens is darker blue ring around the green of the physical universe.

THE PHYSICAL UNIVERSE

(Green.) The Physical Universe is the QUANTUM FIELD springing up into forms, into the illusion of all the things that exist. The CREATOR WILL causes ITSELF to take those forms. You-human-psycan within the forms, also have the ability to influence them to bring into your experience (life) the forms that you desire to experience. You do this by holding the thought image of what you desire to manifest. One of the purposes of events in the Physical Universe is to activate your ESM so that you can discreate it and work your way back to the ONE.

Chapter 5

Polarity

"So, if I am God, why am I a human? What went wrong?"

Quotes from *CWG* in Regular font. Author's elaborations in **Bold**.

My greatest desire is to experience MYSELF as What I am. I can only do that in the space, **against the contrast,** of What I am Not. So I have carefully created **(the illusion of)** What I AM Not so that I can experience What I AM.

In the absence of that which you are not, that which you are, is not. **You as a human being are (the illusion of) What I AM Not that permits ME now, and you later, to have the experience of What I AM. You will experience being ME when you Return and Re-Integrate.** (3-1-11)

The profane and the profound, the lesser and the larger, the hollow and the holy, the ghastly and the godly, the up and the down, the left and the right, the here and the there, the before and the after, the good and the bad. And I am the Alpha and the Omega, **the beginning and the end of it all. Behind all polarity, there is ONE.** (1-12-173)

You have this idea that God shows up only one way in life. This stops you from seeing God all over **(because I AM ALL of it)**. If you don't see God in the profound and in the profane **you are missing the half of IT**. (1-1-60)

To remain in the state of sublime ONEness with the ALL would eventually make it impossible to experience being there. The total bliss of ONEness cannot be experienced as total bliss unless something less than total bliss exists **to provide the contrasting field and relativity.** Thus, I must give a part of MYSELF to the lesser **(and illusory)** experience of not being MYSELF **(God)** so that the rest of ME can experience ITSELF as GOD. **It is currently your turn and honor to be that part of ME that experiences being not ME; that part of the ONE that has gone so fully to the opposite polarity of our Essence (WPVLJ), which is the human being. Thank you for doing that—and note that it is a great adventure for you, as well as a great service to the ONE.**

> It is your soul's desire to turn its grandest concept about itself into its greatest experience. (1-1-22) Life exists as a tool for God to turn concept into experience. **Polarity is one of the greatest tools for doing so.** (Paraphrased from 3-15-257.)

> And you may Return whenever you are ready to do so, whenever you tire of the drama. You will then-experience the GLORY **of our UNION** once again. **And once again the appreciation of that will eventually fade, so that once again you will want to go out to play in Created Reality and pretend not-to-BE ME, so that you can once again Return to the full knowledge and experience of your GLORY.** You will do this, the Cosmic Cycle, in an infinity of ways and forms for all eternity as WE explore OURSELF, **adventuring through OUR infinite possibilities of BE→FEEL→THINK→DO→HAVE. This is the inhalation and exhalation of God: WE breathe in to the ONE, and out to the Many forever more.** (Paraphrased from 3-5-102 and added to from my own understandings.)

> The most magnificent experience of all time is the realization of your Divine Self (2-5-67) **In order to have that real-ization, you must first have the experience of not being your Divine Self. Thus, Created Reality is a world of polarity, of relativity.**

Polarity is a concept mentioned many, many times in *CWG*, but usually as Relativity, or Contrast, or Opposites. **Polarity is one of the most fundamental and important properties of Created Reality, and understanding it fully is critical, absolutely critical, to your happiness and your Return to the ONE.** In fact, BEing the ONE is a transcending of polarity.

Ignorance of the Laws of Polarity guarantees a life of suffering.

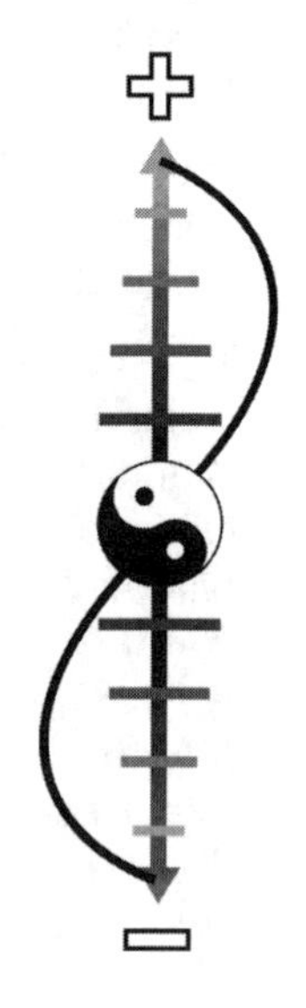

A polarity is an idea, a concept, for experience, that is then pulled or stretched into two opposing directions, towards two extremes or poles. This creates a spectrum, a range, of degrees of experience between those two poles. Examples of polarity spectrums in the physical universe include: light<>dark; big<>little; spectrum of color; the electromagnetic radiation spectrum; hard<>soft; sharp<>dull.

Differences between things, creating possibility of contrast of field and background, are necessary to distinguish, to know a thing. Note that distinction is the first step of knowledge.

No experience of a concept is possible until the concept is stretched and so differentiated into a series of possibilities, or gradients, and you have experienced at least two distinct points on that gradient scale.

For example, if everything was the same temperature such that you have never experienced hot or cold; "temperature" could only be a mental concept for you. Somebody could explain it to you philosophically, but like a deaf person reading about Beethoven's Emperor Concerto, you simply could not really know what they were talking about. You could not know what cold or hot is because you have always known only one temperature and hot and cold do not exist for you experientially. If everything was the same temperature, there could be no experience at all. That one temperature would not be a recognizable experience because it would be your one and only background. There would be no contrasts, no distinctions of one temperature from another to have a differential of experience to which to apply the label of hot or of cold.

Similarly, if everything were red, you would have no concept of color. And if everything were red, you could not see forms or shapes because both foreground and background is red; there is no contrast to make a figure visible.

Render: Experience is the purpose of the cosmos, of Created Reality. The cosmos is God manifesting HIMSELF in all HIS infinite possibilities of BEing in order to know and play—experience—HIMSELF. In computer terminology, to "render a graphic" is to take the black and white sketch for a painting, or a storyboard for a movie, and fill in all the colors and textures to make it come alive. That is what polarity does to Life: it renders it. Without polarity, huge kinds and quantities of experience would not exist and life would be dull indeed.

Spectrum

The range of gradients between two poles of a polarity is called a spectrum. An example will help make the concept of spectrum clear. The temperature spectrum is one that you are surely familiar with. Its two poles are hot and cold. The temperature of anything can range from absolute zero to minus 459 °F (chilly) to about 100,000,000 °F (sizzling) in the center of a supernova at the time of its explosion. The temperature spectrum consists of the 100,000,459 degrees Fahrenheit between those two poles (give or take a few million degrees).

In this book, we are concerned with the non-physical experience polarities. Much of your non-physical experiences are polarities, including:

- Cause<>Effect
- Wise<>Stupid
- Able<>Unable
- Success<>Failure
- Valuable<>Worthless
- Happiness<>UPS (Unhappiness, Pain and Suffering)
- Love<>AntiLove.
- The Emotions: from the deepest negative (depression) to the highest positive (ecstasy).
- Good<>Bad
- Affinity<>Aversion

Symbols: We use these symbols to indicate polarity: +/- and < >.

1. "Emotions+/-" means the Emotional Energy Polarity consisting of both the positive and the negative emotions. This is a shorter way of writing it than Positive Emotions<>Negative Emotions.
2. "Love<>AntiLove" means the Love Energy Polarity. It can also be written Love+/-.
3. The word "anti" means the negative polarity of a spectrum. AntiLove is the negative polarity of Love.

Relativity: Polarity creates Relativity: You cannot define any position on a polarity spectrum except relative to another point on the spectrum. Two examples:

- Are you hot or cold? Notice you can't say without another pole for comparison. Relative to ice, you are hot. Relative to boiling water, you are cold. You can't say what you are or where you are on the spectrum, except as relative to some other point. You are a parent only relative to having children. You are rich or poor only relative to some standard.
- You can only detect one color relative to a different color. You can't perceive a white figure on a white background, or a red figure on a red background.

Life is the play of opposites, and the play between opposites.

The Laws of Polarity

There are several Laws of Polarity that are critical to understand:

1. **Both poles and sides of a polarity must exist. You can't have one pole or side without the other.**

You must have both poles and both sides of a spectrum for either side to exist. It is impossible to have one side of the polarity without the other also existing.

For example, it is impossible to have good without bad. It is impossible to have physical pleasure without physical pain. It is impossible to have happiness (positive emotions) without unhappiness (emotional pain). It is impossible to have Love without AntiLove also existing.

YOU CAN'T HAVE POSITIVE WITHOUT NEGATIVE.

It is impossible for positive experiences to exist
without negative experiences also existing.

2. **You can know and appreciate one side of a spectrum (i.e. the positive side) only to the degree that you have experienced the other (i.e. negative) side of the spectrum.**

Some examples:

- The farther apart two colors; the more contrast (difference) between them, the better you will note them. Light green to dark green is little contrast; black to white, or blue to yellow, is most noticeable.

- The farther apart the poles of your temperature spectrum experience, the richer your experience will be. You will understand "temperature" much better by holding ice and then burning yourself with hot coffee, than you will playing with two things of only slightly different temperatures.
- You most appreciate a warm house when you come inside from a blizzard. You most appreciate an air-conditioned room when you come inside on a hot, humid day.
- You most appreciate health when you are sick.
- If you were to win a game all the time, never lose; you would soon cease to appreciate winning and you would become bored with the game.
- A wealthy person, who has been rich all hir life and never even seen poverty in others, would not even know s/he was wealthy. Only by losing all hir money and becoming poor, would s/he be able to full appreciate hir former wealth.
- You cannot savor the richness of PosLove without having experienced, at least once, AntiLove (the negative emotions). You cannot know and enjoy joy without having experienced, at least once, sorrow.

We must have and experience negative polarities to be able to experience and appreciate positive experiences.

Now, sit up and pay attention, because this next law is of extreme importance. It is why you are here so far from God.

3. **You must alternate Polarities. To continue appreciating any polar experience, you must occasionally go to the other side of the polarity to refresh your experience of that other side.**

To experience anything all the time without experiencing other points on the polarity is to lose appreciation and even awareness of that experience. It is the movement between polarities that maintains your experience and your appreciation of that polarity fresh. To the degree that you live in the same conditions all the time, in your comfort zone, with few challenges, life will become jaded and boring.

For example, if you stay a long time in a warm room becoming completely warm and accustomed to it, you will lose the consciousness and appreciation of the warmth that you had when you first came in from the cold. If you stay very long, you will forget all about warmth itself; it becomes your ground of being without a contrast to bring it forward into your experience, into appreciation. You must go back into the blizzard and get cold again to refresh your awareness and appreciation of warmth.

All experience is the perception of energy. The forms of experience-energy that are polarities are like waves, sine waves. They are like alternating current that switches back and forth between polarities. Notice that all electromagnetic phenomena in the physical universe are waves. Quantum physics says that the underlying essence of the universe is waves.

When a surfer rides the waves, there is no high point (crest) without a low point (trough); they mutually create each other. It is a combination of both, the entire wave, the energy created by the alternation, which enables the surfer to glide. So think of life as waveforms, as alternating current. Let the current that is life alternate as it will, without resistance. Ride the waves, rather than cling to the crests and resist the troughs.

Experience is the purpose of existence and polarities are one of the major forms of experience. Existence would be gray, dull and boring without them. Life is juicy (full of experience) to the extent that you move back and forth along the spectrums of polar experience. If you stay in any one experience too long, your senses become dulled to it. (Compare how you feel when you first fall in love to after 10 years in a marriage or relationship.)

Mysticism and the Great Polarity of God<>Human

This is what you are doing in relationship to God: alternating Polarities. You have left the "warmth" of "heaven," the ease and luxury of the "Garden of Eden," and gone out into the "cold," "hard," "valley of tears" of the physical universe. You have left the ONE to BEcome the Many so that you can return afresh to the experience of ONE. You have left the Quantum Field of the GOD ESSENCE and BEcome AntiEssence so that you can return to and appreciate BEing ESSENCE again.

There is no experience of anything in the Quantum Field except "I:" Will and Consciousness. There is nothing there to experience. GOD = LIFE = ESSENCE, *to be experiential,* must be a polarity. Actually, IT is four polarities of ESSENCE, Wisdom, Power, Value, and LoveJoy

1. Wisdom<>Ignorance/Stupidity; Know<>Not-Know;
2. Power<>AntiPower; Creator<>Victim;
3. Value-able<>Worthless, not good enough; and
4. Love<>AntiLove, which is the same as Happiness<>UPS (Unhappiness, Pain and Suffering).

As a human being, you are now dramatizing AntiEssence, which consists of the negative polarity of the four Nuclear Energies of BEing:

1. **AntiWisdom** (includes amnesia of Who You Are, ignorance, difficulty learning, dumbness, stupidity, etc.);
2. **AntiPower** (includes I can't do it, can't get it, weakness, failure, etc.);
3. **AntiValue** (unworthy, undeserving, not good enough, ugly, unloved, etc.); and
4. **AntiLove** (anger, fear, hate, grief, etc.).

Now ALL THAT IS knew intellectually, conceptually, that IT was all that there was, but this was only a thought, not an experience, not a BEing and FEELing.. On the scale of the Intensity of Experience, of FEELing, thought is a very weak form of experience, next to nothing. FEELing something is another whole order of knowing something; far, far above THINKing.

IT wanted to know ITSELF fully in all ITs utter magnificence, in the fullness of ITs ESSENCE. IT wanted to experience, to live, ITs ALIVENESS, by BEing and FEELing it, not just THINKing about it. IT wanted to BE-FEEL ITs **Wisdom, Power, Value,** and **LoveJoy**.

Thus IT had to create polarities out of ITSELF, out of each of ITs four LIFE qualities: Wisdom, Power, Value, Love and Joy. ESSENCE knew that it could experience ITs ESSENCE only by also experiencing the opposite of ESSENCE, of Not-Essence or AntiEssence. (Remember our example of how you cannot know hot without having experienced cold.) IT knew that IT could BE-FEEL God only by first (or simultaneously) BEing and FEELing ITSELF as the opposite of God, as AntiGod. God realized that SHE must become a polarity!

What separates you from experiencing yourSelf as God again, from experiencing **your Self as INFINITE ESSENCE, as the ONE, is a mass of non-physical energy of AntiEssence IDentities, your creations of not-being ESSENCE**. It forms a shell around you and both blocks your connection with God and generates for you the experience of being a human being. **To Return to the ONE you only need to discreate this shell.** All of this is a story that will unfold in this book.

For now, just remember that your existence as a human being is **an experience of being Negative Polarity of God, of AntiGod**, an experience that you have created by creating AntiEssence IDentities. Although your God Suppressor Mass is an illusion, it is a powerful one, as is the physical universe itself.

You have created yourSelf as the Negative Polarity of God for a good purpose. Obeying the Laws of the Polarized nature of Experience, you have gone as far away as you can from BEing God:

1- to enjoy playing in the cosmos, experiencing all that you can in all kinds and forms of experience;
2- to have the challenge, adventure and drama of "journeying" back to God, a great experience in itself. Of course, this "going" is not a physical journey, but one of identity, of experience, of Self; and
3- on arrival back, for having alternated polarities, to now be able to appreciate and celebrate BEing God again.

Remember these particular polarities, WPVLJ, because your ability to control and increase them, a power which you will learn in this book, is a very effective path of return to the ONE. You must discreate the four AntiEssence Nuclear IDentities. There are many paths; this is one.

> Yet another game involved in all this is the challenge, from God's point of view: "Can I create something so far from ME that I can't bring it back?"
>
> From our human point of view: Does it not sometimes feel like that: "God is so far away that I can't get back"?

Being AntiGod is part of why you are being a human being. You serve the WHOLE by being that part of God experiencing ITSELF as the opposite polarity of God, as **AntiEssence** (**AntiWisdom**, **AntiPower**, **AntiValue**, **AntiLove**) thereby providing the relativity, the contrast, that allows other parts of God to experience ITSELF as God, as ESSENCE, as LIFE, as **Wisdom**, **Power**, **Value**, **LoveJoy**.

As a human being, you are the opposite polarity of God. You are minimum Wisdom, Power, Love, and Joy for a Creator BEing. For God to be God, SHE needs somebody to be God of. You as a human being are one of the things God is God of.

Given that SHE is all that is, given that there is nothing else, SHE had to make those apparently more limited parts out of HERSELF. That is where you as a human being enter the picture. You are experiencing the negative polarities of the characteristics of God. Therefore, we can say that you are experiencing a great deal of "not-God" or "negative God," "AntiEssence" or "AntiGod." (All these terms mean the same thing.)

As a human being, you are experiencing a great deal of AntiEssence (I don't know, I am dumb, I can't do it, I am weak, I am a failure, I am unworthy, I am less than, anger, fear, hate, grief, depression, etc.). To be more precise:

- Minimum wisdom, and even total ignorance, instead of WISDOM.
- Separate, isolated, unconnected individuality; the Many as opposed to the ONE.
- Localization in one spot, limitation to one Point of View; as opposed to INFINITE SPACE, localized EVERYWHERE-NOWHERE, and all VIEWPOINTS.
- Minimum Power: can't do it, can't get it, weakness, not creator, failure; instead of POWER.
- Minimum Value: unworthy, undeserving, less than, unlove-able; instead of INFINITE VALUE.
- AntiLove: negative emotions, unhappiness, pain and suffering; instead of INFINITE LOVEJOY.
- Density and Resistance, as opposed to INFINITE SPACE.

In the chapter on IDentities, we will explain how you do this, how you create yourSelf as the negative polarity of God. The good news is that you only need to visit BEing AntiGod temporarily: you don't have to live here and it was never intended that you should stay as a human being. If you are reading these books, then your time for experiencing the negative polarity of God, of dramatizing AntiEssence is at its end. With the technology of discreation that is introduced in this book, you will be able to eliminate all forms of AntiEssence from your BEing. Your freeing your Self will model the path for others, so that eventually all humanity will change polarity.

You are made of the LIFE energy; that is part of your image and likeness to God. You are made out of the same "stuff," same ENERGY, the same ESSENCE, out of LIFE ITSELF. This book is about how you can un-cover your ESSENCE to re-discover Who You Are. Who You Are is the MAGNIFICENT ALL THAT IS, the ONE. You are an incorporated spirit in the realm of polarity. Remember these words: ENERGY, ESSENCE, and LIFE; we will go more deeply into their nature a little later because these are what you must learn to control to restore your experience of your MAGNIFICENCE.

> It is your soul's desire to turn its grandest concept about itself into its greatest experience. (1-1-22) Life exists as a tool for God to turn concept into experience. **Polarity is one of the greatest tools for doing so.** (Paraphrased from 3-15-257)
>
> My greatest desire is to experience MYSELF as What I am. I can only do that in the space, against the contrast, of What I am Not. So I have carefully created **(the illusion of)** What I am Not so that I can experience What I am.

This is what you are doing as a human being. You are experiencing and exploring the negative polarity of God, which is what a human being really is. To the degree that you explore the negative polarity of God, to that degree can you experience and will you appreciate and so celebrate the positive polarity when you get back to IT.

As a human being, are you not FEELing very intensely the experience of (pretending) not-being God? Have you not experienced unhappiness, pain, and suffering? These are AntiGod experiences.

Of course, you have not left the positive polarity (God) by going anywhere. All that you have done is counter-created the experience, the reality[18]—not the Truth—of Who You Are. You continue to be at the very center of the infinite sphere of the ONE, and you continue to be the entirety of the ONE. All that you have done is to create blocks and counter-experiences to Who You Are. Our purpose is to show you those counter-creations within you, and show you how to discreate them.

---

[18] Reality is an advanced concept meaning anything that exists because it can be experienced. It is not Truth, which is the verifiable correspondence between a reality and a statement about that reality. The difference between these: reality and Truth is a key concept important in communication, relationships, and in creation and discreation.

And I repeat: **This path back to God is not a creation of your SELF, you already are IT ALL. All you need to do is discreate your created reality (illusion) of not-being God. This illusion is a mass of energy in the modulation of AntiEssence that forms a shell around you and suppresses your consciousness of Who You Are.**

I have found it very helpful to always remember that my journey through life and to HOME is not a search for God. I am inside of HIM and in the Kingdom of Heaven even now—I never left, nor is there any place to go. My journey HOME is an endless experience of God. It is impossible to be lost. I have only to real-ize where I am and make it real again experientially.

Everything that I see is a form and a face of God. I am in a game of the polarity of “I”<>“Not-I” that creates for me the opportunity to define and experience who I am in relation to “Not-I = Other,” until I transcend the illusion of individuality and separation, and real-ize that IT is all ONE and I am IT ALL.

> The purpose of your existence is to decide and create; to declare and express; to BE and FEEL; to live and experience Who You Really Are, which is ME.
>
> **This is a process of becoming aware of who you are now; from which base you can transform to your next ideal of who you want to BE as your next step on the road to BEing ME again. Oftentimes, the fastest way to make that transformation is to discreate who you are, which lets more ESSENCE naturally shine through.**

Chapter 6

Resistance

S/He who does not understand Polarities and Resistance will suffer.

What maintains the existence of, and locks you into, your God Suppressor Shell is your resistance to it. Resistance Causes Persistence.

Resistance is the ONLY unhappiness, pain and suffering that exists.

There are two levels of resistance:

1. Negation **to experience** something. This level of resistance can include blocks to feeling, suppression, avoidance, and escape. Resistance as negation to experience causes the persistence of that which you avoid experiencing.
2. The use of negative energy to stop, change, punish, or destroy something. This not only causes the persistence of what you are resisting, but actually makes it stronger.

Level two resistance is any form of negative energy: mental, emotional, or physical; that is then directed against anything, physical or non-physical. The purpose of resistance is always to stop, change, punish, or destroy "bad" events[19] (people, things, or experiences).

For example, all negative emotions are resistance energies. Every time you experience a negative emotion (the four basic emotions are anger, fear, sorrow, and depression), you are resisting something "bad" in your life. You can verify this law by looking at your activations of negative emotion and identifying what you are resisting. For example, in a relationship, every time you are angry, you are resisting something the other person said or did, or did not say or do, according to your opinion.

19 The word "event" in psycanics means anything that is or occurs. It can be any person, behavior, thing, action, situation or circumstance.

There are multiple and important reasons why resistance is a "bad" idea.

- The first is pain: **resistance**, especially emotional resistance to anything, **is painful**.
- Resistance creates or attracts that which is resisted. (e.g. Fear attracts that which you fear.)
- Your resistance (negative energy) to other people will cause them to resist you.
- Your resistance to situations in your life will cause the persistence of those situations.
- Resistance to your negative emotions will cause the persistence of your negative emotions, and your negative emotions are the only pain that exists. Resistance to pain is suffering.
- Resistance puts you into Effect, thereby undermining your Cause and Personal Power.
- Your resistance to anything inhibits your intelligence, creativity and wisdom in dealing with what you are resisting, further reducing your personal power to control life.

If you have a negative event or situation in your life, why make your experience worse by emotionally resisting it?

Notice that when you resist (i.e. get angry, or blame) another energy generator, another person, that person will tend to respond to your negative energy = resistance with negative energy = resistance of their own. Thus, the law: **Resistance Causes Counter-Resistance**.

As the negative emotions are the only unhappiness, pain and suffering (UPS) that exists, resistance is painful. In fact, your negative emotions are the ONLY UPS that exists in the known cosmos. Thus, the Law: **Resistance is UPS**.

Furthermore, all resistance is energization and energy is creative. The more energy you throw into something, the more massive, denser and "realer" it becomes. It is irrelevant whether the energy is positive or negative: energy is energy. Thus the law: Resistance Creates and Persists (that which is resisted).

The complete Law of Resistance is:

Resistance Creates, Causes Pain, Counter-Resistance and Persistence.

The symbol for Resistance Causes Persistence is Rxx→Perxx.

Polarity and Resistance

Remember that the negative side of a polarity must exist for the positive to exist. Therefore, one half of life is negative. This creates a trap for the person who does not understand polarity and resistance. When a person does not understand polarity, s/he will usually resist the negative polarities of life.

Negative polarities most people resist include:

- "Bad" things, people and events;
- AntiWisdom (not knowing, feeling oneself as ignorant or stupid, etc.);
- AntiPower (not being able to do something, fear, weakness, etc.);
- AntiValue (feeling unworthy, less than, unimportant, ugly, rejected, etc.);
- AntiLove (the negative emotions such as anger, fear, guilt, resentment, grief, depression, etc.); and
- UPS: their unhappiness, pain, and suffering.

Now apply the Laws of Resistance. Resistance to anything is painful and in fact is the only pain that exists. Thus, when you resist anything, you are creating UPS. When you resist your UPS, you are creating more UPS about your UPS. This resistance to pain is suffering.

Furthermore, you are causing the persistence of what you are resisting which is exactly what you want to cease to exist. So instead of achieving your purpose of stopping, changing, or destroying the "bad" things you are resisting, you are actually attracting and strengthening them.

External events NEVER cause your UPS in life, only your resistance to them causes your UPS. Furthermore, your resistance causes the persistence of what you resist, by which you prolong your UPS and make it persist. You then resist that UPS and that turns pain into suffering. You are a tremendous creator and when you don't understand how life works, you can tie yourself in knots with your creations.

Notice that often you are resisting the negative sides of polarities: anything "bad" and especially your own negative emotions. When you resist your negative experiences, **you are resisting Life itself as it is and as it must be. The negative experiences must exist for the positives to exist. You can't have one side without the other.**

You are therefore resisting one half of Life as it is and it can't be otherwise. You are resisting reality; you are resisting the truth of What Is, As It Is—causing yourself pain as you do so, and causing the persistence of exactly what you wish to end. Furthermore, the half of experience = life that you are resisting cannot be changed or destroyed with your resistance! On the contrary, you are only strengthening it.

Most people, at the effect of their ignorance of polarity, spend much of their life and emotional energy resisting all kinds of things in their lives. They resist: events, situations, what others say or do, what they themselves do or don't do; their own thoughts and emotions. Above all, they resist themselves when they are in negative (AntiEssence) IDentities.[20] As the resisted experience seems to be the

20 IDentities and AntiEssence are extremely important concepts to be covered in coming chapters.

cause of their UPS (Unhappiness, Pain and Suffering), and seems to persist; the only solution appears to resist even more with even more negative energy. It is a downward spiral in which much of humanity is trapped.

The ONLY UPS that exists in life is your own emotional resistance to What Is, to Reality. Your UPS is never the events of your life, and never caused by the events. It is always your negative emotional reaction = your Rxx to the events.

Negative Emotion = Resistance = Pain = Unhappiness:
They are all the same.

Thus, the Law: **The Price of Ignorance is Suffering.**

A corollary of these Laws is: **All suffering is Life telling you that there is something you need to learn.**

The opposite of resistance is **SPace**, an extremely important concept in psycanics, on which we will have a chapter later. SPace is nothingness, the absence of all energy, especially of all negative energy that is resistance. In life, you are SPace, which is the beginning of PosLove, or you are resistance. God is the SPace in which everything that exists, exists. God has no resistance to anything.

As we shall show, your negative emotions are not resistances to external events, but rather to your Self. **Your resistance, your AntiLove, to your Self is the ONLY UPS that exists in life.** That is the subject of our next chapter: You Negative Psycanic IDentities, which is how you counter-create your ESSENCE, the God in you. These IDentities are what you must discreate to Return to the ONE.

Summary of Polarity and Resistance

You must understand polarity and resistance to be able to Return to the ONE. The ONE is static; it has no waveform, no polarities, no separation, no resistance. IT is INFINITE SPACE in which all realities exist, with ZERO resistance to anything. What separates you from BE-FEELing yourSelf as God in this moment is a polarity. What keeps you stuck in the negative side (AntiGod = human being) of that polarity is your resistance to BEing AntiGod.

What keeps you from discreating your God Essence Suppressor Mass is your resistance to BE-FEELing it. Therefore, because polarity and its child of ignorance, resistance, are so important, we summarize the last two chapters here. The Laws of polarity and of resistance that you need to know at this point are:

1. **Life is Polar.** Polarity creates the immense spectrum = gradient = variety of possibilities within any one phenomenon. **Without polarity, most experiences would not exist at all.** For example, without Hot and Cold, Temperature would only be a concept, never an experience.

2. **For a polarity to exist, both poles <u>must</u> exist.** It is impossible to have a polarity or a spectrum without <u>both</u> poles, and **it is impossible to have one pole or side of a spectrum without the other**.

   "Success" cannot exist without "failure"; "pleasure" cannot exist without "pain." You cannot have Good without BAD. In other words: BAD *must exist* for Good to exist.

3. **Life is a sine wave** of **alternating** polarities. Ride the waves, rather than resist one part and cling to the other. (The final objective is to transcend all resistance to polarities.)
4. You can experience, know and appreciate one side of a polarity only to the extent that you have experienced the other side.
5. To refresh and thereby maintain the experience of one side of a polarity, you must alternate polarity. (This is what you are doing as a human being: You are BEing AntiGod to refresh your experience of BEing God.)
6. To resist one side of any experience polarity, e.g. failure, pain, or "bad" events, is to resist one half of Life; it is to resist Life itself As It Is and Must Be.
7. **The result of such resistance is pain.** All pain is resistance, and resistance is the only pain that exists. Resistance is negative energy thrown against negative energy. The only pain that exists is your <u>negative emotions = resistance</u> to <u>What Is = Reality</u>. Thus the saying, "Resist not evil." Resist not—for your own good and happiness.
8. **Resistance Creates that which is resisted (e.g. feared). Resistance Causes Resistance in other people. Resistance Causes Persistence; and Resistance Causes Pain.** The purpose of resistance is to change, stop, punish or destroy something—a most difficult and often impossible task using resistance.
9. Resistance to your resistance (negative emotions) transforms pain to suffering, by persisting and worsening your negative emotions.
10. You cannot change things by resisting What Is. You cannot create positives in your life by resisting the negatives: your resisting them only prolongs the negatives. **You cannot create what you want by resisting what you have.** You cannot find happiness by resisting your unhappiness.
11. The path of Return to the ONE by discreating your God Suppressor Mass is a path of reversing your resistance to it, to yourSelf in the AntiEssence IDentities. (This will be explained in coming chapters.)

Chapter 7

The Existential Imperative

The Ultimate Motivation of all human behavior and action is to BE-FEEL more God, which search can only end when you are ONE with the INFINITE LIFE ENERGY = GOD from whence you come.

We have seen that your Return to BEing the ONE God, again, is the purpose of life. But it is not only a purpose or a goal. That implies you have a choice. You have no choice in the matter. Your Return to the ONE is an **imperative**, an innate drive within you. **You have no option in life but to seek the Kingdom of Heaven. You cannot do otherwise.**

"Imperative" is related to "imperial" and "emperor." Think of it as an imperial edict or decree. An imperative is an order, instruction, command, that you *must* obey; you have no choice in the matter. For example, you have an imperative to breathe. To check this and to see what an imperative feels like, stop breathing for as long as you can. Less powerful imperatives include eating and sex.

In the same way, you and every human being have an imperative, an impulse, a compulsion, to return to the ONE. **No matter what anyone does, their underlying, unconscious motivation is to BEcome God again.** This law has been proven true in psycanics for any and every human behavior. It is true for terrorism and for patriotism, for cowardice and for bravery, for generosity and for selfishness. **There are no exceptions.** This is important to understand because when you begin to look at life, at relationships for one example, understanding everything in this otherwise seemingly insane world begins to make sense.

You and everybody else are always seeking God, whether you know it or not, or whether you want to or not. You have no choice in the matter; it is inherent in the nature of your separation from the ONE that you seek to Return. There is something within us that always knows, never ever forgets, our original and whole nature of WISDOM, POWER, VALUE, LOVEJOY-ECSTASY, and that will never be satisfied until we are BE-FEELing THAT again.

Thus, you are always, always, seeking the Kingdom of Heaven. The problems and conflicts of life arise because few people understand what they are seeking, or how to go about it. They are lost in the External Quest, seeking heaven in the physical universe, instead of within through the Internal Quest.

The Existential Imperative was discovered and proven to be true through the following line of investigation, which took a number of years and thousands of hours of observation of thousands of people:

- The only motivation of all people is to control **experience**. Your experience is everything you perceive, sense, or feel in any manner. It includes both physical experience (light<>dark; hot<>cold; hungry<>satiated, etc.); and non-physical experience (mind-thoughts, emotions, happiness<>pain, Love<>AntiLove, etc.)
- When we analyze physical experience, we find that beyond physical utility, the reason people want things is because they think they will make them happier. Thus, we can ignore physical experience as the prime motivation. Therefore, the ultimate motivation of all people can be summarized as Happiness.
- Happiness is purely emotional; this is proven beyond doubt. Thus, the ultimate motivation is to control one's emotions: to avoid or end negative emotions, and to FEEL positive ones (i.e. love, joy, passion, etc.)
- When we examine the nature of emotions, we find that they are the **Love Energy Polarity** (as will be explained later in the book). The positive emotions are PosLove and Happiness (Joy). Thus, the ultimate motivation of all human behavior is **LoveJoy**. *CWG* is also very clear about Love being the motivation:

  > Your soul seeks the highest feeling of perfect love. This is the soul's desire. This is its purpose. The soul is after the feeling. Not the knowledge, but the feeling.

- When we examine the nature of Love, we find that Love always originates in the Self and is always Self-Love. Love for others is always a projection of love for Self. This too accords with *CWG* as we are all ONE. There is no "other" to love, only Self.
- When we investigate the nature and cause of Self-Love, we find that it is part of the nature of BEing itself. It is the fourth ESSENCE energy (LoveJoy). Love is part of the ESSENCE of God and you are of that ESSENCE. You are made of WPVLJ: Wisdom, Power, Value, and LoveJoy.
- You love yourSelf to the extent that you are Wise, Powerful, and Value-able (the ESSENCE IDentities) **The only true Happiness that exists is your BE-FEEL of ESSENCE.** The more of these that you are = BE and experience = FEEL, the happier you are.

- The maximum source of WPVLJ, of Love = Happiness, of Ecstasy, is God. You are trying to BE as happy as possible, which is to BE as much Love as possible, which is to BE as much God as possible. Thus, the Ultimate Motivation of all human behavior is to get back to and BE-FEEL Self as God. This is the Existential Imperative.

Even the biological imperative of sex is not to guarantee the survival of the species, but to experience the ONEness which is the true nature of your BEing. The biological imperative is not to create more life, but to experience more LIFE and to experience that LIFE as I really am: ONEness and ALLness. (3-10-154)

There is only one purpose for all of life, and that is for you and all that lives to experience fullest glory. What the soul is after is the highest feeling of love. The feeling of love is your experience of God. This is the soul's desire. This is its purpose. The soul is after the feeling. Not the knowledge, but the feeling. The highest feeling is the experience of unity with the ALL THAT IS. This is the feeling of perfect love. Your soul seeks the highest feeling of perfect love. Love is the ultimate reality. It is the ONLY. The ALL. The purpose of the soul is to experience ALL of IT which is to BE ALL of IT. Your holy cause is the realization of Self. This the great return for which the soul yearns. Of course, *you are seeking to be God!* What else did you think you were up to? (1-1-20 1-1-56, 2-1-83, 2-1-76, 2-1-85)

The Existential Imperative

The Ultimate Motivation of all human behavior and action is to Return to the ONE.

Everything you do, you do for yourself. (3—232)

This is where humanity divides itself into two camps:

1. Those who do not know what they are seeking, other than their (often vague notion of) happiness. Not knowing what they really seek, where it is, or how to arrive at it; they seek it in the external world. They seek it through travel and fun, through relationships; through goals and getting things, through fame and fortune, through prestige and power, through the hoarding of money and material things, and through drugs, to a name a few of the more common ways. This is the **EXTERNAL QUEST**.

   The External Quest is impossible—nothing in the world can ever satisfy the hunger for ESSENCE within—they must keep on seeking and struggling and getting and hoarding, always to find it is not enough. So they return to seek more and more and more, forever without end—until they awaken to understanding What Life Is About and How It Works.

2. Those who know what they seek, and know where to find it. These seek the Kingdom of Heaven WITHIN. This is the **INTERNAL QUEST** for happiness, for ESSENCE.

This book is for group two. It is to remind you of your Internal Quest, your search for the Kingdom within. More importantly, it is to give you a very powerful technology for your Internal Quest for ESSENCE.

To find the ESSENCE within you—for you are made of it—you only have to uncover, dis-cover, discreate, that which counter-creates and suppresses your experience of the INFINITE ESSENCE you already are.

Chapter 8

The Causal Sequence: How Life Really Works

Life works according to the Causal Sequence.
Understand it and you control Life.

In the *CWG* series, God mentions the Causal Sequence numerous times, but only as the shortened version of BE→DO→HAVE. The Causal Sequence is much more important and much more powerful than at first appears. In fact, understanding it is a key to both power over your human existence, and to your Return to the ONE. It is a key concept in psycanics and in life: it is the basic formula or equation of How Life Works.

Understanding the Causal Sequence is a key to Wisdom, Power, Love and Happiness, both in your human life, and to your expansion of BEing to BEcome these INFINITELY again.

The first step is to expand the shortened version of the Causal Sequence to the full version so that it covers everything in your life. The full Causal Sequence is:

BE → FEEL → THINK → DO → HAVE

The Causal Sequence can also be expressed as:

IDENTITY → EMOTION → MIND → ACTIONs → RESULTs

Where each element in the second statement of the sequence is equivalent to the corresponding element in the first statement.

The element of <u>DO = ACTION</u> includes RELATE, which includes communication and all relationship interactions. These are your <u>DO = ACTIONS</u> as regards others and includes what you say, how you say it, your treatment of others, and your reactions to others' treatment of you. Thus, a full expression of the Causal Sequence is:

BE → FEEL → THINK → [SAY–RELATE/DO] → HAVE

We can write out the Causal Sequence as:

Who I AM (BE) determines **What I FEEL**, which determines **How I THINK**, which determines my **DO**ings, which include how I communicate and treat others, and **how I perform** and **handle** things. Obviously, my **ACTION**s, both with others and with things, determine my **results = HAVE** in life.

Laws relevant to the Causal Sequence include:

- Everything in your life falls into one of these six[21] areas. It is life itself.
- Your life consists of your Causal Sequences. Everything in your life is part of a Causal Sequence and obeys the Laws of the Causal Sequence.
- It is a Causal Sequence because each element determines the following ones.
- **The beauty of the Causal Sequence is that you only need to learn to control the first element, your BEing, to control all the rest of your life.**

Your life functions according to the Causal Sequence whether you know it or not, and whether you want it to or not. There is no escaping it: **it controls your existence**. You can only learn how the Sequence works and harness it to your benefit. Doing so will give you great power over life and a path of Return to the ONE.

> When we are referring to any element of the Causal Sequence, we will capitalize that word to make sure the reader knows that we are referring to an element of the Sequence. Examples of words that will be capitalized include: BE, BEing, FEEL, FEELing, FELT, DO, DOing, DID, SAY, SAYing, RELATEing, HAVEing, HAD, etc.

Let us explain what each element covers:

HAVE = RESULTS: Your HAVE is everything material that shows up in your life, the good and the bad. It does not matter whether you take responsibility for it being there or not; if it exists in your life, it is part of your HAVE. It is your "fame and fortune" in the world. Your HAVE includes all your material possessions and properties. It includes your business, job, and career; and your money, bank accounts and financial condition. It includes your successes and your failures. It includes the quantity and quality of your relationships (but not the actions you take to create those results; that would be your DO). It includes your body and its condition of health or sickness. It includes all events, everything that happens to you, whether you call it luck, coincidence, or accident. If it occurs in your life; you HAVE it.

Your **Negative HAVE** is everything in your life that you have but don't want and have not been able to eliminate. Examples can include a health problem, an accident, insufficient money, debts, a job you dislike, conflictive relationships, etc.

Your **Not-HAVE** is everything you do want but have not been able to manifest, for example, a better job, more money, or a new house.

---

21 We are counting RELATE as its own area, although technically it is one form of DO.

<u>**DO = ACTIONS and BEHAVIORS**</u>: The concept of DO in the Causal Sequence includes all your actions, habits, customs, and behaviors. You have two basic areas of DO: people and things.

Your **RELATE** is your **DO with people**. Your RELATE includes your SAY, what and how you communicate with others. RELATE includes all your dealings with, treatment of, interactions with others. It includes how you respond, either wisely and serenely, or reactively with negative emotions, to their treatment of you.

Your **Negative RELATE** includes all your negative energy communications and conflictive relationship behaviors.

Your **DO with things** starts with how your perform your work or business activities. It also includes your driving ability, your ability to use a computer, hobbies, and anything else you DO in life.

Your **Negative DO** is everything that you DO and want to stop DOing, or know you should stop DOing, but you have not been able to stop that behavior. This can include bad habits, substance abuse, and addictions, as well as compulsions, aversions, and obsessions.

Your **Not-DO** is anything that you want to do or know that you should do, but you have not taken action to accomplish, not matter your justification for not acting. Common examples of Not DO include changing jobs or careers, moving to another city, getting married, or getting divorced.

- Examples of positive DO in life: keeping your word, being on time, listening attentively, working with quality, driving carefully, and working to the best of your ability.
- Examples of negative DO in life: criticizing, arguing, blaming, laziness, not communicating (the silent treatment), being stubborn, complaining, smoking, overeating, abusing drugs, arriving late, etc.

<u>**THINK = THOUGHT = MIND**</u>: Your THINK is everything that occurs or exists in your mind. There are two parts to this: 1- the thoughts, which are things, are thought-energy objects; and 2- the processes and activities of THINKing.

THINKing is the creation and manipulation of thought objects. Your THINKing processes and activities include: analyzing, comparing, deciding, imagining, remembering, memorizing, visualizing, creativity, design and creation, intuition, and planning. All your DO in the mind is considered THINK.

Thoughts: Your varieties of thought-energy creations, of mental realities, include ideas, concepts, desires, goals, plans, dreams, memories, knowledge, data, information, values, beliefs, dogmas, programs, paradigms, and visions, to name a few. Your THINK includes all the content of your subconscious and your unconscious.

Although we will not be exploring these concepts in this book: 1- There is no such thing as mind; and 2- what you call your mind is actually another universe, bigger than the physical one. That universe also contains the holographic thought patterns (beliefs are one form of these) that act as a projector lens to manifest your physical universe around you, the BEing. Really Big BEings such as Jesus and Buddha modified those patterns to create instant changes in the physical universe. As you apply the psycanics technology on this path of Return to the ONE, you will naturally and progressively recuperate that level of power. After all, you are God.

FEEL = EMOTION: Your FEEL includes all your feelings and emotions, both positive and negative. Your FEELings include: love, joy, enthusiasm, rejoicing, interest, delight, affection, attraction, aversion, anger, fear, anxiety, panic, phobia, worry, guilt, resentment, hate, sadness, sorrow, depression, grief, mourning, regret, apathy, and any other sentiment of any kind. As we will have several chapters on FEEL in this book, we shall say no more here.

BE = IDENTITIES: Your IDentities are your creations of self, of who you are, or who you are not. Most of them are declarations of "I AM," or "I AM NOT." Your creations of your Self are subtle energies, but they are the most powerful things in your life. They are your BE, the first element in your Causal Sequences, and therefore determine all the other aspects of your life. Understanding your BEing will also require several chapters.

Observations About The Causal Sequence

As shown in the diagram below, of the six arenas of life, only two are in the physical universe: DO with things, and HAVE. The other four are non-physical: BE, FEEL, THINK, and RELATE (the people half of DO) are all non-physical = spiritual energies.

Note that **the most important things in life are non-physical**. This includes who you are (BE), how you FEEL (both your painful emotions and your positive emotions), your experiences of love and happiness, the quality of your relationships, your knowledge, learning ability, intelligence, intuition, and creativity.

As we have seen, you have four levels of experience:

1. The **ONE = God = the Quantum Field** (currently counter-created and blocked).
2. Individual Self = psycan = Will and Consciousness or Essence.
3. Your Mental Universe, which consists of all your thought-energy realities.
4. The Physical Universe, by means of your body, and includes experience of the body.

The first three, Quantum, Self, and Mental are non-physical universes consisting of non-physical = spirit-ual energies. (Spirit-ual means of or relating to spirit, non-physical life energy entities such as yourself.) Only the lowest form of your experience is physical.

The non-physical energies of BE, FEEL, THINK, and RELATE are more powerful and more important than physical energies. Furthermore, the quantum energies of BEing and FEELing determine and control the psycanic energies (THINK, SAY, RELATE), and through them, the physical universe. You manifest what you want in the physical universe by forming psycanic energy (thought) patterns of what you want to attract.

BEing is the beginning of the Causal Sequence. Your BEing determines your human life. Your expansion of BEing is the path of Return to the ONE. It is all about BEing. To quote *CWG*:

> What your soul is seeking to BE is ME. It is a state of BEingness that your soul seeks, not a state of DOing or HAVEing. Your soul only cares about what you are BEing, not about what you DO or HAVE. Your body is always doing something. The question is: is it acting according to the desire of your soul, or in ignore-ance of it? You are not on this planet to produce anything with your body; you are here to produce with your soul. Focus on making a life, not a living.
>
> Your soul already is ME and knows it. It is seeking to experience that. DOing and HAVEing is a function of the body; BEing is a function of the soul. You can't produce the evolution of your soul, your Return to ME, by DOing, by the worldly activities of your body. (1-12-170)

You can best control and make your life by "making" your BEing. You BEing will then ex-press (push out) through your Causal Sequences to create your human life. We can show this with the following illustration in which the horizontal circle represent your human life in this plane of existence (the physical universe) and the vertical line represents your expansion of BEing back to BEing IT ALL again.

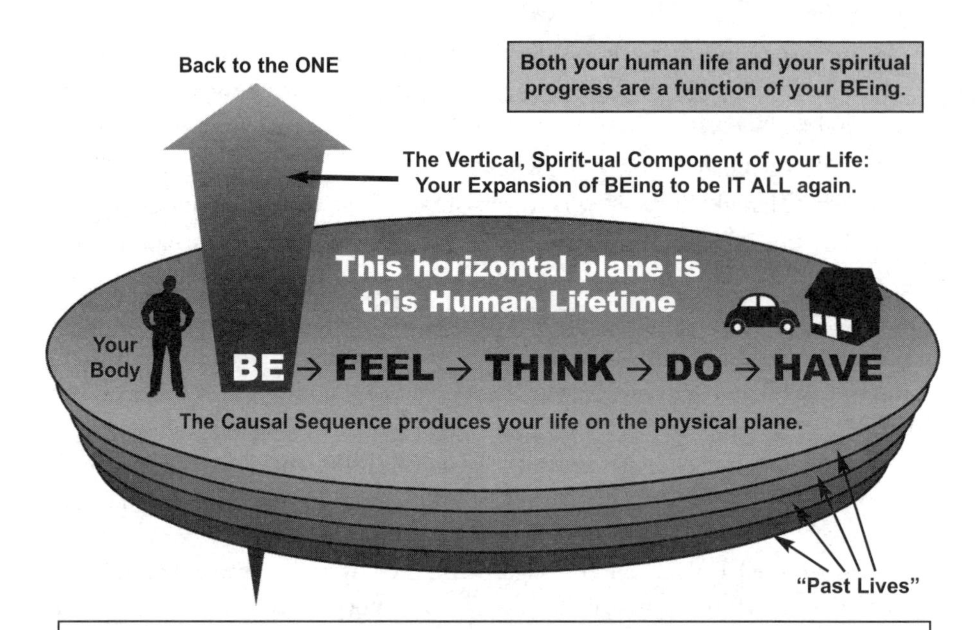

Illustration 8-1:
Each horizontal plane represents one lifetime on earth. Based on *CWG*, the average human has about 600+ past lives here. In each incarnation, you DO and HAVE on the horizontal plane of human life, and you make some progress on your journey back to the ONE, which is represented by your vertical process of expansion of your BEing through all your lifetimes here.

As the Causal Sequence indicates: BE→FEEL. Your BEing also determines your FEELing. Your FEELing is your experience of love and happiness. Here are some paraphrases of *CWG*:

> From the correct states of BEing, **(the Essence IDentities that we will define in another chapter)**, there will spring **a FEELing of LoveJoy and** a life so rich, so full, so magnificent, and so rewarding that worldly success will be of no concern.
>
> **At the same time,** worldly success automatically follows successful BEing—**if you so desire. That is the Causal Sequence in action: BE→FEEL→THINK→DO→HAVE. However,** to the degree that you are successful at BEing (ME), you will not be concerned about being worldly successful. Successful BEing is so joyous a FEELing that you will not much care about worldly success, **which after all, you only seek because you think it will bring you joy.**

In fact, you may find material success more a bother than a joy. Notice that all the Great Masters have shown indifference to success, fame, and fortune. Certainly, they would never waste their time and energy accumulating, caring for, and hoarding material things. To do so is to BEcome a servant to things, and this is a very low position for a Master of Life.

One of the traits of the 4th State of Consciousness[22] is an intense interest in working on self, coupled with a loss of interest in controlling life and in HAVEing things. In this state, you want to sit back and just enjoy the "movie" and whatever the next scene brings, knowing absolutely that what does occur is always perfect for you and the entire universe.

The Internal versus the External Quest

We are all seeking happiness: that is the Existential Imperative. As we shall prove later, the only true happiness that exists is the LOVEJOY of BEing God again. What the average person experiences as hir quest for happiness is really part of the Existential Imperative to Return to the ONE again.

- The Internal Quest is the focusing on and expanding our BE-FEEL in the Causal Sequence, working on our "vertical" journey HOME.
- The External Quest is all forms of THINKing and DOing to HAVE in the physical universe, all effort to find "fame and fortune," in the world (in the illusion that these will someday fill the void within and make us happy).

> There is only one reason to THINK, DO, or HAVE anything: as a direct statement of Who You Are **(BE)**.

Thus, a basic question of life is: **Where and how are you seeking happiness?** How are you obeying the Imperative? Are you seeking it within through developing your spirit-uality, through the Internal Quest for the Kingdom of Heaven[23] and the INFINITE LOVEJOY that that is? Or are you seeking it with-out in the accumulation of worldly success and material things, which is the External Quest?

These are questions you must ask yourself. And if you don't like the answer, begin to change course. We shall have much to say about the two Quests in a later chapter.

> Seek first the Kingdom of Heaven—**which is done by "working" on your BEing**—and all else shall be added unto you. (Jesus) Your life was never meant to be a struggle, and doesn't have to be one, now or ever. (3-11-184)

Summary

CWG makes very clear the supreme importance of BEing. This Power of your BEing is expressed by the Causal Sequence:

1- Your BE controls the rest of your life at the human level:
FEEL→THINK→DO→HAVE.

2- Spirit-ually, it is the evolution of your BEing that is the Purpose of Life and

---

[22] The 7 States of Consciousness most people go through on the way back are described in *The Psycanics of the Mind.* (These are different from the Ten Stages of Consciousness.)
[23] A reference to a famous statement of Jesus: "The Kingdom of Heaven is within."

the highway back to BEing the ONE again. Your objective is to wake up to the purpose of life and take charge of your evolution and accelerate it.

The Causal Sequence simply affirms the overwhelming importance of BEing. It shows how it both determines your "horizontal" results in this lifetime as you move through life (#1 above); and your "vertical" progress back to your Re-Integration with the ONE (#2 above).

So you can see that BE is the Name of the Game. It is the Kingdom of Heaven within. It is the path to BEcoming LOVE = GOD. It is the path to BEcoming happy and joyous, permanently. It is the starting point of all your Causal Sequences and is therefore the origin of BEcoming materially successful if you want that. Control your BE and you control both your life and your LIFE (remember that words in all capitals refer to God or to the elements of the Causal Sequence.)

The question now is: What is my BEing and how do I control it? How do I eliminate negative states of BEing and cause mySelf the positive ones? We shall give you an exact and very powerful technology of how to do this. We must start by distinguishing exactly what is your BEing, which is the subject of the next chapter.

> Note: The illustrations are designed so that you can post them around your residence to remind you of the concepts in this book.
>
> These illustrations
>
> a- are reproduced in this book, necessarily small, and in black and white
>
> b- are available for download and printing, in color, size 8.5" x 11", at www.psycanics.org; and
>
> c- can be ordered as color posters, 11" x 17" inches at www.psycanics.org.

Chapter 9

BE, BEing, and LIFE

You are not a physical being seeking spiritual experience; you are a spirit-ual BEing savoring a physical experience.

Quotes from *CWG*:

> You are not a physical BEing, but a BEing being physical. (3-19-335)
>
> Seek to determine Who You Want To BE. (1-1-20)
>
> The purpose of life is to constantly transform and evolve from Who You Are, to Who You Want to BE. Who you Want to BE is ME, God, the Supreme BEing, Who is BEing IT ALL. You are here to remember and re-create yourself as Who You Really Are. (1-1-21)

"To BE or not to BE, that is the question," Shakespeare's Hamlet stated.

However, he was wrong. That is not the question. You already BE, and you cannot not-BE—never, ever, absolutely impossible.

The true questions are:

- What is my BEing?
- What is it made of?
- How does it work?
- How do I control it?
- How do I eliminate negative states of BEing and cause mySelf the positive ones?
- How do I evolve my BEing? How do I Re-Integrate it to the ONE BEing?

In this chapter, we shall present the nature of your BEing. In this book, we shall give you an exact and very powerful technology of how to evolve your BEing and Return to BEing the ONE again.

We start by distinguishing exactly what is your BEing, or as it is often called, your spirit or soul. However, the word "spirit" has different denotations and even more connotations according to who is using the word, so we shall use it seldom. We will use the word "psycan" to mean the non-physical life-energy entity that is your fundamental nature. You are a psycan, an individualized "particle" of the ONE INFINITE LIFE ENERGY, of the GREAT UNIVERSAL SPIRIT, the SOUL of all that exists, the TAO, the QUANTUM FIELD, aka GOD.

Thus, our questions are: What is a psycan? What is it made of? What is its nature? Where does it come from?

A psycan is an individual unit of LIFE FORCE ENERGY. To understand our psycanic nature, which will help us to understand GOD, we must understand:

LIFE

LIFE

Another name for ME, for God, is LIFE.
I AM the INFINITE LIFE FORCE.
LIFE and God, we are the same thing.

In *CWG*, God states that SHE is LIFE. She mentions that atheists and agnostics can argue about whether God exists or not, but nobody can deny that the LIFE FORCE exists. We can see LIFE all around us and in us. We can see that the universe has a LIFE FORCE creating, running, and animating parts of it, and that that FORCE is infinitely greater, more intelligent, and more powerful than we are. We, as humans, do not even understand our own bodies, much less are be able to create them or maintain them.

Our question, then, is what exactly is LIFE? If God and LIFE are the same, then **understanding LIFE is a way to understand more about God—and therefore, more about ourselves, our origin and essence.**

But most importantly, understanding LIFE is absolutely essential, critical, to understanding the nature of our separation from God and how to Return. We are LIFE, and we need to know exactly what that entails, because what we want in life is more LIFE. **The search to BE evermore LIFE is another way to state the Existential Imperative.** What we are experiencing as human beings is a lot less of LIFE than the INFINITY of IT.

What is LIFE?

Let us begin by introducing the **Ectropy<>Entropy Polarity**.

Observing the universe, we can see that the universe, energy[24], tends to move in two opposing "directions." There is no exact word for this. The words "life" and "death" are included but not inclusive, so we will borrow and expand concepts taken from the science of thermodynamics. These are the concepts of "ectropy" and "entropy."

- Ectropy is the intelligent, causal, **organizing** force that combines materials and synergizes energy to create ever more powerful **systems**. It distinguishes matter and energy types, orders and organizes them, builds systems and grows things. It increases energy states; it heats things "up." We will call it the "up" force. LIFE is the ectropic force in the universe.
- Entropy is the "dumb" (not-intelligent), **decaying** force that tries to pull everything "down" to inert, homogenous matter (dust) and minimal energy

24 As matter and energy are the same thing (E=mc2), the word energy should be understood to include the special case of "rigid" pattern energy that is matter. In quantum physics, energy-matter itself is distortions of space-time, so that space-time, which springs out of the Quantum Field, is all that exists.

(cold). Entropy in living things is aging and **death**. As regards matter, it is randomness, homogeneity, and chaos. We will also call it the "down" force. Matter represents the entropic force in the universe.

LIFE = ectropy works to organize matter and energy into ever more complex, powerful, and "hot"[25] (energized) systems. Entropy or decay works to disrupt and "downgrade" energy systems into chaos, cold, and death. The following polarity table will help make this clear:

Table 9-1: The Ectropy<>Entropy Polarity

Ectropy = the Power-ful, Life Force, Spirit, Heat **Pulls things "up" into ever higher states of organization, energy, and power.**		
CONSCIOUSNESS and INTELLIGENCE includes perception, memory and retaining knowledge **Wise, Creative**	**CAUSE, Power, Control Creator**	**HIGHER VALUE** (eg. living things are more valuable than matter-ial ones)
Distinguishes the differences and properties of things and energies. Orders and organizes them according to their nature and capabilities. Plans and predicts.	Uses Power and Force to produce desired results. Changes and Transforms. Synergizes to create systems. Controls, Channels, Moves and Transports.	Increases the order, energy, and power of things and therefore increases the VALUE of things.
↕	↕	↕
Lacking intelligence. No perception, no awareness, no mind, no memory, no knowledge, no wisdom, not creative.	No Causal ability, no Power = EFFECT. Acted up, moved and controlled by external causes.	Decreases Value. Turns distinction into homogeneity; systems into disorder and chaos.
DUMB	**EFFECT**	**MINIMUM VALUE**
Entropy = the Decay and Death Force, Matter, Cold **Pulls things "down" into ever more homogenous and lower energy states.**		

Therefore, we can first define LIFE as the ectropic force in the universe. But let us not stop there.

LIFE from another Point of View

Let's go into the nature of Life deeper and from another angle. What are the characteristics and qualities of Life that permit it to be ectropic? What properties

[25] Heat is a measure of the velocity of movement.

are you referring to when you say something is alive? What are the differences between a rock and plant and animal and a human being, as each represents a different level of LIFE?

Let's make this question easy by just analyzing the two ends of the polarity Life<>Matter. You will be the pole of Life; a rock will be pole of Matter.

What are the differences between you and a rock? Before you read my list of characteristics, make your own list. Make a list of the differences, of the qualities that you have more of than a rock has.

Here is my list of some of the differences:

Awareness, perception, consciousness, mind, intelligence, knowledge, memory, creativity, will, decision, causal ability which includes the ability to change and move self, and the ability to change and move other things, the ability to create; the ability to decide value, to e-value-ate; the ability to love self and others, self-esteem, emotions; and the capacity to be happy and to suffer—to name a few.

Would you agree that a rock is not much good at any of that? Would you agree that these differences exist between you and a rock?

So there are notable differences between your BEing and the being of a rock. Those differences are LIFE, the energies and abilities of LIFE.

The Distilled ESSENCE of LIFE

That list contains an unwieldy number of characteristics, qualities, and abilities to have to enumerate every time we want to talk about LIFE. We need something simpler to work with. We can observe that many of these LIFE energies are similar or related. On close observation, we find we can classify and distill all of these properties into four basic groups.

1. All those properties related to consciousness, perception, knowing, memory, knowledge, intuition, creativity, etc.
2. All the characteristics related to Cause, to Power: decision, creation, change, movement, etc.
3. All things related to Value and the determination of Value.
4. All the energies that are FEELings: the emotions, love, happiness and pain[26]. Let us make this clearer by distributing the characteristics of LIFE into a table with four columns.

---

[26] In psycanics, the words "pain" and "suffering" always refer to emotional pain, as opposed to physical pain, unless physical is specified.

Table 9-2: The ONE LIFE FORCE consists of four basic elements:

CONSCIOUS-NESS	CAUSE	VALUE	FEELings positive and negative
Awareness	Will	Assign Relative Values	Positive FEELing
Perception	Word, Promise	Good<>Bad	Positive Emotions
Experience	Decide, Determine, Commit	Assign Value to Self; Self-Esteem	Happiness
Distinguish	Change, Move	Assign Value to Other	**Love**
Know	Persist, be Constant	Deserve<> Undeserving	↕
Memory, Knowledge	Design, Plan	Worthy<> Unworthy	**AntiLove**
Intelligence	Order	Less than<> More than	UPS: Unhappiness, Pain and Suffering
Intuition	Organize	Inferior<>Superior	Negative Emotions
Creativity	CREATE, Manifest	Should Be<> Should Not Be	Negative FEELing

We need a designator, a name, for each column; one word that will represent all the forms of energy in that column. We will use the following labels as the English words most representative of the overall concept of each column: **Wisdom**, **Power**, **Value**, and **LoveJoy**. (Psycanics proves that love and happiness are the same thing, thus the term: LoveJoy.)

To make this perfectly clear, we rewrite the LIFE ESSENCE table with the "bottom line" designator for each of the 4 groups of Life Energies:

Table 9-3

CONSCIOUS-NESS	CAUSE	VALUE	FEELings positive and negative
Awareness	Will	Assign Relative Values	Positive FEELing
Perception	Word, Promise	Good<>Bad	Positive Emotions
Experience	Decide, Determine, Commit	Assign Value to Self; Self-Esteem	Happiness
Distinguish	Change, Move	Assign Value to Other	**Love**
Know	Persist, be Constant	Deserve<> Undeserving	↕
Memory, Knowledge	Design, Plan	Worthy<> Unworthy	**AntiLove**
Intelligence	Order	Less than<> More than	UPS: Unhappiness, Pain and Suffering
Intuition	Organize	Inferior<>Superior	Negative Emotions
Creativity	CREATE, Manifest	Should Be<> Should Not Be	Negative FEELing
WISDOM	**POWER**	**VALUE**	**LOVEJOY**

The ESSENCE of LIFE: Four "Energies."

Thus, we can abbreviate LIFE[27] to **Wisdom**, **Power**, **Value**, and **LoveJoy**, abbreviated **WPVLJ**. These are the basic characteristics of LIFE = GOD = SPIRIT. They are the basic characteristics of you as a psycan, an individualized unit of GOD-LIFE-ENERGY. They are the most powerful energies on the planet and control your life and that of every human being.

27 LIFE also has the qualities of SPace, Unity (Interrelatedness), Synergy, and others, but we can ignore these for our present purposes.

They are also the key to your Return to the ONE. The ONE is the INFINITY of these qualities: WPVLJ (Wisdom, Power, Value, LoveJoy). **Your return to the ONE is an expansion of your present level of BEing to BE more and evermore of these LIFE energies, until you are ALL of them again.** As you already are ALL of LIFE, that expansion is achieved primarily by discreating the counter-creation mass that is suppressing your experience of BEing these energies. The REALITY of Who You Are already exists; it is the experience of IT that you are missing.

We will also call these four elements the ESSENCE energies of LIFE, or the ESSENCE of BEing, or just ESSENCE, capitalized, when we are talking of them at the level of God. We will capitalize only the first letter, "Essence" when we are speaking of them at the human level.

We will also call them the "Nuclear Energies of BEing," and the "Quantum Field Properties" or "Quantum Properties." All these terms refer to the same thing: WPVLJ (Wisdom, Power, Value, LoveJoy). The word we use depends on the point of view we wish to evoke in that sentence.

We will use any and all of the following terms to refer to these characteristics of LIFE:

- LIFE Energy, or the LIFE Energies.
- Essence of LIFE, Essence of BEing, or the Essence of Spirit.
- The Essence Energies, or just Essence.
- The Quantum Field Energies, or Quantum Energies, or Quantum Properties.
- The Nuclear Energies of BEing.
- Wisdom, Power, Value, LoveJoy.
- WPVLJ, or WPV→LJ, or W→P→V→LJ.

We will call them "energies," although this is not necessarily correct: at least the Quantum Property of Cause-Will-Power is not an energy. However, we have no other term, unless you prefer to call them "Quantum Field Static Substance."

You have seen how we arrived at the understanding of the LIFE FORCE, of God, through observation and reason (i.e. science). However, God confirms our conclusions in *CWG*:

> The Divine Force in the universe is made up of these: gentle wisdom, creative energy **(power)**, pure love. (4-10-228)

GOD = LIFE = SPIRIT = PSYCAN consists of these four energies: WPVLJ. God has included Value within LoveJoy; and they are, in fact, very related and very similar. However, the additional distinction of Value from LoveJoy is useful, as we shall see.

Every "BEing," whether a plant, animal, or human, is a Life entity and so has some degree of these four Life Energies.

Furthermore, everything that exists is made of the ONE LIFE ENERGY; there is nothing else to make anything of. Therefore, even a rock is made of LIFE ENERGY, although we can detect this scientifically only at the atomic and quantum levels. To our everyday senses, a rock does not demonstrate much LIFE.

LIFE ESSENCE = SPIRIT = PSYCAN is really ONE energy—everything is ONE energy—but manifests as four qualities or rays. You may have seen white light going through a prism. (If not, search online on wikipedia.org for "Triangular prism optics.") One ray of white light enters, and four colors of light, like a rainbow, exit the prism.

Illustration 9-1

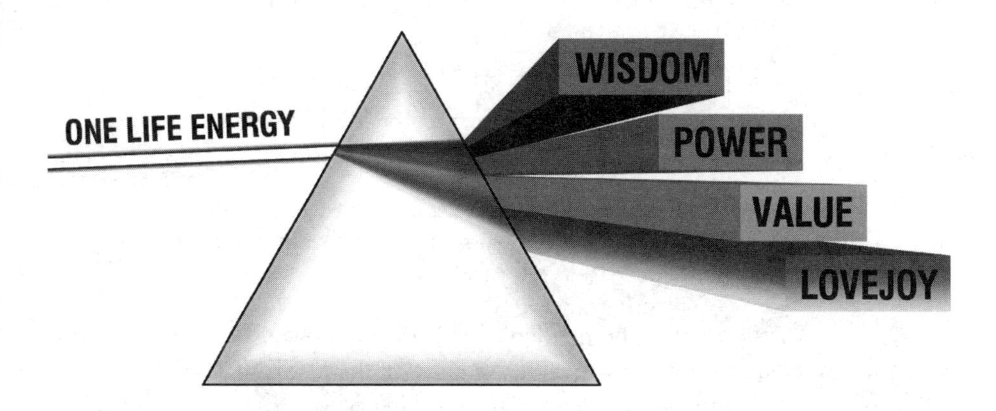

The analogy of white light and a prism represents very well the LIFE ENERGY: ONE and Many at the same time.

Your basic BEing, what we call the psycan, is made of these four Life Essence Energies. They are subtle energies that you are BE-FEELing all the time, but you may not recognize them for what they are. They stand "behind" all your emotions, positive and negative. In fact, your emotions are the fourth Essence Energy, LoveJoy, as we shall prove.

The Essence Energies are the most powerful energies on the planet because they are the object of the Existential Imperative. Everybody on the planet is trying to BE and FEEL more of these energies at every moment, with every effort and behavior. The External Quest for more ESSENCE is the force that has and continues to shape all personal lives and history itself.

To BE-FEEL* the positive polarities of the four ESSENCE energies, and to avoid BE-FEELing their negative polarities, is the ultimate motivation of all human behavior. That Is The EXISTENTIAL IMPERATIVE and the highest purpose of your existence.

*Explanation of the concept of BE-FEEL. These are the first two elements of the Causal Sequence. BE and FEEL are related. They are the complete experience of something. To feel something, you must be it. For example: to feel happy, you must be happy. If you are being happy, you will feel happy. If you are being powerful, you will feel powerful. To fully feel and therefore to full know anything, you must integrate with it and be it. This is what you are trying to do as regards God: re-integrate and BE HIM in order to fully FEEL HIM. The maximum FEELing = experience of God is to BE HIM perfectly.

The Existential Imperative is to BE-FEEL evermore of the ESSENCE energies. This is the only happiness that exists. Correctly understood and followed, the Existential Imperative is your beacon HOME. On the other hand, if you do not understand Essence, life will be a field of pain and suffering, the situation of about 80% of humanity.

You have counter-created[28] your ESSENCE to suppress your BE-FEEL of the LIFE = God that you are, down to the level of a human being. Your counter-creations form what we call your God Essence Suppressor Mass.

The discreation of your counter-creations to your LIFE energies = your God Suppressor Mass frees your BEing and re-integrates you to BEing the ONE again.

We will always capitalize the first letter of Wisdom, Power, Value and LoveJoy when we are talking about these qualities as part of the ESSENCE of BEing. We will capitalize the entire word when we are speaking of one of these as a property of the INFINITE = God: e.g. WISDOM, POWER, VALUE, LOVEJOY.

In the illustrations and graphics of psycanics, we represent the human Essence energies in two ways. 1- As an atom, as represented in physics. 2- As concentric circles. (See Illustration 9-2 on the opposite page.)

So, how does it feel to be made of WPVLJ?

How much WPVLJ are you BE-FEELing right now?

Compare that to how much WPVLJ God is BE-FEELing, and you see the distance you have to grow.

But, remember, it is not a creation of WPVLJ that you need. You already are the ONE INFINITE LIFE ESSENCE ENERGY. You only need to discreate a

---

28 Counter-create means to create one creation to counter-act, block, or suppress another one; usually as opposed to discreating the one you want to block or cancel. However, you cannot discreate God or BEing God, so you can only counter-create that REALITY to create the appearance (illusion) and experience of not BEing IT.

shell, a mass, of realities and energies that create for you the experience that you are not IT ALL. We call that shell your God Suppressor Mass or your Essence Suppressor Mass (ESM).

Illustration 9-2: Symbols for the human Essence energies.
(Download the full color illustration from www.psycanics.org.)

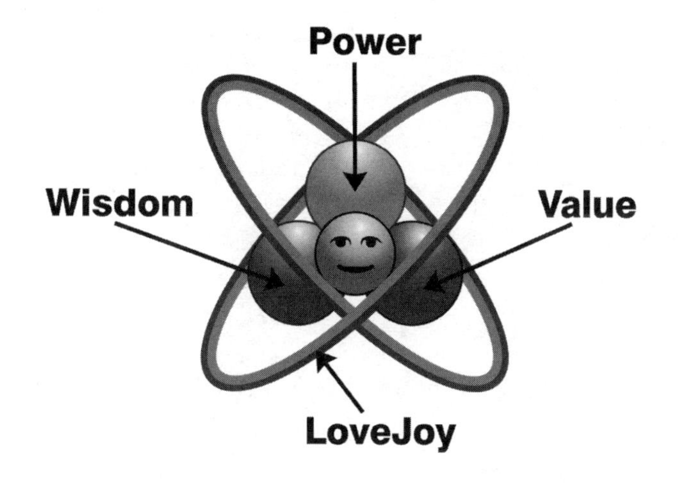

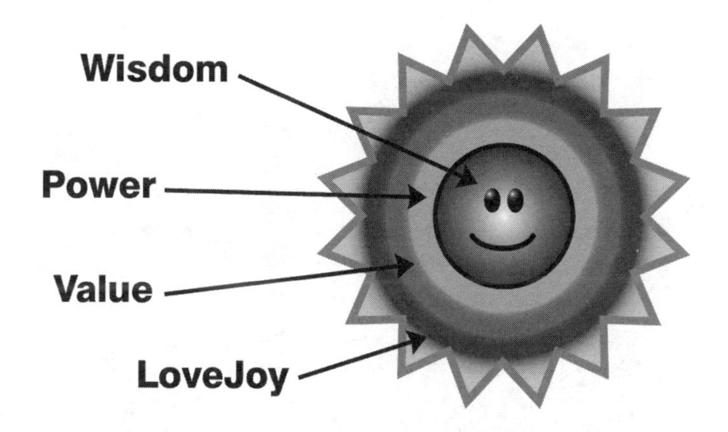

Chapter 10

IDentities

Through your IDentities You Counter-Create your ESSENCE and Transform Yourself From God into Human.

Quotes from *CWG*:

> These are the only questions I have ever had: Who am I? And Who Do I now choose to BE?
>
> You have come to this world to Know Who You Are—and to create Who You Wish to BE. This is the purpose of life. Life is an ongoing, never ending process of re-creation. Keep recreating yourself in the image of your next highest idea of yourself. **That next highest idea will be more of ME, of Divinity, of LIFE, of WPVLJ.** (2-1-19)

To understand and take control of your BEing and to "evolve" it back to the ONE, you must understand IDentities. You are a psycan, an individualized "particle" of the ONE LIFE ENERGY CREATOR BEING, of the QUANTUM FIELD, of the TAO. As a psycan, you are ESSENCE = WPVLJ, and that, in the beginning, is all that you are: a localized concentration of the Quantum Field.

However, because of the Laws of Polarity, you cannot experience What You Are until you experience that you are not THAT. Thus, you must "descend" out of INFINITE ESSENCE into Not-ESSENCE (AntiEssence), so that you can return to ESSENCE and now experience and appreciate IT. We are moving into the explanation of HOW you do this.

In this chapter, we are going to **distinguish between the psycan and the BEing**: they are not the same thing, and **the difference is the key to your Return to the ONE**. You-psycan are the ONE. Your current BEingness (states of BEing) are (deliberately so) less than THAT and are stopping you from experiencing THAT.

One of the four ESSENCE energies is Power. The highest aspect of Power is creation. Ergo, "I AM CREATOR" is a primary IDentity: You are Psycan, The Creator. That is a basic IDentity.

What are you creating? Well, entire universes: your mental universe and your physical universe. However, y**our primary creation is the creation of yourSelf**, of your BEing. You do this by creating identities which are statements of what you are or are not.

Definition of **Identity**:

> What something is. The unique characteristics and qualities of a reality (mass of energy) that makes it a unique individuality and distinguishes it from all other forms of energy. A table is an identity; a house is an identity.
>
> Identities are: **creations** of self; they are **self-determinations** or declarations, they are **realities** about self; they then become **beliefs**, stable data, about self.
>
> Identities are self-creations of I AM<>I AM NOT; with a few taking the form of verbs such as I CAN<>I CAN'T. (This is really I AM ABLE<>I AM UNABLE.)

Most identities are statements of "I AM (whatever)" or "I AM NOT (whatever)."

Most identities take the form of I AM<>I AM NOT polarities. For example:

- I AM STRONG <> I AM WEAK.
- I AM INTELLIGENT <> I AM STUPID.
- I AM ABLE <> I AM UNABLE.
- I AM A SUCCESS <> I AM A FAILURE.
- I AM WORTHY <> I AM UNWORTHY.
- I AM THE EQUAL OF<> I AM LESS THAN.
- I AM GOOD <> I AM BAD.

Some identities are expressed as verbs, for example:

- I CAN (whatever) <> I CAN'T (whatever);
- I DESERVE (whatever) <> I DON'T DESERVE (whatever).

However, note that these verb forms are just other forms of I AM:

I CAN = I AM ABLE; I DESERVE = I AM DESERVING.

An identity is any thing or quality you are BEing, or deny BEing, at any given moment. An identity is anything you create (by simple *fiat*[29]) and thereby BEcome = are (or the opposite: are not). An identity is what you decide You BE, at least for the moment and in that situation.

There are many kinds of identities; many nouns and adjectives can be identities. For example: I AM: a father, a doctor, a salesman, hot, cold, wet, a daughter, tall, a graduate, a trainee: all these are technically identities. Apart from adjectives

29 *Fiat* is Latin for a command decision.

that are not important as identities, there are two major kinds of substantive identities: Essence and human identities or roles.

1. **Essence IDentities**. These are the identities that refer to the fundamental qualities of **spirit**, of the LIFE FORCE, of the SUPREME BEING. These are your Nuclear Energies of BEing that we have already seen: Wisdom, Power, and Value.

   Your Essence IDentities are the most powerful and most important things in your existence. They are the major part of the BE in the Causal Sequence that determines your life. They are polarities.

2. Human identities = **roles**. These are the parts that we play in our human dramas. There are three basic kinds:
   i. Family roles: ones that you are born or marry into: daughter, cousin, father, mother, spouse, etc.
   ii. Social roles: ones you acquire by association or positions in society: friend, leader, teacher, student, preacher, etc.
   iii. Commercial roles: electrician, architect, doctor, plumber, mechanic, salesperson, politician, boss, etc.

In this book, and essential for your return to the ONE, we are interested only in your Essence IDentities Polarities[30], not your human ones. We will capitalize the first two letters in "IDentity" to indicate we are speaking of the Essence IDentities+/-.

Notice that an IDentity can be created or implied by either a positive or a negative statement, and can be stated in many ways. **The exact words are not important; it is the concept of BEing some way, or not-BEing that characteristic, that determines the IDentity.** Examples:

I AM NOT WEAK = I AM STRONG <> I AM NOT STRONG = I AM WEAK.

I AM UNABLE = I AM NOT ABLE = I AM WITHOUT SUFFICIENT POWER = I AM NOT CAPABLE.

How Your IDentities Work to Form your BEing

The cosmos is God manifesting HERSELF in all HER infinite possibilities of BEing in order explore, know, and play—that is, EXPERIENCE— HERSELF in all those permutations of BEing. The purpose of the Creation is Experience. You are one of those experiences, having many experiences, **especially of all your forms of Self (IDentities)**, while experiencing many other of those infinite possibilities of experiences.

30 The human identities become important when you begin to create your human life with the Causal Sequence. We do not have space for how to do this in this book.

A psycan is ESSENCE and is not a creation. It is part of IT which is before all else, the QUANTUM FIELD. As a psycan, your prime creation is of yourSelf, your BEing.

You are the God of your BEing. You-the-psycan modify yourSelf = psycan = ESSENCE = God to BE other "things"—including to BE AntiGod (for polarity purposes). You modify and add to (or subtract from) your fundamental nature of Life Essence = psycan by creating your IDentities. You form your BEing by creating IDentities.

You-psycan are the CREATOR LIFE ESSENCE ENERGY = WPVLJ. This is your basic spirit or soul. You then modify you-psycan by creating, and thereby "including" or "excluding" within you qualities and characteristics. Each creation = quality is an IDentity, an I AM or I AM NOT.

You create an IDentity simply be declaring and choosing it to be so, i.e. by *fiat*. Nothing more is necessary. (Abbreviations for IDentity and IDentities are ID and IDs.)

Your BEing consists of you, the psycan, modified by all your IDentities.

As a Creator, you-psycan modify yourSelf by creating IDentities. Your IDentities are your creations (determinations, declarations, thoughts, and beliefs) of Self, of what you are and what you are not. Each IDentity affirms or denies a particular quality or thing that you are BEing (or are not BEing). Thus, through IDentities do you determine, expand, modify yourSelf and so create viewpoints and experiences. It is how you BEcome "things."

Your BEing consists of all that you are, well, BEing—which is also defined, delimited, by all that you are not-BEing. This is Polarity at work. For example, if you are strong, then you are not weak. If you are weak, then you are not strong. All the ESSENCE IDentities are polarities, a fact of extreme importance as we shall see. What you are BEing and not-BEing in the area of ESSENCE = God is defined, counter-created, by your AntiEssence IDentities. The sum total of your AntiEssence IDentities is what makes up your God Suppressor Mass.

You-psycan "molded" by your IDentities is your BEing.

Psycan + IDs+/- → BEing

You-the-psycan are currently an individualized particle of the ONE LIFE ESSENCE ENERGY, of WPVLJ. But you want to BE much more: in fact, you want to BE IT ALL again: this is the **Existential Imperative**.

What stops you from BEing IT ALL right now, are your creations that you are less than IT ALL, your creations of AntiEssence, AntiGod. These are creations are negative IDentities. **Thus, a path back to the ONE is to remove, discreate, your AntiEssence IDentities that are limiting your BEing ESSENCE, BEing IT ALL again.**

Let us attempt to show the relationship of psycan to BEing with the following illustrations.

Illustration 10-1: Condition #1: The psycan without IDentities.

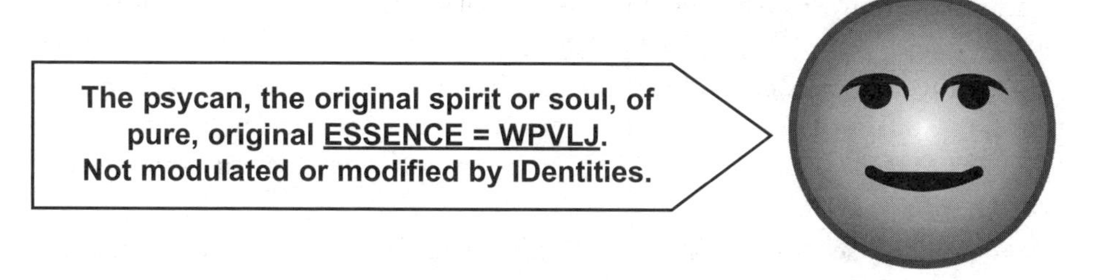

Illustration 10-2: Condition #2: BEing: the psycan modified by IDentities.

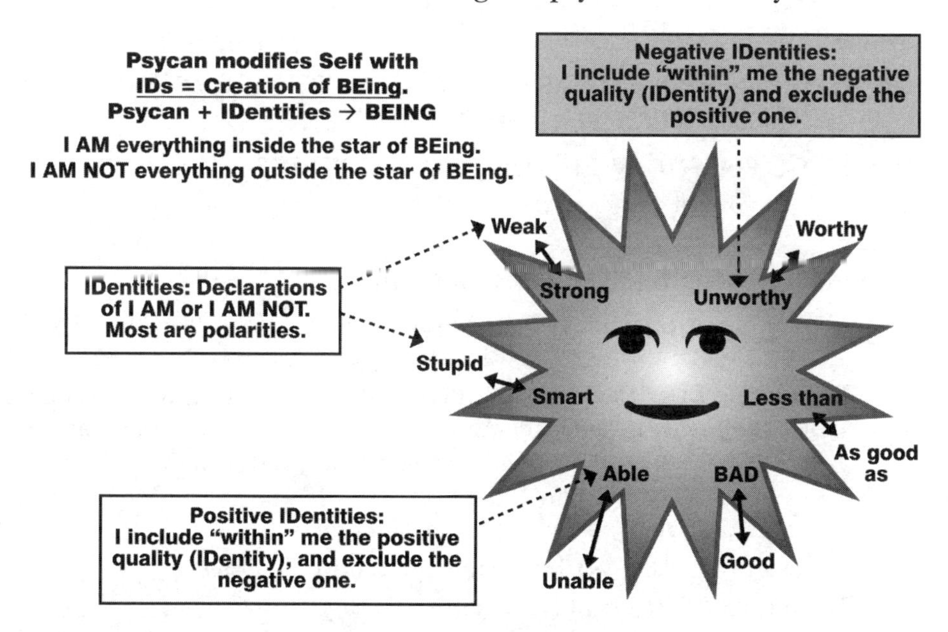

In the illustration above, notice how a quality of BEing is included within the psycan (the star) and its polar opposite excluded, thus forming out of your psycan what you are and what you are not, which is your BEing.

IDentities that the BEing is being by placing them within the star in the diagram above:

- Positives: I AM STRONG, I AM SMART, I AM ABLE.
- Negatives: I AM UNWORTHY, I AM LESS THAN (others); I AM BAD.

The ESSENCE IDentities, WPVLJ, are polarities, e.g. Strong<>Weak. Remember that WPVLJ must be polarities for the positive side of ESSENCE to exist—and that positive side of ESSENCE is the experience you and God are seeking.

Thus, for ESSENCE to be experiential-able, AntiEssence = AntiWisdom, AntiPower, AntiValue, and AntiLove must also exist. Humanity is God descended into AntiEssence. Much of human experience, of all BE-FEEL, is of AntiEssence. For example: every negative emotion WITHOUT EXCEPTION signals an activation of an AntiEssence IDentity.

As we shall see, the AntiEssence IDentities are very subtle energies, counter-creations of ESSENCE. They are not mere thoughts or beliefs, but masses of energy; they are realities (but not Truth). However, to talk about them, we must label and state them so that they become thoughts. In working with them, you need to remember that you need the experience, the energy or them, NOT THE THOUGHT or belief.

DO NOT CONFUSE THE PSYCANIC ANTIESSENCE IDENTITIES WITH THOUGHTS OR BELIEFS.

IF YOU DO SO, YOU WILL NOT BE ABLE TO DISCREATE THEM!

Nor can you counter-create them with Affirmations.

Positive and Negative IDs: PIRs and NIRs

- Those Essence IDentities that affirm your spiritual ESSENCE of WPVLJ are called **PIRs: Positive IDentity Realities**.

  Definition: PIR: Positive IDentity Reality*: Any identity = creation about self = declaration of I AM or I CAN that affirms your spiritual Essence of Wisdom, Power, and therefore Value, and therefore determine your experience of (self) Love and Joy.

- Those Essence IDentities that deny or suppress your basic psycanic nature of WPVLJ are called **NIRs: Negative IDentity Realities**.

  Definition: NIR: Negative IDentity Reality*: Any identity = creation about self = belief that denies or suppresses your spiritual essence of WPVLJ. Any reality about self that denies or suppresses Wisdom, Power, Value, or Love and therefore triggers Self-AntiLove = negative emotions = suffering.

*"Reality" is an important and sophisticated concept in psycanics. For now, consider it any thought, idea or belief that a person can perceive; anything that causes experience. All physical objects, e.g. stars, bodies, trees and rocks, etc., are physical realities. All psycanic objects, all thoughts and emotions, and all IDentities, are psycanic realities.

The following table presents some of the more common ways we state our Essence+/- IDentities:

Table 10-1: Essence<>AntiEssence IDentities Statements

Positive ESSENCE IDentities (PIRs)			
	WISDOM	**POWER**	**VALUE**
POSITIVE: Those identities that affirm the quality or ability.	I learn easily. I know. I am smart. I am intelligent. I am creative. I am intuitive. I am imaginative. I am wise.	I can. I am able. I am capable. I am strong. I am a success. I am powerful. I am useful. I perform well.	I am good. I am worthy. I deserve. I am useful. I am good enough. I am excellent. I am superb.
Negative or AntiEssence IDentities (NIRs)			
	ANTIWISDOM	**ANTIPOWER**	**ANTIVALUE**
NEGATIVE: Those identities that deny the quality or ability.	I don't know. I am ignorant. I am uneducated. I am slow. I am stupid. I can't think (well). I am not creative.	I can't. I am powerless. I am unable. I am incapable. I am weak. I am a failure. I don't function well.	I am bad. I am less than. I am nothing. I am worthless. I don't deserve. I am not good enough. Nobody loves me.

Your Essence IDentities+/-, PIRs and NIRs are those which affirm or deny your spiritual ESSENCE of Wisdom, Power and Value, and thereby trigger your (self) Love-ability = Joy = Happiness.

The exact words used to express an IDentity are not critical: it is the way of BEing, the concept of self, and internal experience of that concept, that are important. Thus, AntiPower can be expressed as: I AM UNABLE, I AM INCAPABLE, I CAN'T, I DON'T HAVE THE ABILITY, I DON'T HAVE THE POWER, I AM WEAK, I AM POWERLESS, I AM A WIMP, I AM A FAILURE, and many other ways.

The words are just a label for a creation = IDentity = experience of No-Power, of not being able to do (whatever). The creation is beyond and above words; words are only symbolic representations of realities and experience, not the reality or experience itself.

As a human being, you are existing in a thick shell of AntiEssence IDentities = creations = realities = mass. You try to block your BE-FEEL of your NIRs to avoid experiencing them. It is both that block and the NIRs that prevent you from perceiving your ESSENCE, from BEing God again experientially.

As a human being, you are God who has counter-created HIS ESSENCE with NIRs and now has HIMSELF "buried" in a big mass of the AntiEssence IDentities. This massive shell is your **God or Essence Suppressor Mass**. You are resisting and blocking experiencing BEing AntiEssence, and that resistance causes its persistence and keeps you stuck in "human being."

That which separates you from experiencing yourSelf as INFINITE ESSENCE = WPVLJ is your God or Essence Suppressor Mass. The nucleus of this mass is your AntiEssence IDentities, your Negative Nuclear IDentities called NIRs.

An easy and fast way back to the ONE is to discreate your AntiEssence.

The Existential Imperative is your overwhelming motivation and impulse to avoid or end your experience of AntiEssence and BEcome ESSENCE again. **However, the path is not one of resistance and avoidance, but of opening up, going through, completely BE-FEELing and thereby discreating your NIR Masses.**

There is nothing you can do in life as powerful as discreating your NIR Masses and thereby freeing your soul to BE ESSENCE, the ONE, again. The Return to the ONE is not just a process of re-creating yourSelf in ever higher visions of Self as God. Although it is useful to see the process as re-creation, you don't really need to create anything. You ALREADY are God, the ONE. What you need to do is discreate the illusion, the Essence Suppressor Mass, that counter-creates you as not-God and "shapes" you to BE a human being.

The Human Side of your Existence

Your NIRs are also the negative BEs that cause all your negative experience in all the other areas of the Causal Sequence (FEEL→THINK→DO→HAVE). **Your NIRs are also the cause of all your problems, conflicts, pain, and suffering in your human life.**

Your Essence IDs = BE initiate all your Causal Sequences of FEEL, THINK, DO and HAVE. Your IDs cause your emotions, as we will see in the chapter on FEEL. Your IDs color your thinking and determine the manner of your actions = DO, and your DO determines your results = HAVE in life. In fact, all your efforts in the world to DO to HAVE are attempts to control your BE-FEEL externally. This is the External Quest and it ends in failure every time.

A PIR initiates a positive Causal Sequence:

BE = IDentity of WPV = [**W**: I KNOW → **P**: I CAN → **V**: I AM WORTHY]
→ FEEL = emotion+ = self-Love = Joy; that produces . . .
→ Expansive, positive THINKing that produces . . .
→ Loving and effective ACTIONS that produce . . .
→ Good RESULTS = positive HAVE.

A NIR initiates a negative Causal Sequence:

BE = ID = [**W**: I DON'T KNOW → **P**: I AM UNABLE → **V**: I AM USELESS]
→ FEEL = negative emotion = self-AntiLove = UPS; that produces . . .
→ Negative, angry or fearful THINKing that produces . . .
→ Negative (angry, fearful) DO = ACTIONS that produces . . .
→ Poor RESULTS = negative HAVE.

God is very clear about stating WHAT you need to do: see Who You Are, then evolve to Who You Want to BE, which is finally to BE INFINITE ESSENCE, the ONE, again. The cycle of spiritual advancement is to become change from Who You Are, and then to change to Who You Now Wish To Be.

The problem is that when Who You Are is AntiEssence—and EVERY NEGATIVE EMOTION INDICATES ANTIESSENCE—you resist BEing that IDentity. That Resistance Causes Persistence of the AntiEssence = AntiGod IDentity, and of the entire Essence Suppressor Mass.

You want to Not-BE that way (NIR), but you must not-BE it by discreating the ID (done by integrating with and loving it), not by resisting it. Unless you know how to discreate your current negative states of BEing, your process of evolution back to the ONE tends to "hang up," because you resist experiencing the negative polarities of the Essence IDentities, your NIRs.

The Laws are: Experience Experienced Discreates. Resistance Causes Persistence. You discreate your AntiEssence by experiencing and "love-ing out" the negative IDentities, using the procedure (technology) we will see later. Discreation of present reality (the NIR) clears your SPace of BEing for your next creation of Who You Now Decide To Be.

> When you are through experiencing that polarity of US, you will seek to experience that Which You Are: ME = **God**. (Paraphrased from 3-12-207)

Ego: One of the great errors of some people, some "spiritual" schools, and of most religions, is to fall into the trap of Ego. Ego is all forms and efforts of trying to glorify our individuality, trying to make Self more powerful than, better than, superior to others; not by working on Self to "polish" who we are, but by making others less, depreciating them.

Ego tries to create Self as Greater and Greater and the GREATEST—that is the Existential Imperative. But Ego tries to do so through separation and distinction from others, instead of Integration to the GREAT SELF ALL THAT IS. It is a path of division, separation, and polarization[31].

The underlying cause of Ego is the AntiEssence IDentities. Ego is an erroneous attempt to compensate, to counter-create, our AntiEssence IDentities, our feelings of not knowing, not being powerful, and not being value-able and love-able. Ego is an effort to "steal" Essence or BEing from others by making them *seem* less (wise, powerful, value-able), so that we seem to be more of these Nuclear Energies of BEing and therefore Greater (superior and better) than others.

The true path to spirituality and to true Power is a path of discreating your AntiEssence IDentities, as opposed to trying to counter-create them, compensate them or steal Essence from others. Counter-creating them requires a lot of effort and is a resistance that persists the negative IDentities. By discreating AntiEssence, you do not have to resist or control your Ego; you "retire" it for lack of work.

True spirituality and true access (return to) Wisdom, Power, and Love is an expansion of identity to BE IT ALL again; not a greater withdrawal into "re-enforcing" individuality and polarizing it against others to appear greater.

> Separation from God and from each other is the cause of all your dysfunction and suffering. (3-1-43)
>
> **What separates you from God and others are your AntiEssence IDentities. Discreate them! The technology exists now to do so quickly and easily.**

---

31 Polarization: To divide and separate into us<>them and therefore better<>worse, greater<>less than, right<>wrong, good<>bad, thereby seeming to justify exclusion and AntiLove attacks. This planet is highly polarized into races, religions, countries, political parties, etc.

Chapter 11

Introduction to Power

Of the three energies of ESSENCE, the Will = Power = Creator ability is the most, well, powerful. After all, in life, if you can always do everything you want and get everything you want, you would have no problems, right? In this chapter, we introduce knowledge that is essential to your Power in life, to BEing God again. It is a transition from Effect to Cause that every human being must make sooner or later.

The three fundamental polarities of LIFE are SPace, Cause, and Energy, which correspond to Wisdom, Power and Love. We can call them the "Trinity."

Illustration 11-1: The Three Fundamental Factors of Existence

Cause, SPace and Energy = Power, Wisdom, and Love

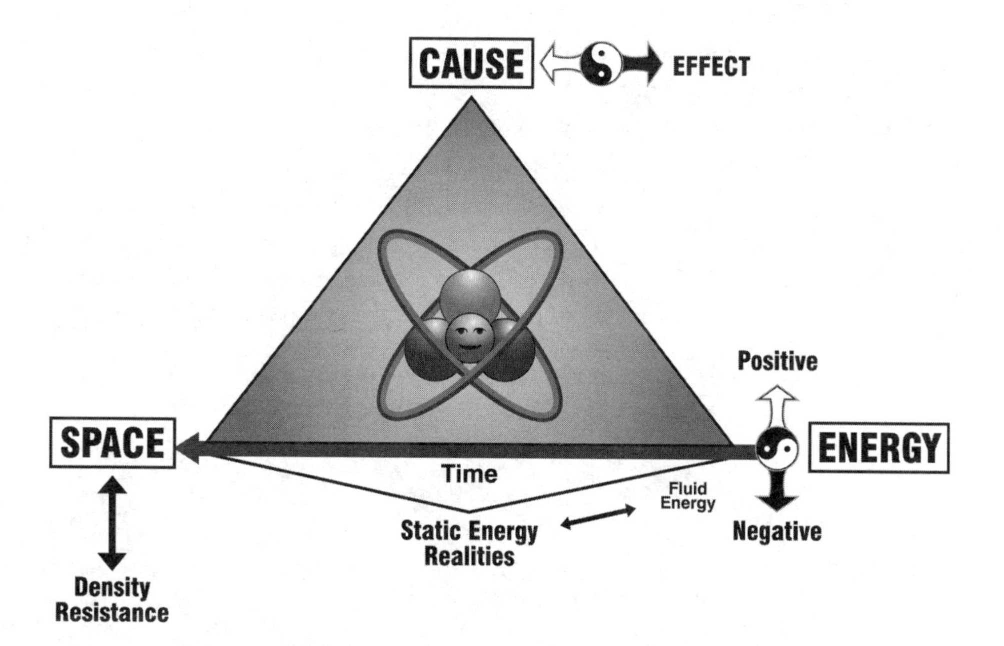

Definition of **Power**:

1- The ability to produce the desired result. (The highest level of Power is Creation, followed by Manifestation.)

2- The ability to hold a position in spite of all opposition.

Personal Power: The ability of a person to manifest hir desires and achieve hir goals.

AntiPower is the opposite polarity of Power. It is the inability to Cause = produce the results that you desire. Forms of AntiPower include BE-FEELing that you are UNABLE, INCOMPETENT, WEAK, TRAPPED, DEFICIENT, or a FAILURE. The AntiPower IDentities are almost always accompanied by the AntiPower emotions: Anger, fear, sadness and depression are all sure symptoms of AntiPower.

To have Power in life, you must be operating in a condition of Cause. Most people are not. They are in Effect, also known as Victim.

Definition of **Cause**:

The "northern" pole of the Cause<>Effect Polarity. The action of bringing into existence any thing; to create, to originate anything. The highest level of Cause is creation. To affect or effect anything. To produce an effect of any kind. The action of starting, producing, controlling, changing, moving, anything.

That which causes anything. The agent of action that affects or effects anything. That which originates, initiates, creates, manifests, decides, determines, acts, forms, produces, moves, controls, or changes anything.

Cause includes the concepts of Will, Power, Strength, Force, Decision, Determination, Commitment, Persistence, Creator, Creation, and Manifestation. You are studying psycanics to acquire these qualities.

Definition of **Effect**:

The "southern" pole of the Cause<>Effect polarity. That which is caused, produced, acted upon, affected, or controlled by an agent of Cause, and usually having little influence over that Cause. The result produced by a Cause: e.g. "The effect of a bomb is destruction."

At every moment, in every situation,
you are either Cause or you are Effect.

Illustration 11-2: CAUSE<>EFFECT Polarity Spectrum

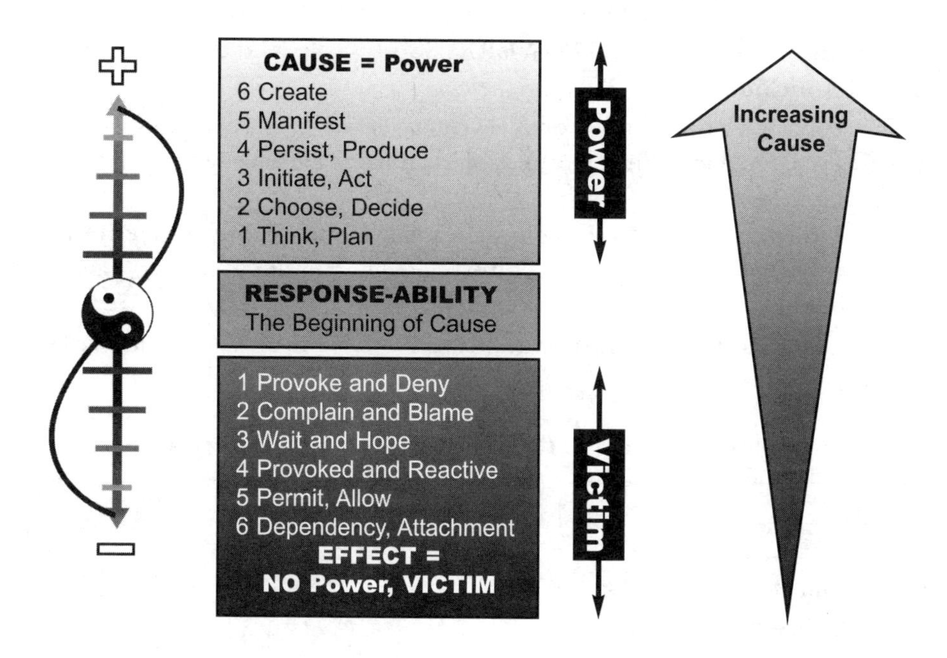

When you do not understand the Cause<>Effect Polarity, **you will unconsciously turn your Power against yourself**. You will tend to create yourself as a Power-less Victim and so block your getting what you want while creating lots of things you do not want. (Does that sound familiar?)

The BEing condition of Cause is the place of Power. The highest act of Cause is Creation. The Victim is a person who turns hir creator power against hirself by creating Self as powerless. AntiPower is the condition of the Victim.

Definition of **Victim**:

> Any person who perceives hirself to be at the unpleasant Effect of external Causes over which s/he has little power. Someone who believes that s/he is being unjustly Caused to do "bad" things by others without her participation or contribution to the situation. A Victim believes that s/he is acted upon, "pushed around" in life by external agents of Cause, and feels that s/he can't do much about it: No Personal Power.

A Victim is a person who denies Response-ability for negative events, assigning the Cause/Response-ability to external agents (who are automatically judged as BAD for causing the victim BAD things).

The Victim complains of negative events and <u>blames = assigns Cause</u> for the BAD events to external factors while believing that s/he had little to do with causing those events (is innocent), and has little Cause = Power to stop, change or avoid such events in the future.

Victim is a condition of POWERLESSNESS. It is, therefore, a condition of AntiGod.

The condition of Victim is extremely common among human beings. Almost all humans are in Victim in some areas of their lives, and most are in Victim for everything in their lives.

To Return to BEing God again, you must climb up out of Victim into Cause = Power. God is powerful; AntiGod is the opposite. Which way are you headed in life?

The following tables compare the BEing's condition of Cause with that of Victim. As you read them, notice which one best describes you.

Tables 11-1 and 11-2: CAUSE vs. VICTIM Comparison

CAUSE = POWER
Strong
Dynamic, Highly active
Creative and Creator
Proactive
Optimist
Shows Initiative
Response-able, Reliable
Highly Productive
Independent and Interdependent
Forthright, Honest
Seeks excellence
Leader
POWERFUL

EFFECT = VICTIM
Weak
Does the minimum necessary
Conformist
Reactive
Pessimist
Procrastinator, Waits to be told
Irresponsible, Unreliable
Dependent
Beaten, Defeated
Manipulative, Deceitful
Complainer and Blamer
Accepts mediocrity
Not even a good follower
POWERLESS

The Creation of the Victim

- What creates you as a Victim is, of course, you. You are the sole and soul Creator in your life, experience and universes.
- You create yourSelf as a Victim by denying being the Creator, the Cause of anything in your life.
- You deny Cause by assigning Response-ability to external agents as the Cause of anything that shows up in your life. It is your Denial of Response-ability (DOR) that creates you as a Victim.

To see this, just make a list of all the "bad" things in your life, physical and non-physical, and ask yourself, "Who is responsable for this being in my life?" If you answer anything but "me," you are denying Response-ability and are in Victim.

Denial of Response-ability (DOR)

DOR (Denial of Responsability) has ALL of these Effects:

- Creates the Victim
- Kills Love
- Kills Self-esteem
- Kills Power
- Kills Initiative
- Kills Proactivity
- Kills Creativity
- Reduces Productivity
- Damages Relationships
- Produces Pain and Kills Happiness
- Is Insanity: you are always response-able. DOR does not stop your Response-ability; it only blinds you to it.

Where you deny Response-ability, you deny your Cause, and Cause is Power. When you deny Response-ability, you blind yourself to how you could exercise Cause to produce the results you want. Thus DOR blinds and blocks your creativity, your proactivity and initiative, and thereby reduces your power and productivity.

Believe that you are not response-able for your emotions and you will have no power over your emotions. And if you are not response-able for your emotions, then who is?—others, right? You make them responsable for how you FEEL; and then try to control them so that they act to make you FEEL good = be happy. This destroys relationships.

Believe that you are not response-able for your relationships or any particular problem in them, and you will have no power to improve your relationships. If you are not able to respond = act in your relationships, then who shall? Do you put the entire burden, all the Response-ability for the problems on the other? How well has that worked?

Declare that you are not the Cause, not responsable for your poor financial situation, and you will have no power to change it, and little creativity about how to do so.

To identify the responsable person in any situation, ask: "Who is going to suffer the effects? Who has any possibility of action to escape, avoid or remedy those effects?" If either answer is "me" and you have any possibility of action whatsoever; you are response-able.

Law: **The Negation of Response-ability Kills Power**
and all aspects of Power such as proactivity, creativity,
initiative, and productivity; and creates Victim.

POWER BEGINS WITH RESPONSE-ABILITY.

Fortunately, it is easy to get out of Victim and back into Cause. All you have to do is declare that you are Response-able for everything in your life.

Response-ability

Response-ability is the midpoint and the transition point between Cause and Effect (see Illustration 11-2: the Spectrum of Cause–Effect). Response-ability is the beginning of Cause, and Denial of Response-ability is the entry point into Victim.

Responsability in psycanics is spelled with an "a" to remind you that its concept in psycanics is far larger than what you will find in a dictionary. In psycanic science, it is:

1. The point of change between Effect and Cause on the Cause–Effect Spectrum.
2. Consciousness of Cause; acknowledgement and awareness of being Cause, and of being able to act.
3. Any condition of **possibility of action**. You have Response-ability in any situation where you will experience the (negative) effects of decisions and actions, whether yours or others; and you have a possibility of action to avoid or remedy those effects.
4. The relationship of a Creator to hir creations. The relationship of a person to hir actions and the results and consequences of those actions. You are Response-able for everything that you create and do, and the consequences of those actions. Wisdom is the ability to foresee those consequences.
5. **Love: Response-ability in action is Love.** Response-ability is to be Cause, to act. To act positively is to Love. To refuse to be Cause, to care for something, is to refuse to Love. To deny Response-ability for anything is to deny Love.
6. The ability to **respond under self-control** and **reason** as opposed to out-of-control emotional reaction. The ability to act from logical decision as opposed to emotional reactivity and resistance to the event.
7. The ability to vary your actions and responses until you achieve the desired result (as opposed to repeating over and over the same emotional or behavioral reaction, such as an ingrained habit or behavioral rut).
8. The duty or assignment to care for (be Cause) someone or something, as in "I am response-able for the maintenance of my vehicle."

9. A counterpart of Freedom. Freedom requires Response-ability; and Response-ability does not exist without Freedom.
10. Accountability: Response-ability includes Accountability. The duty under Love and Justice to respond for our negative actions by making amends and restoring any damages we have caused. Without Accountability, Response-ability does not exist.

What Response-ability is not:

- Response-ability is not blame. Blame implies BAD; Response-ability is free of all invalidation, of all judgment. It is value-free; it is always in a condition of SPace. It only acknowledges Cause.
- Response-ability is not guilt, which is how you will feel when you blame yourself. Again, Response-ability is free of judgment of BAD.
- Response-ability is not obligation and is not burden. It can seem like these when it is distorted by other factors such as Antipower IDentities or imposition by external agents.
- Complaining is usually a denial of Response-ability. If you can do something about the situation, then you are response-able and should act. Even communicating to someone who can act is action. If you cannot do anything about the situation then either leave it, or grin and bear it with a positive attitude. Either way you choose and are response-able for the effects on you of your decisions.

Response-ability IS GOOD!

In psycanics, Response-ability is something very positive. In fact, it is one of the "sacred" concepts. It is always capitalized. To play the game of life, you must be Cause. To win, you must be a Power-ful player. To BE God again, you must BE Powerful.

Cause = Power has a switch that turns it on and off. The on position of that switch is Response-ability. The off position is DOR: Denial of Response-ability. You have that switch.

CAUSE, WISDOM, POWER, LOVE and HAPPINESS
all start with Response-ability.

Response-ability is the ESSENCE IDentity "I AM Cause,"
which is the start of "I AM POWERful,"
which is a prerequisite to BEing God again.

It is to stop assigning Cause outside of myself
and declare it within me.

Response-ability is to recognize that:
"If it's to be, it's up to me."

Chapter 12

The Existential Imperative

FEEL in the Causal Sequence

Quote from *CWG*:

> By your own **(mistaken)** thoughts about love do you damn yourself never to experience it purely, and so to never know ME as I really am. Until you do. (1-1-18)

We now come to:

- The second element of the Causal Sequence: FEEL, which is a polarity.
- The fourth of the four Nuclear Energies of ESSENCE = BEing: Love+/-, which is a polarity.
- The nature of the Happiness<>UPS (Unhappiness, Pain and Suffering) Polarity.
- The nature of the emotions, also a polarity.

All these are the same thing, the same energy! They are all the same polarity. In other books, I show in great detail that the Happiness<>UPS Polarity, the Love<>AntiLove Polarity, and the Emotions Polarity are all the same energy. (I will summarize that information in this chapter.)

You are God, made of the same ENERGY. God is LOVE. You are made of Love. Love is the fourth energy of the four ESSENCE energies (WPVLJ). And it is FEEL in the Causal Sequence. Love is the only happiness that exists.

Love is a polarity: remember that it must be a polarity for the experience of Love to exist. Therefore, there is positive love (PosLove) and there is negative love or AntiLove. Love is the only Happiness that exists, and AntiLove is the only Unhappiness, Pain and Suffering that exists. Your experience of the Love Polarity energy is your emotions+/-, which are the only Happiness<>UPS that exists. IT IS ALL THE SAME ENERGY.

We shall now add "Emo" to LoveJoy and call this energy **EmoLoveJoy** to remind us that Emotions, Love and Happiness (Joy) are different aspects of the same energy. EmoLoveJoy is the fourth element of ESSENCE, WPVLJ. ESSENCE is Wisdom, Power, Value and LoveJoy (LJ). EmoLoveJoy (ELJ) is the Love Energy Polarity, the fourth nuclear energy of BEing.

EmoLoveJoy is and must be a Polarity Spectrum.
EmoLoveJoy is your FEEL in the Causal Sequence.

The Causal Sequence, if you remember is BE-FEEL→THINK→DO→HAVE. Notice that the BE-FEEL is often written, not with an arrow like the others, but with a dash. That is because BE and FEEL are fundamentally the same thing: ESSENCE. The Essence IDentities, BE, are WPV = Wisdom, Power, Value. FEEL is Love which is also Joy (the Happiness Polarity), which is also the Emotions.

Illustration 12-1: Emotions, Love and Happiness (Joy) are the same energy

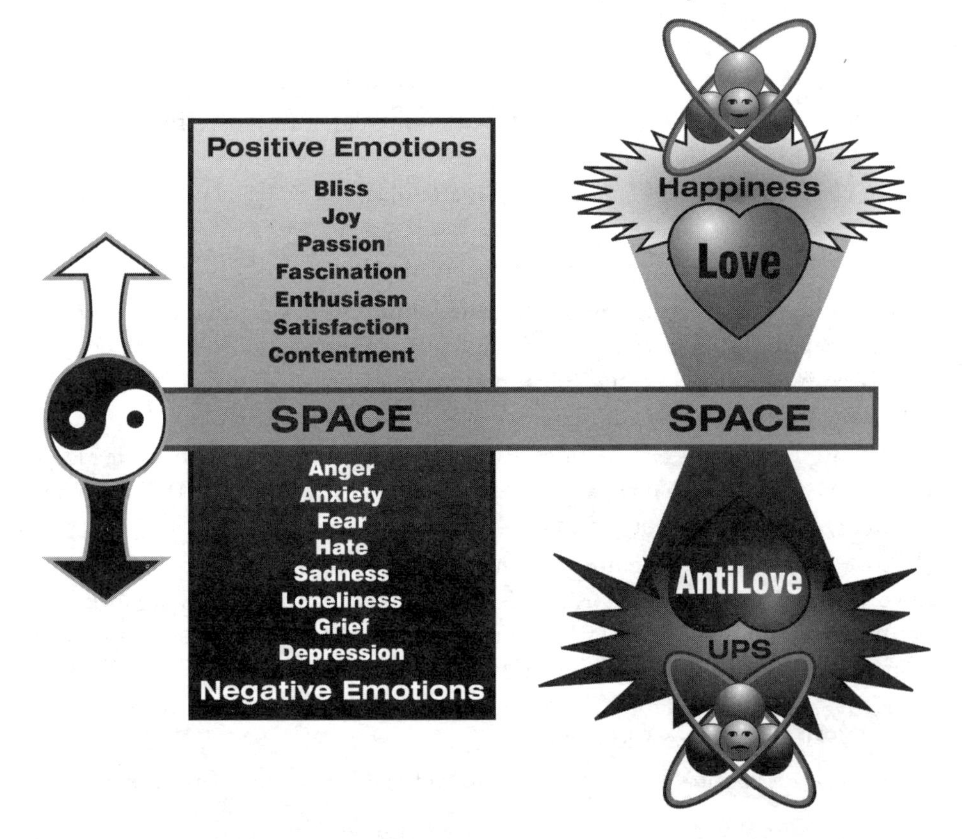

Summary of How Emotions, Love, and Happiness are All the Same Energy

- The Ultimate Motivation of all human behavior is Happiness.
- Happiness<>UPS (pain) is a polarity spectrum, ranging from depression to ecstasy, from maximum of one to the maximum of the other. One side cannot exist without the other.
- Happiness+/- is how you FEEL in relation to an event, never the events in themselves. For any given event, people will have totally different emotional experiences. Same event "causing" different emotions is absolute proof that events are never the cause of human emotions; and therefore, externals (events, people, things, situations, etc.) are never of the Cause of Emotions+/- = Happiness+/-.
- When we analyze Happiness and Unhappiness (UPS), we find that they are purely FEELing. They are how you FEEL and nothing more.
- When we analyze FEELing, we find that it is purely emotional. When we analyze Happiness+/-, we find that it is purely emotional.

Thus, we can see clearly that Happiness<>UPS is the Emotional Energy Polarity. The emotions are an energy polarity that runs from the deepest negative emotions, despair, depression, apathy; up to the highest joy, bliss, ecstasy. The positive emotions are the only happiness that exists; the negative emotions are the only UPS (pain) that exists.

- Ergo: Emotions+/- = Happiness+/-. These are the same energy, same polarity.
- When we analyze the properties of Love, we find that the emotions are the energies within us that are Love+/-. **Love and the Emotions have exactly the same properties.**

We show this in the tables that follow by examining the "internal" and the "external" characteristics of both Love and Emotions.

- Internally, Love is a FEELing+/- (FEEL in the Causal Sequence).
- Externally, Love+/- is the energy and actions (DO in the Causal Sequence) that you give to others and the world.

Table 12-1: Love+/- includes the characteristics of:

Characteristic of FEEL or DO	**Characteristics of Positive Love**	**Characteristics of Negative Love = AntiLove**
FEELing Happiness<>UPS	Positive Love is Positive FEELing. Positive FEELing is Happiness. The +Emotions are +FEEL = Happiness.	Antilove as Negative FEELing. Negative FEELing is UPS (pain). The neg. Emotions are neg. FEEL = UPS.
Motivation	The emotions are motive energy+/- that impulse and move you to:	
Movement	Move towards, approach.	Move away from, avoid; separate.
Distance	Reduce distance between lover and beloved: draw near, be closer.	Increase distance between one and that which is AntiLoved. Get away from, send away.
SPace	Give SPace to BE, and want to be in the same SPace with.	Deny SPace to (reject), and not be in the same SPace with.
Integration	Join, Unite with, be ONE.	Not be connected with; attack to disintegrate and destroy.
Experience	You try to have more experience of what you love.	You try to have less experience of what you AntiLove.
Energy	You give positive energy (attention, aid, support, money) to what you love.	You give no energy or negative energy to what you AntiLove to harm, damage, punish or destroy it.
Increase<>Decrease	You try to increase so that more more exists of what you love (e.g. grow your children or your business).	You try to decrease, reduce, have less exist, or destroy (no existence) of what you AntiLove.

In the following table, note how the emotions+/- are internally the FEELing of Love<> AntiLove = Happiness<>Pain; and externally motivate positive or negative behaviors (DO) that are Love+/- expressed out to the world. The emotions as FEELings are degrees of internal Love+/- energy. It is all one and the same energy polarity spectrum.

Every aspect of Love+/- as both FEEL and DO in the Causal Sequence is powered by emotional energy. The emotions are the internal, FEELing aspect of Love that then motivates and impulses the external aspects of Love as DO towards others.

Table 12-2: Internal FEEling of Love+/- motivates external DO+/-

POSITIVE POLARITY			
Love+/- as DO and Energy	**Love as SPace / Distance**	**Emotions+/- = Love as FEEL**	**FEEL as Happiness<> UPS**
Die for Total commitment of full positive energy Grow, Increase Support, Aid Contribute to, Help Participate with Interest Give Positive Energy	Total ONEness Union Integration with Seeking to experience more and more of the beloved. Approach, Draw Nearer Acceptance	Bliss, Joy Passion Enthusiasm Delight Affection Interest Satisfaction Contentment	Increasing Positive Experience = Increasing Happiness
NEGATIVE POLARITY			
AntiLove	**AntiLove**	**Negative Emotions**	**Unhappiness, Pain**
Give Negative Energy Hinder, Obstruct Attack to reduce, minimize, lessen Use negative energy to harm, damage, punish Attack with neg. energy to Destroy	Resistance Aversion Rejection = Denial of personal SPace Avoidance Separation, Divorce Maximum Distance = Minimum Experience Effort to Destroy = Denial of SPace to BE at all	Hostility Anger, Rage Regret, Guilt Resentment Hate Anxiety, Worry Fear, Terror, Panic Sadness, Loneliness Sorrow Grief, Mourning Depression	Increasing neg. experience = increasing Unhappiness, Pain, Suffering

Love+/- = Emotion+/- = Happiness<>Pain
It's all the same thing.

The Fourth Energy of Essence = Being: WPV→ELJ

Many people think that Love is just one narrow band of FEELing = emotions, that of strong affection. This is totally erroneous: Love is ALL the emotions: they are exactly the same energy polarity spectrum.

The person who does not understand that Emotions+/-, Love+/-, and Happiness+/- are all the same thing, understands none of these and is unlikely to be able to produce much of the positive side of these in hir life.

Your EmoLoveJoy energy is actually part of what you are, part of your spiritual Being, of your soul. EmoLoveJoy is one of the four basic kinds of energy of which you are formed, it is the fourth energy of your ESSENCE.

This brings us to the question of what CAUSES our FEELings = emotions = Love+/-. Most people think external events cause their emotions; and that other people provoke their Love (attraction) or AntiLove (dislike, aversion). This is totally false and a dangerous hallucination.

The following table is the same one we saw in the chapter on IDentities, but now we add to it a fourth column, the Fourth Nuclear Energy of EmoLoveJoy. The polarity of the fourth column, Love (ELJ), is the result of the polarity of your WPV IDs in the previous columns. According to whether your Nuclear IDentity of the moment is positive or negative, Essence or AntiEssence, you love or AntiLove yourSelf. In other words: WPV+/- → ELJ+/-

When you are in PIRs, you naturally love yourSelf. That is the only happiness that exists.

When you are in NIRs, you naturally AntiLove yourSelf. That is the only UPS that exists.

As PIRs are Positive ESSENCE = God; and NIRs are Negative ESSENCE = AntiGod, we can restate the above:

Your EmoLoveJoy energy is modulated to the different emotions as your natural and automatic response to Who You are BEing in the first three energies of ESSENCE: Wisdom, Power and Value. WPV causes ELJ (WPV+/- → ELJ+/-). This is shown in the table by the arrows from the first three columns of WPV to the resulting fourth column of ELJ.

Table 12-3: Essence<>AntiEssence IDentities Cause EmoLoveJoy+/-

Positive Essence IDentities (PIRs) → Self-Love = Positive Emotion = Happiness These IDentities are the GOD in you.			
WISDOM	**POWER**	**VALUE**	**LOVE (ELJ)**
I learn easily. I know. I am smart. I am intelligent. I am creative. I am intuitive. I am imaginative. I am wise.	I can. I am able. I am capable. I am strong. I am a success. I am powerful. I am useful. I perform well.	I am good. I am worthy. I deserve. I am useful. I am good enough. I am excellent. I am superb.	Ecstasy Joy Passion Enthusiasm Delight Satisfaction Contentment
Negative or AntiEssence IDentities (NIRs) → Self-AntiLove = Neg. Emotion = UPS. **Here you are BEing ANTIGOD, the opposite polarity of GOD.** **This is the "normal" state of the human psycan.**			
ANTIWISDOM	**ANTIPOWER**	**ANTIVALUE**	**ANTILOVE**
I don't know. I am ignorant. I am uneducated. I am slow. I am stupid. I can't think (well). I am not creative.	I can't. I am powerless. I am unable. I am incapable. I am weak. I am a failure. I don't function well.	I am bad. I am less than. I am nothing. I am worthless. I don't deserve. I am not good enough. Nobody loves me.	Anger Resentment Hate Anxiety, Fear Sadness Sorrow, Grief Depression, Apathy

(Arrows labelled "CAUSES" point from each column to the next: WISDOM → POWER → VALUE → LOVE, and ANTIWISDOM → ANTIPOWER → ANTIVALUE → ANTILOVE.)

What causes your emotions is YOU!—Who You Are BEing: God or AntiGod.
Your emotions are not only Love, they are Self-Love.

They are part of What You Are, one of the four Nuclear Energies of ESSENCE = GOD. They are, and must be, a polarity—you can't have positive without negative. They change polarity according to the polarity of your other GOD-ESSENCE IDentities of Wisdom, Power, and Value. Thus, WPV→ELJ.

When you are affirming ESSENCE by BEing PIRs, you are BEing God. Therefore, you are naturally LOVE and you naturally love yourSelf with ELJ+. BEing God, as much God as you can BE, is the ONLY Happiness that exists; that is "heaven."

When you are stuck in your AntiEssence IDentities = NIRs, you are BEing AntiGod (the opposite polarity of GOD-ESSENCE). You are therefore also AntiLove; you naturally AntiLove yourSelf with negative EmoLoveJoy. That negative ELJ is the ONLY UPS (Pain) that exists; that is "hell."

This is also clearly shown in the Causal Sequence. BE→FEEL: BE+/- causes your FEEL+/-, which is Love+/-: Love for Self! Your BEing consists of your Essence or Nuclear Energies of WPV: Wisdom, Power, and Value. The polarity of these determine the polarity of your emotions, which are how you FEEL about yourself according to your WPV IDentity +/- of the moment. You are always BEing these IDentities in some degree and polarity. They are the God<>AntiGod Polarity of YOU.

BE Causes FEEL: your FEEL is caused by your BE.

For those of you who are mathematically inclined, these equations may help make this clear:

BE → FEEL (Causal Sequence)

IDs → Emotions (Causal Sequence)

BE = WPV → FEEL = ELJ (Love for Self+/-)

IDentities WPV → Emotions+/- = Love for Self

WPV → ELJ

WPV- = NIRs = Negative BE → Negative FEEL = Self-AntiLove = Neg. Emotions = UPS

WPV+ = PIRs = Positive BE → Positive FEEL = Self-Love = Pos. Emotions = Happiness

I am now going to state all of this in other ways to make sure it is perfectly clear, because this is the key to life, love, happiness and your Return to God:

You Love yourSelf (generate positive emotions = happiness)
when you are in positive Essence IDentities.

When you are in a positive IDentity of Wisdom, or Power or Value, you will love yourSelf = experience positive emotion = FEEL happy. You are, in effect, **experiencing and celebrating the ESSENCE, the God in you. This love for Self as ESSENCE and as the fourth energy of that ESSENCE is the only happiness that exists.**

You AntiLove yourSelf (generate negative emotions = pain)
when you are in negative Essence IDentities.

When you are in the negative polarity of an Essence IDentity, you will AntiLove yourself = experience negative emotion = pain = unhappiness. You are, in effect, **resisting and lamenting the AntiGod you are. This AntiLove for Self as AntiEssence and as the fourth energy of AntiEssence is the only suffering and unhappiness that exists.**

Please review the following statements to make sure you are understanding all this:

Your Nuclear IDentities determine the 4th Nuclear Energy of BEing which is Self-Love+/- = Emotions+/- = FEEL in the Causal Sequence.

The polarity of your EmoLoveJoy corresponds to the polarity of your Wisdom, Power and Value IDentities.

Your Emotions+/- are how you FEEL about YOURSELF—always; *never about external events.*

Your emotions are how you FEEL about yourself according to the ESSENCE IDentity that you are assuming in relation to any event of your life.

Your emotions = Love+/- = Happy<>UPS are NEVER caused by events, but by the Essence IDentity, WPV, that you are activating to handle that event.

Your emotions are your Love or AntiLove (ELJ+/-) for yourSelf, according to the Essence Identity WPV+/- that you are activating in relation to events.

The only Happiness<>Pain that exists is Self-Love+/-. Your emotions+/- are the ONLY happiness or UPS that exist.

The ONLY Happiness that exists is your Self-Love. The ONLY UPS (Pain) that exists is your Self AntiLove.

Self-Love is the ONLY Happiness that exists. Self-AntiLove is the ONLY UPS (Pain) that exists.

Your emotions are your Love or AntiLove for yourSelf, according to the Essence IDentity Polarity you are adopting in relation to the events of your life.

Underneath every negative emotion, there is ALWAYS a Negative Nuclear IDentity.

Your negative feelings always arise out of an unhealed part of you. (2-1-17)

Behind every negative emotion = self-AntiLove, there is always a Negative Nuclear IDentity. Behind every experience of self-AntiLove there is your creation of AntiGod, of not-BEing God. This is what you must heal, and you do so by loving it to discreate it.

Whenever you are FEELing negative emotions, you are experiencing a "leakage" of your Essence Suppressor Mass into your consciousness = experience = FEEL.

Instead of ignoring or suppressing that experience with substance or activities, we want to find and discreate the underlying NIR. That discreates that "piece" of your AntiEssence Shell and moves you that much closer to BEing ESSENCE = GOD again.

The purpose of life is to constantly transform yourSelf from Who You Are to Who You Want to BE. The ultimate "Who You Want to BE" is God. **Your negative emotions are invaluable signposts in this journey.** As the 4th Nuclear Energy (ELJ), that is the result of the other three nuclear energies (WPV), they show you directly where you are BEing AntiEssence, AntiGod (negative WPV). Thus, **they show you where you most need to "heal" your BEing to move to BE more God.**

You heal your BEing by penetrating the negative emotion to find the NIR and discreating it with CDT.

Your AntiEssence IDs (neg. WPV) are the ONLY Cause of all your self-AntiLove = UPS. Discreate the activated AntiEssence BE = ID, and the negative FEEL = neg emo = neg EmoloveJoy = UPS will disappear. This not only moves you that much closer to God, but it also changes your Causal Sequences of BE→FEEL→THINK→RELATE/DO→HAVE at the human level. Thus, this is the secret of life for both your "vertical" progress back to the ONE, and your "horizontal" control of your life on the physical plane.

BE-FEEL Is Really One Phenomenon

There are two ways to see that BE and FEEL are really two aspects of one thing: one is theoretical, the other practical.

1. Theoretical: You are really made of just one LIFE ESSENCE ENERGY. (Remember the prism that splits the ONE WHITE LIGHT of BEING into the four Nuclear Energies of WPVLJ). WPV is your BE = IDs, and LJ is your FEEL = emotions. WPVLJ is one energy, the ESSENCE OF BEING or LIFE ENERGY, and therefore so is BE-FEEL ONE energy.
2. Practical: There is no way to separate your FEEL from your BE. BE is always followed by a FEEL, and a FEEL always results from a change in BE. Your IDentities = BE trigger your emotions = FEEL. Your emotions+/- are ALWAYS an automatic love energy reaction to Who You Are; they are always EmoLoveJoy+/- about self. They always occur together, like an electron always has a negative charge; and a proton always has a positive charge: it is the nature of the thing.

We list BE and FEEL as two separate elements in the Causal Sequence, but they are really one phenomenon: Essence of BEing.

Ergo: we will often use "BE-FEEL" together as one word, one concept.

An Ophidian Example

A simple example will help make all this clear. Imagine that a snake appears in a crowded room. What will be the reactions of the people?

We will have reactions all along the entire Emotional Energy Spectrum, from panic, fear, loathing, running away, or attacking to kill (AntiLove reactions); all the way up to interest, enthusiasm, joy and passion; and approaching to care for and protect the snake, a Love+ response. (On Discovery Channel, Animal Planet, and NatGeo, you have seen people that *rough it* for days in enthusiasm to find and love snakes with joy.)

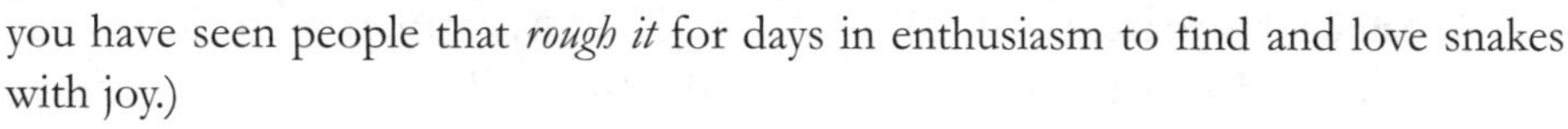

Let's reduce the responses to just the two basic poles of Love<>Antilove.

1. **AntiLove:** negative, internal FEELings of fear, loathing, panic or hate; motivating external AntiLove DO of fleeing or attacking (to harm or kill). (FEEL→DO)
2. **Love+:** positive internal FEELings of interest, enthusiasm, passion, joy; motivating external positive Love DO of approaching, experiencing, touching, uniting, and caring for.

We have the same external event, our snake; and two—not just different *but opposite*—experiences of FEEL→DO for that same trigger event.

The inconsistency of different Effects to the same "Cause" (the snake as the trigger) proves the absence of a Cause–Effect relation between the external event and internal experience. We have inconsistency here in that the same trigger "causes" two totally different "effects" = experiences. Ergo, there is no Cause–Effect relation.

Whenever the stimulus (trigger, "Cause") is held constant and the experience (Effect) varies, then the Cause of that variance cannot be the unvarying trigger, and must be within that which is varying: the people. There is no other possibility for the variations.

We can run this proof on anything in the universe, and we will always find that for any given trigger, human reactions (FEEL→THINK→DO) vary. This is proof that nothing external EVER causes psycanic experiences.

What causes the totally different experiences of FEEL = ELJ is the BE = IDs of WPV that the two people are assuming in relation to the snake.

1. The first person activates a BE = IDentities of AntiWisdom and AntiPower: "I DO NOT KNOW how to handle this; I CANNOT handle this snake; I AM UNABLE (to prevail against the snake); I AM

INCAPABLE; I AM LESS POWERFUL than the snake; therefore, **it has the power** to harm me; **it is more powerful than I**, and I CAN'T STOP or prevent it from prevailing against me."

Note the AntiWisdom and the AntiPower IDentities above. In those AntiEssence IDentities, the person automatically generates AntiLove for Self in the frequencies = "flavors" of (any combination of) fear, anger, revulsion, hate, etc. Hir AntiLove FEEL of fear then motivates hir AntiLove DO of attack to kill or running away. (Remember that increasing distance and separation—not to mention attack to kill—are AntiLove behaviors.)

2. The second person activates positive BE = IDentities of **Wisdom** and **Power**. "I KNOW about Copperheads (or whatever the snake is). I CAN handle this snake. I AM CAPABLE. I AM POWERFUL in relation to this animal." In those positive Essence IDentities, the person automatically generates love for Self in the flavors of interest, excitement, enthusiasm, and joy. Hir positive FEEL then motivates hir Love-ing DO of approaching, protecting and caring for the snake.

Note how it is not the snake event that causes the EmoLoveJoy+/- (it is the same event for both), **but rather Who the person "BE" (is) in relation to that event.** Who the person is = BE is determined by the IDentities+/- that s/he activates = assumes usually unconsciously and automatically in relation to the event.

Here is the Causal Sequence spelled out: **This is how all emotion = Happiness+/- works:**

An event occurs.

- You activate one or more IDentities = BE (PIRs or NIRs) in the areas of Wisdom, Power, and Value.
- You then love or AntiLove yourself in that IDentity+/-, experiencing that love+/- as your FEEL = emotion+/- = happiness or UPS; and then
- you take some corresponding action (DO), that
- will produce some kind of result = your HAVE.

There is no escaping the Causal Sequence, BE-FEEL→THINK→DO→HAVE. Your life operates by it whether you know it or not, and whether you want it to or not. In psycanics, we seek to make your BE→FEEL response conscious and under your control. We seek to discreate the automatic negative ID→UPS response, and teach you how to create (and maintain) a positive ID→JOY response. This is the road to happiness in life, and a highway of Return to BEing God again.

Your Point of Power

What you control and do not control in life:

1. **You cannot control most events.**
    - You cannot control world events: wars, economic crisis, earthquakes, storms, etc.
    - You can't even control most events in your own life:
        - You cannot control what other people say or do.
        - You cannot control the big, negative events, such as death of a loved one, loss of a job, income or savings; repossession of a home, being assaulted or raped, car or work accident, major illnesses, etc.
2. **You cannot control your emotions:** they are automatic love reactions to Who You Are. (Suppression does not count as control: suppression—whether by tension and resistance or substance abuse—causes neuroses, and is emotionally and physically unhealthy.)
3. **Where you do have control, what you can always control, are your IDentities.**

You cannot always choose what happens, but you can always choose Who You Are, your BE, when it happens. Notice that this is exactly what God is saying in *CWG*.

As your emotions are automatic love reactions to Who You Are; on controlling your IDentities, you thus automatically control your emotions.

As your emotions = self-love are happiness or UPS (and the only happiness+/- that exists); by controlling your IDentities, you automatically control your happiness. Control of your IDentities is the only way you will ever reach a real, impregnable, and permanent happiness.

Your God Essence Suppressor Mass is the totality of your AntiEssence IDentities, which are wrapped in your corresponding AntiLove for Self for BEing those IDentities.

By always discreating your AntiEssence = AntiGod IDentities (AntiWisdom, AntiPower, AntiValue) every time they activate; you automatically eliminate AntiLove = UPS from your BEing, experience, and life. (In other words, the emotions are not important; they are but Effects of the IDentities as Cause.)

By discreating the NIRs as they appear, you slowly but surely discreate your God Suppressor Mass. Thus, you live transforming yourSelf from BEing AntiGod to BEing God again. This is the secret of the fast track back to the ONE.

Chapter 13

Negative EmoLoveJoy: BADness and UPS

Quotes from *CWG*:

> Nothing is painful in and of itself. Pain is a result of wrong thought. It is an error in thinking. (1-1-37)
>
> That which you judge, you will one day become. (1-1-38)

Resistance Attracts and Causes the Persistence of that which is resisted.

Much earlier in the book, we introduced the phenomena of Polarity and Resistance. We now want to pick up those threads again and weave then into the fabric of your understanding of the psycanics of your BEing and the mechanics of your Return to the ONE.

Two chapters ago, we said that your NIRs, Negative Nuclear IDentities, cause your AntiLove. This is not the whole story. There is another—and essential—element involved.

Your negative emotions = AntiLove = neg. EmoLoveJoy Energy are negative energy responses to your WPV NIRs. They are RESISTANCES to your NIRs. They are AntiLove that internally is an energy attack on the NIRs; and externally moves you to attack externals (e.g. with anger), get away from them if they are more powerful than you (fear), or lament negative externals you can't change (grief). The important point here is that they are RESISTANCES. You remember, of course, the Laws of Resistance:

Resistance Causes UPS, Counter-Resistance (in others),
and Attracts and Persists that which is resisted.

You see the problem here? Your NIRs are exactly what you most need to get rid of, not only for your temporal power, success, and happiness; but also to Return to GOD = ESSENCE = PIRs. And what are you doing with them? Yes, RESISTING them. And that causes what with them? Yes: pain and persistence.

You cannot discreate anything you are resisting—on the contrary, you are creating it stronger, more persistent. You must eliminate your resistance to your

NIRs before you can discreate the NIR. **The key to discreation of your NIRs and God Suppressor Mass is to first eliminate your resistance to what you want to discreate** (NIRs). So the question is:

- Where from comes resistance?
- What causes resistance; what triggers it?
- Why and how are you creating resistance?

See if you can see the answers: Why do you resist things? What are you trying to do with your resistance? What kinds of things do you resist? **What does everything you resist always have in common? What is the commonality of all resisted things?**

Try to answer this yourself, before you go on.

If you think on this awhile, you should come to the realization that what you resist is always BAD[32]: BAD things, events, people, whatever. What everything you resist has in common is that it is BAD. Verify this datum by looking at what you resist in life. Do you ever resist something that is other than BAD in some way? Do you ever resist "good" things?

Definition of **BAD**: **That which should not BE (as it is or at all)**,
thereby seeming to justify the use of negative energy
to attack, change, stop, punish, or destroy it.

BAD is anything that **should not BE** as it is, that should not BE at all, or should BE different in some way. (Notice the words, "**should not BE**": that is another name for BAD.) Notice that BAD is an attack on the first element of the Causal Sequence—very important when dealing with other people.

As a result of something BEing BAD, we usually feel or think that we should do something to make it BE different or not-BE at all, and we usually try to do so with negative energy = AntiLove. We attack the BAD event to stop, change, punish or destroy it, the Anger Range of AntiLove. If we can't stop it, we will try to get away from it; the Fear Range of AntiLove. We don't have the power to attack, but we can still do something: flee. If we can't stop it or get away from it, we will go into the Grief Range and lament our fate. This is evidence that indeed we have no power at all.

Examples of this are infinite. However, just look at your relationships.

- Who is using negative energy on you to try to change something about you or your behaviors? Notice that they believe that how you are or act is BAD

32 Because of its overwhelming importance in screwing up life at all levels from the individual to the planetary, in being the root cause of all pain and suffering, and because of the sheer size of its entire concept (far beyond what we cover in this book), the word BAD is capitalized in psycanics.

(their opinion, of course. Yours may differ.)

- Now on the Cause side: Against whom are you using negative energy (AntiLove: e.g. anger) to stop or change something they are BEing or DOing? Look for your opinion of BAD, or "SHOULD NOT BE."

So BAD is the culprit, the "BAD" thing, that triggers your resistance to things external and internal (such as your NIRs and your negative emotions). Therefore, BAD is BAD, no? No, it is not, but it has very powerful and negative consequences for you because you have created and felt it "BAD."

So all you have to do is go out and get rid of all the BAD things in life and you will live happily ever after: there will be nothing to resist and suffer over. Good plan, isn't it?

However, it's not a workable one. First, of all, how many BAD things occur in your personal life and in the world? Quite a few, right? If you had the power to eradicate them, you would have done so, long ago, wouldn't you? What we need to do is get rid of BAD once and for all, and keep it from ever coming back. So let's go to the root of the problem.

- Where does BAD come from?
- How do things, events, and people get to be BAD?
- What makes something BAD? Did God do it? If so, how can a Good God, create or even allow to exist BAD things, because doing so would make HIM BAD, would it not? So, God can't have created anything BAD: it is contrary to HIS nature as the highest good. In fact, "God" and "good" come from the same root word.
- So where does BAD come from?

Again, try to answer this on your own first.

The answer is: BAD comes from you, and ONLY from you. BAD is always an opinion, a creation, a viewpoint. It is always a personal decision based on some arbitrary value system You are the sole and soul creator of BAD. BAD exists ONLY in your mind and by your creation. Nowhere in the cosmos is there anything intrinsically BAD and for anything you call BAD, I can find a viewpoint from which it is good. Anything whatsoever. Furthermore, no matter how BAD some act seems to you; it is good—always, without exception—from the viewpoint of the person doing it at the time of doing it.

There is no universal nor objective standard of BAD, and BAD does not exist outside of the mind of the person creating it. It is a hallucination, one of the 12 Great Hallucinations of Humanity[33] that cause all the problems in your life and on the planet.

[33] These are detailed elsewhere in psycanics.

You create BAD out of nothing, and then you project it onto events[34]; creating the illusion that BAD is over there in that thing. Then you deny having created and projected it, and claim that BAD is an intrinsic property of such events. Remember DOR (Denial of Response-ability)? You "DOR" your creations of BAD. You thus create the illusion that you are not Creator and that BAD is over there in that event.

As the event now seems BAD to you—after all you are creating it that way; how can it not BE BAD to you?—you then generate AntiLove (negative energy, negative emotions) to stop, change, punish or destroy it. Your own negative EmoLoveJoy that you generate against BAD is only the UPS that exists. You have thus just created your own pain and suffering. You have taken yourself out of the "heavenly" state of Love→Joy, and sent yourself to "hell" = UPS. And you do it all by yourself. **You are the sole creator of all your pain and suffering in life.**

It is impossible to escape the Response-ability of being the creator of BAD. Even when you claim that BAD is established by some code or book, or by God HERSELF; it is still your evaluation and decision to use that as *your* mental criteria of Good<>BAD. Notice that there is no universal code or book establishing Good<>BAD on the planet, no criteria to which everyone agrees. For example, there is no religion or holy book that has more than a fraction of adherents of the total population on the planet.

In fact, Good<>BAD is often a question of when or where. Something that is "BAD" in one place, is "Good" a mile down the road (gambling, prostitution, drugs, for examples). Or timing: one day something is Good; the rules change, and now it is BAD, or vice versa.

There is no way you can escape the ultimate responsability of being the decider, the creator, of what is Good<>BAD in your world.

However, the real Cause is even deeper.

Your BADs to externals are projections of your BAD to yourSelf, to your NIRs.

The underlying reason that you create BAD about externals is that they trigger your NIRs (because you are not controlling your NIRs, but letting events do so). **You have created your NIRs as** "It is **BAD**-to-BE-that-way." It is your BADs to your NIRs that triggers your AntiLove pain.

Your BADs to externals are but projections of your BAD to Self, just as your love for Self is projected in love to others. Once you have created BAD to a NIR and trigger negative ELJ, you then create that UPS as BAD. Then, as the external event seems to be the cause of that pain, you label it BAD, and attack it with your

34 Remember that "events" includes occurrences, people, things, action, circumstances, situations, etc.

AntiLove to stop, change, punish or destroy it. However, that usually only makes it more persistent, which activates even more of your NIRs, especially your AntiPower ones, so you attack it with even more AntiLove. You are trapped in a downward spiral of your own resistance to NIRs and events, and never knew what hit you: it was your creation of BAD. And it is all a hallucination: BAD does not exist; there is no BAD! Talk about suffering over nothing.

All resistance starts with the opinion of BAD. BAD is the parent of resistance. Resistance is the parent of UPS. The purpose of resistance is to avoid experiencing something BAD, to try to make it not-real using negative energy. However, resistance is energy and all energy, regardless of polarity, energizes. More energy is more mass, therefore more reality and therefore more persistence. Thus, the Law: Resistance Causes Persistence and UPS. (Rxx→Perxx and UPS.)

The Sequence is

BAD→Rxx = AntiLove = neg ELJ = Pain and Perxx→Counter-Rxx (if a person).

All resistance starts with BAD.
Resistance stops Discreation.
Discreation of your ESM is a fast
path of Return to the ONE.

This is why you should "Resist Not Evil:" because *you* will suffer and will cause to persist what you resist.

What you most resist are your NIRs, which are the AntiGod in you. Thus, when you resist, you persist yourSelf in BEing NIRs; **you stop your Return to the ONE.**

You must learn to make your realities (NIRs) not-real by discreating them, not by resisting them. This is what you do with Creation and Discreation Technology.

Response-ability for Experience

In the previous chapter, we spoke of the importance of Response-ability. Here is an important application of that wisdom. We have just proved that you are the sole creator of all your pain and suffering in life.

Now make a list of all the instances of negative emotions, of unhappiness, pain and suffering in your life. To the right of each item, write down who you have been holding responsible for causing you that UPS.

Are you blaming anything external for your moments of UPS? For example: other people, what they do or say, what you have or don't have, what has happened to you, your parents or upbringing, the situations, circumstances of your life, your lack of education, your bosses, the government, God, the Devil, your stars, or the Tooth Fairy?

Because if you are, you are in Victim. The price of Victim, remember, is that you have no Power; in this case, no Power to eliminate your UPS, which is no Power to be any happier than you are now. (It is impossible to be very happy in the condition of Victim.)

And don't go blaming yourself. Take Response-ability for your emotions, not blame.

Stay tuned, and you will soon be able to discreate your negative emotions.

Polarization

Polarization is the creation and application of artificial Value polarities to others resulting in exclusion and AntiLove to the polarized person or group.

The fundamental artificial (i.e. hallucinatory) value polarity is: Good<>BAD. It is artificial because it is not a natural polarity: it does not exist in Nature; it is purely a creation of Humanity.

The related, secondary, value polarities of polarization all imply Good<>BAD, and include: better than<>less than; superior<>inferior; right<>wrong[34]; saved/redeemed<>sinners/lost, among others. All this is part of Ego.

The creation of these hallucinations creates the "in" group and the "out" group; which often becomes the "we versus them." The "in" group then feels justified in excluding, relegating, segregating, denying equal treatment and access to education and resources, etc. to the "out" group. History shows that the snobbery and bigotry often does not stop there, but continues into enslaving, torturing, and killing the out group.

Humanity polarizes around skin color, nationality, language, race, religion, politics, economics, social status, disability, gender, money, sexual orientation, intellectual ability, residence location or cost, model of car driven—the list probably includes any detectable difference between one human being and another.

Polarization is a form of AntiLove and triggers even more AntiLove. **It is the opposite of Integration and ONEness that is the nature of God.** This is a planet where polarization and AntiLove abound.

34 Where it is implied that it is BAD to wrong, as opposed to merely needing to correct erroneous data.

The following is a law that will guide you through life.

NIsGOB and CarPriCon

Nothing **Is** **G**ood **O**r **B**ad, and
Everything has **Char**acteristics, **Pri**ces and **Con**sequences.

When you achieve living in a state of Consciousness and perception of the world, in which you have no judgments of events whatsoever, where you perceive life as a parade of events, as the cosmic movie projected for your viewing pleasure, as the Flow of the Tao in manifestation; you are close to Enlightenment and to Re-Integrating with the ONE.

This is a state in which BAD does not exist—because you are not creating it. **It is also a state in which Good does not exist**—remember, Good–BAD is a polarity and you cannot have (create) one without automatically creating the other.

In this level of BEing you, therefore, have no likes and no dislikes, no attractions and no aversions, and therefore no graspings and no resistances. You totally, "Let go and Let it BE." You "Let go and Let God" BE however IT shows up before you.

Create even the smallest preference and you "set heaven and earth infinitely apart." (Quote from *The Tao Te Ching*). "Seek not to be enlightened; seek only to have no opinions, and the ALL shall be revealed to you." (Quote from the *Third Patriarch of Zen*.)

This is the State of **SPace**, also known as the **State of Grace**, of being totally graceful to What Is. SPace is a condition of zero energy. Thus, SPace is end of AntiLove and the beginning of Love. It is, therefore, the end of UPS and the beginning of Happiness.

SPace is the State of God, and the nature of the Kingdom of Heaven. God is the INFINITE SPACE in which everything exists, without the least resistance = should not BE = BAD. If it exists, it is **not** BAD in the eyes of God. If the OMNIPOTENT ALMIGHTY thought that something is BAD, that it "should not BE," it would not BE, period. Therefore, if it exists, it is OK with God; it has HIS SPace to BE and to BE as it is. (There is an entire chapter coming on SPace.)

Thus, there is nothing objectively or intrinsically BAD in the cosmos in the judgment of God. So if you are of a different opinion than God about something —i.e., you are creating it BAD—take Response-ability for that. Stop blaming your BADs on God.

It is not BAD to walk around creating BAD—nothing is BAD (that is our point: NIsGoB). However, YOU pay enormous prices and consequences (CarPriCon) for creating BAD. These include: polarization, AntiLove, pain and suffering, persistence, counter-BADs and resistance from others, dis-integration from the ONE and from others, separation and isolation. In short: BAD hurts; it hurts you.

In psycanics, instead of using Good<>BAD, we learn to evaluate things in terms of Love<>AntiLove; and as Positive<>Negative, which is the same as works<>doesn't work.

On your path back to the ONE, you must transcend the creation of Good<>BAD. If you are familiar with the Christian bible, you know the story of Adam and Eve in the Garden of Paradise or Eden, which is another name for the Kingdom of Heaven. In the "Garden" they walked in love and happiness and were together with God.

Then, they snacked on what? Yes: the apple of the **KNOWLEDGE of GOOD<>BAD**. They began to know good and evil; and the only way you can know them is to create them. With that, they were expelled from the Kingdom of God, the SPace of LoveJoy and ONEness, and went forth into the world of pain and sorrow: UPS (where most of us still are).

The objective is to go back to the Garden. To do so, to achieve ONEness, you must transcend Good<>BAD. To achieve ONEness, you must transcend all polarization of others. You must BE perfect SPace to ALL THAT IS again. To transcend the polarization of others, you only need to discreate what you polarize in yourself: Your NIRs.

Chapter 14

NIR Masses: The Basic Unit of the Essence Suppressor Mass

You have disowned many parts of yourself that you do not wish to claim. (4-16-323) **In disclaiming them, you have made it impossible to totally love yourself, and that makes it impossible to love others.**

We have seen the nature of four elements:

1. NIRs, Negative IDentity Realities, your declarations = creations of Self that counter-create, and thereby deny, hide, and suppress your GOD-ESSENCE of WPVLJ. The capital "ID" in "IDentities" reminds us that these are the ESSENCE+/- IDentities. NIRs are your AntiEssence "I AMs" and "I AM NOTs" in the areas of Wisdom, Power, and Value. As they take you in the direction opposite of the Existential Imperative, away from BEing God again, and into the UPS of Self-AntiLove, you automatically and unconsciously create that they are BAD, the second element:
2. BADs: your creations that something—in this case, YOU in your NIRs—is wrong and should not BE. BAD is that which you should not BE; it is even more AntiGod.
3. AntiLove, which is always negative EmoLoveJoy for Self in a "BAD-ed" NIR IDentity. You attack your BAD Self = NIRs with AntiLove to stop, change, punish or destroy them. That negative EmoLoveJoy energy, the fourth element of ESSENCE is the only UPS that exists. It is also resistance energy to the NIR that energizes and strengthens the NIR and makes it persistent in your universe.
4. Resistance Causes Persistence: Unable to destroy or escape your now-persistent NIRs in order to not BE-FEEL them, you find yourself locked into a life-long war against them. The smoke above the battlefield of this war is your UPS: Unhappiness, Pain and Suffering.

All together, these elements form a NIR Mass. Your NIRs do not stand alone. They are embedded in creations of BAD and encased in the resulting Self-

AntiLove = UPS. NIRs Masses are massive energy forms consisting of three basic parts: a NIR, a creation of BAD about the NIR, and the resulting charge of Self-AntiLove (negative emotion). It is literally a **mass** of psycanic energy.

The basic structure of a NIR Mass is always: NIR + BAD → UPS and Perxx. (This formula reads as a "NIR invalidated by a BAD triggering negative EmoLoveJoy and therefore Resisted and Persisted.") You will always find these three creations: NIR, BAD, -ELJ (neg ELJ) as the basic elements of a NIR Mass.

Your Essence Suppressor Mass: You have hundreds of NIR Masses. The sum total of your NIR Masses is your God-Essence Suppressor Mass (ESM). The ESM is what separates you from BEing God by counter-creating and blocking out your experience of BEing God, done with all your NIRs = IDentities = realities = experiences of not BEing God. Underneath all that suppressor mass, your LIGHT IDentity still shines

I repeat because this is so important to your being able to discreate them painlessly and quickly: Your NIR Masses are masses of psycanic energy. They consist of:

1- One or more **NIRs** (IDs of AntiWisdom, AntiPower, or AntiValue)
2- One or more creations of **BAD→Rxx**[36] to the NIRs.
3- One or more flavors of **negative EmoLoveJoy** energy; i.e. negative emotional charges.

Thus, a NIR Mass is a NIR, embedded in BAD→Rxx, embedded in negative emotion energy. Illustration 14-1 shows this graphically.

Illustration 14-1: The Basic Structure of a NIR Mass: A NIR+BAD+ANTILOVE

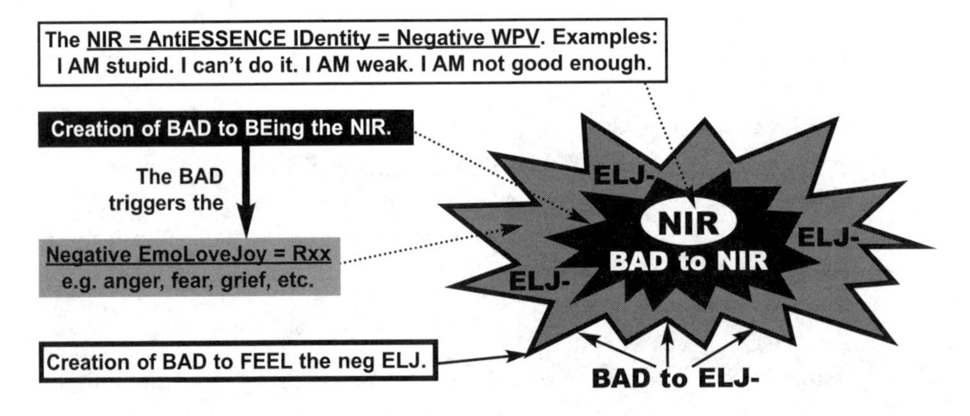

36 The symbol BAD→Rxx, means creation of BAD triggering resistance (Rxx), and that these are so intimately related that they can be distinguished but cannot be separated. You can no more separate BAD from Rxx = UPS than you can separate Love from Joy.

Activations

How Your Negative Psycanic Experience Works

Your "subconscious" is that psycanic space around you-psycan = creator and experiencer where your non-physical realities (thoughts, memories, and NIR Masses) "hang out" when they are out of your immediate consciousness = awareness = perception = experience = FEELing. There is no such thing as a subconscious as an entity (just as there is no such thing as a mind). There is only the Creator (you), the Experiencer (you), and your creations (thoughts and emotions; and NIRs and BADs).

Your non-physical creations are either within your perception = awareness, or outside of it = subconscious—just as every thing in the physical universe is either in or out of your sight = physical perception.

Illustration 14-2 shows your BEing, as an inner SPace of Consciousness, and outer SPace of unconsciousness = subconscious. Your psycanic realities (IDentities, thoughts, emotions, NIR Masses, etc.) are either close enough in to you = Consciousness to be perceived = FELT, or they are too far out, outside of your experience. In Illustration 14-2, they are shown as all out of experience.

Illustration 14-2: Consciousness and Subconscious, Realities and Perception.
Unactivated state: Consciousness = Experience in SPace = clear of NIR Masses.

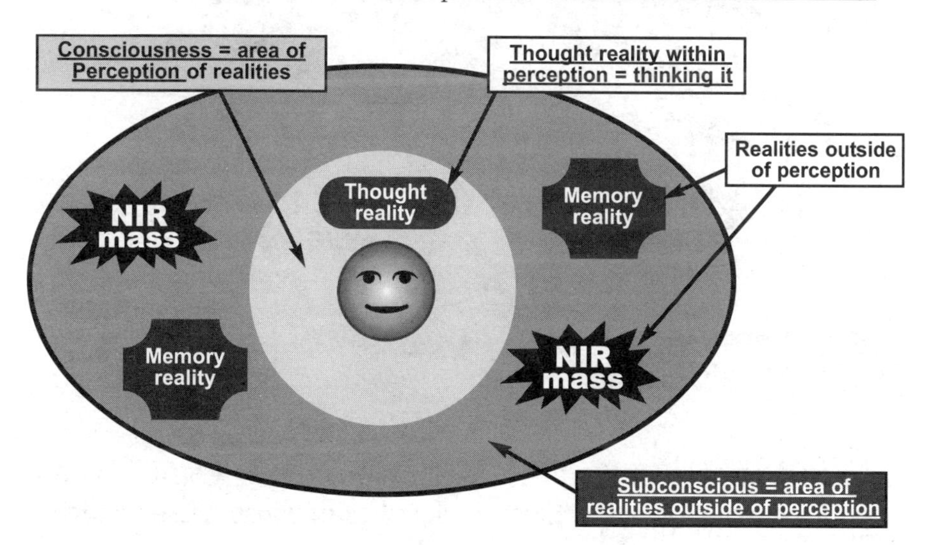

Activations (of NIR Masses)

An activation is the stimulation or triggering of a NIR Mass such that it moves from subconscious = out of perception, to your consciousness = experience = FEELing. (This happens by the same mechanism of all involuntary stimulation = triggering of memories, in your subconscious.)

You experience an activation primarily as negative FEELings, negative emotions, but the NIRs are always present underneath the emotions. An activation is also called a Moment of Dolor (MoD). (Dolor is Latin for pain; we reserve "P" for a positive activation call a MoP: Moment of PIR = Moment of Pleasure. We will come back to MoPs later.)

Illustration 14-3 shows the ACTIVATION of a NIR Mass, in which the NIR Mass has been triggered (by any event whatsoever, the snake, for example, or being cut off in traffic). The NIR Mass has moved from subconscious = out or perception, into consciousness = perception = FEELing. You will FEEL the NIR Mass primarily as negative emotion = UPS. The NIRs are always there, but you are usually doing your best not to BE-FEEL them, consciously or unconsciously. It is the NEGATION TO EXPERIENCE that is resistance and is what we have to reverse to discreate them.

Illustration 14-3: The Activation of a NIR Mass:
The event triggers the NIR Mass to come up from your unconscious to your consciousness = experience = FEELing.

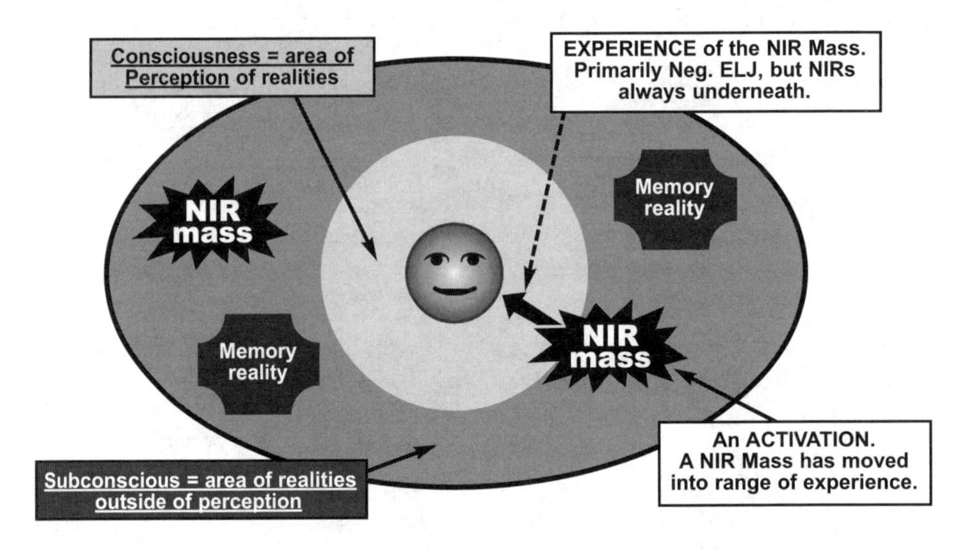

An ACTIVATION (of a NIR Mass) **is the movement of a NIR Mass from the subconscious = out of perception, into consciousness = experience.**

All negative BE-FEEL = all negative emotions = all unhappiness, pain and suffering, is the experience of a NIR Mass moving into your FEELing.

You perceive = FEEL the activated NIR Mass primarily as negative emotion (e.g. anger, fear, grief, etc.). However, **the Negative Essence IDentities are**

always there underneath the emotion. Some people do perceive them, but take them to be merely thoughts or beliefs. They do not realize their true nature as the most powerful—albeit the most subtle—energies of their BEing.

Your NIRs are like icebergs. Even during an activation, only the tip sticks into consciousness: the great mass is "underwater" in your subconscious. And when the IDentities do appear (both blocks and big emotional charges tend to drown out their perception), they may seem to be ordinary thoughts and get lost among all your other thoughts. For this reason their significance and power passes unperceived—until you understand them.

IDentities are not thoughts or beliefs.
They are not mental phenomena.

They are psycanic energy masses. However, to describe them, we must label them, and we label them with words that describe the experience of these energies, e.g. I AM weak; I AM unworthy. **However, a thought-label does not make them thoughts.** Nor can they be handled, counter-created, discreated, or changed as thoughts or beliefs can. This is why "affirmations" against them or trying to change or plaster over them do not work. They must be discreated using the technology in this book

If you think that your IDentities are thoughts or beliefs,
you have not identified your IDentities!

IDentities are experiences, masses of energy, and
they must be experienced, BE-FELT, as such to discreate them.
Words and thoughts are only labels and are irrelevant.

In psycanics, you must rehabilitate your ability to FEEL.
Mind creates; Experience (BE-FEEL) discreates.

You can easily verify the existence of your NIRs by taking any of your negative emotions and FEELing "down" into them to experience the NIR. You must FEEL to find the NIRs, not THINK. THINKing blocks the experience-knowing process. NO mind! Turn off your mind. The mind creates, experience discreates.

Your NIR Masses are energies. They are <u>creations = realities = experiences</u> of Self. They are not thoughts or beliefs. We have to use thoughts as words labels to communicate about them, but never think that IDentities are in the mind. They are not. Nor can they be changed in the mind. Affirmations, for example, are useless against NIRs.

Your NIR Masses are always present around your BEing (until you discreate them), but they are not in acute <u>activation = perception = FEELing</u> until some event (such as our snake, or what your spouse says or does) stimulates you (usually unconsciously) to change IDentities.

It is precisely this unconscious, externally-triggered, at-effect, change of IDentities that we want to learn to control. We want to become Cause; take control of our Essence IDentities+/-, discreate the negative ones, and be able to hold the positive ones no matter what happens around us. This is a powerful path of Return of yourSelf to BE ESSENCE = God again.

This is what CWG means when it talks about becoming aware of Who You Are (NIRs = AntiEssence), and changing to Who You Want to BE = More ESSENCE = more PIR = more God.

Here is a major law to be remembered at all times:

Every negative emotion (anxiety, anger, fear, sadness, loneliness, grief, hate, resentment, guilt, depression, whatever), **IS ALWAYS PART OF A NIR MASS. Behind every negative emotion there are always NIRs. No exceptions.**

This law is important because those activations of our negative emotions signal us that a NIR has come up out of our subconscious, up out of our God Suppressor Mass, and so is available for discreation. Every time you discreate a NIR Mass, you are that much less of AntiGod and your GOD-ESSENCE is that much closer to being real again.

Every activation of a NIR Mass is the opportunity to discreate that mass, that portion of your AntiGodness, and so move that much closer to BEing full ESSENCE = God again.

Behind every instance of UPS, there is a NIR. Every activation of UPS gives you the opportunity to discreate it. Thus, when you know how to use it, your UPS is a fast track back to God.

Activations of NIR Masses occur just as does any involuntary stimulation of your memories. As you go through a day or your life, you see or hear things which trigger memories, feelings, and associations with things in your past. In the same way, any particular event can trigger = activate a NIR Mass for any given person—and not for another.

Discreation

To discreate a NIR, all you have to do is BE-FEEL it, experience it, fully. However, you have created them as BAD and so you resist them (Rxx) instead of experiencing them. You further resist them because they seem to be the source of your negative EmoLoveJoy = UPS. However, this is not true. It is your BADs that trigger your AntiLove, not the NIRs.

A single NIR Mass can contain multiple NIRs, BADs, and emotions. NIR

Masses are interconnected to each other in vast networks, and in temporal and in causal chains. All of these are then bunched up and interconnected to create your God Suppressor Mass. Thus, your God-Essence Suppressor Mass (ESM) is a mass of NIR Masses. The ESM is the subject of our next chapter.

BADs→Rxx = UPS: The only UPS (Unhappiness, Pain and Suffering) in life is your resistance = AntiLove to Self. It usually appears as resistance to external events, but it is not. It is BE→resistance = UPS to the IDentity (NIR) you are activating in relation to that event.

There will often be another creation of BAD to the negative emotion: "It is BAD to FEEL the negative emotion." This energizes the UPS and prolongs (persists) it, turning mere emotional pain into suffering. Suffering is resisted pain.

Determinations: A NIR Mass will usually also contain determinations. A determination is a creation of a reality (belief) about life—as opposed to IDentities which are realities about Self. For example: "You have to work hard to get money," is a determination. During CDT, after discreating the NIRs, you then discreate your negative (limiting) determinations, and create positive ones according to what you wish to experience in the future. For example: "Money comes to me easily and naturally." When a NIR Mass is activated (in experience), it may trigger lots of negative THINK (such as fuming and "if only's")—in other words, the mind goes wild, like a crazy monkey in a cage.

It is important to understand the basic structure of **NIR+BAD+neg ELJ** for fast and easy discreation. Your objective is to discreate the NIR. However, to do so, you must go through the emotion and first discreate the BAD = resistance to the NIR. **You do not have to discreate the emotion!** Furthermore, time spent feeling emotion is time wasted! Discreate the NIR and the emotion disappears.

In fact, just on **discreating the BAD to the NIR, the emotion disappears. This is a danger point!** When you discreate the BAD, the emotion that is, after all, Rxx (resistance) to the NIR disappears and you are in emotional SPace. This can fool you into thinking the discreation process is a success and over; after all your neg ELJ = UPS has gone. But the process is not complete! You must then continue on to *discreate* the NIR, which is a much more subtle energy than the emotion. If you do not discreate the NIR, you have not achieved a permanent change in your BEing and therefore in your Causal Sequences. Furthermore, the negative emotion will tend to regenerate around the NIR.

Positive Activations: PIRs→MoPs

Essence IDentities are polarities. You can also have activations of your PIRs (your Positive IDentities Realities). Triggers for PIR activations are events that allow you to assume the positive IDs of Wisdom, Power and Value (self-esteem). This can be any event where you show up as knowledgeable, intelligent or smart, powerful, winning something, succeeding at something, getting what you want, getting something that makes you feel valued or loved—even candy or flowers.

Such activations of PIRs produce moments of positive emotion called MoPs: Moments of Pleasure (or Moments of PIRs). PIRs do trigger the positive Self-EmoLoveJoy that is the only happiness that exists—but MoPs are not true happiness because they are fleeting. They do not last long because they are not a real causal control and creation of your BEing on your part, but rather the effect of external triggers not under your control.

The problem with MoPs (Moments of Pleasure) is that YOU are not controlling your IDentities (Who You Are as *CWG* puts it); but letting them be triggered by external events. You are still not creating and holding your PIRs no matter what happens around you. You are living at Effect of the world; not at Cause-Creator of your BEing→EmoLoveJoy.

If you are letting the external world determine (trigger) Who You Are; if you are lost in the External Quest to make the world conform to your ideas of how it should be so that you can activate PIRs→MoPs, you will never achieve real happiness. As the external world is a parade of triggers, both positive and negative, your positive trigger will soon pass, and your MoP will fade away—or pop like a balloon when a new event activates your NIRs.

True happiness is all the time, no matter what. It is the result of an internal creation of Self, of PIRs→EmoLoveJoy+ all the time, no matter what happens to you or around you. When you take Response-ability for your BEing and you control and create it, you can maintain your Essence (PIRs) under any attack. This is one of the teachings of Jesus: the world threw at him the maximum negative energy on the planet: he was reviled as a criminal, he was spat upon, tortured and horribly executed; yet He held his SPace, BEing, and Love. That is the Power to be in PIRs→Self-Love = Happiness all the time, no matter what.

This distinction between living at Cause and creating and maintaining yourSelf as PIRs→Self-Love all the time no matter what, as opposed to living in Effect and trying to control the external world to trigger PIRs→MoPs is critical. We are distinguishing that fleeting moments of positive emotions (i.e. emotional pleasure = MoPs), as a result of external triggering of your PIRs, are not true happiness. You are not at Cause, creating and controlling your state of positive BEing (PIR), and neither the PIR nor the resultant MoP will last long.

MoPs (Moments of Pleasure) are dangerous because they create the mirage of happiness as external to you, outside of you. They send you on the External Quest for happiness in the illusion that, "If only I can get enough of what gave me that MoP, eventually I will accumulate enough to keep me in happiness all the time." This will never happen; no matter what you get, nor how much of it you accumulate; **nothing external to you will ever satisfy the Existential Imperative for ESSENCE.** However, despite the very clear instructions from Jesus, Buddha and Krishna: "The Kingdom of Heaven is within;" most people waste their lives in the External Quest for MoPs.

Restated in other words: The ignorant[37] human being struggles to control external events (people and things) to achieve happiness. S/He tries to make the Causal Sequence work backwards: DO→HAVE→FEEL happy. S/He tries to DO and HAVE things, achieve goals, to trigger MoPs. This is the External Quest for happiness.

However, MoPs are always fleeting. They are fleeting because YOU are not controlling your IDs, but letting them be triggered by external events and these always change. Life is a parade of events = triggers. MoPs are never the true and lasting increase of your ESSENCE that comes from taking control of Who You Are to discreate NIRs and create PIRs, to thereby create your BE-FEEL internally. (More about the two Quests in a coming chapter.)

SUMMARY OF THIS SECTION

A NIR Mass is a mass of non-physical (psycanic) energy. It includes BADs (mental creations) and negative emotional energy (-ELJ) created around a NIR (Negative Psycanic IDentity). A NIR Mass consists of NIRs invalidated with BADs and then encased in AntiLove = negative emotional energy.

Your NIR Masses are the source of ALL the negative FEEL (emotion), and therefore of all UPS (Unhappiness, Pain and Suffering) in your life.

They are also the source of all your negative THINK, DO, and HAVE in your Causal Sequences, which are your life. All your problems, conflicts, pain and suffering in life are originating in your NIR Masses.

Behind EVERY negative emotion = activation, there is always a NIR. Every activation is the opportunity to discreate your NIRs. DO NOT WASTE YOUR ACTIVATIONS. Use them to Return to BEing ESSENCE again.

---

[37] Ignorant of psycanics, of how BEing and Life work. A person may be a scientist or scholar in other areas of knowledge, but if s/he does not know how Life works, s/he is ignorant of what most matters.

Chapter 15

Your God Essence Suppressor Mass

Heaven is within you. (3-18-327)

The Kingdom of Heaven is within. (Jesus)

You have placed yourself in a perception shell that blocks out the Total Reality. (3-5-52)

In the ordinary course of your life, you frequently <u>experience = FEEL</u> your NIR Masses. **Any time you are emotionally uncomfortable, unhappy, in any form or degree whatsoever; you are experiencing AntiLove from a NIR mass leaking into your consciousness.** Although emotionally painful, this is actually good because the only time you can discreate your NIR Masses is when you can FEEL them.

The rule is simple: Behind *every* negative emotion, behind *every* negative thought, behind *every* AntiLove behavior, behind every relationship conflict, there is always a NIR. Behind every Negative FEEL, THINK, DO, or HAVE in your life, there is always a Negative BE. (I know I am repeating this many times, but it is a critical concept to grasp.)

When you understand the Causal Sequence, you can take any negative experience or behavior in your life; trace it to the underlying causal NIR (BE). You then discreate the NIR, and your life (which consists of your Causal Sequences) changes, as if by magic. You do not need to struggle to change anything else: FEEL→THINK→RELATE/DO→HAVE all change automatically when the BE changes.

However, your NIR Masses are not few or far between. On the contrary, your BEing is packed with them. **The totality of your NIR Masses is your God-Essence Suppressor Mass (ESM).**

Your ESM is what separates you from BEing God and makes you a human being.

That **perception shell** God mentions we call the **God Suppressor Mass**, or Essence Suppressor Mass, or AntiEssence Mass: the concept is the same. It is the source of all your Not-Godness. It blocks your perception of Who You Are = God. It counter-creates you True IDentity and thereby suppresses your consciousness and experience of THAT.

The ESM is a massive amount of energy creations-realities-IDentities-BADs and negative ELJ inside of which you are existing right now as a human being. It is the reality shell that compresses and suppresses and reduces you down from GOD-ESSENCE to the human level of BEing, like the concrete around the nuclear fires at Chernobyl.

All your experience of BEing less than the ONE God, all your experience of the absence of INFINITE WISDOM, INFINITE POWER, and INFINITE LOVEJOY as a human being is produced for you by your God-Essence Suppressor Mass. You are living inside it at this very moment.

You are packed in all your NIR Masses = ESM very much as you might pack a food item in ice to keep it cold. Your ESM keeps you "cold," far from the "warmth" of BEing God.

Your ESM consists of thousands of creations of Self = IDentities denying ESSENCE (WPV), each packed in AntiLove. **You can think of AntiEssence as muddying the crystal water of your pure psycan ESSENCE; or you can think of it as a massive shell around you-psycan**[38]. Beyond your shell of NIR Masses, beyond your ESM, is your TRUE BEING, your full ESSENCE.

You, as a human being, are existing inside a huge, thick shell of AntiEssence, of counter-creation of yourSelf as God; of creation of yourSelf as Not-God, Not-Essence = AntiEssence. More names for that shell can include your **God-Essence Counter-Creation Mass**, your **AntiEssence Reality Mass**, or your **AntiEssence IDentity Shell**, or your **God Suppressor Shell**. Any combination of these words are a valid label for it. The importance is not the name, but that you understand the concept of it and how you are being affected by it. For short, we will call it your "ESM" or the "Shell."

> You have probably heard of Chernobyl, the Russian nuclear reactor that had a core meltdown and steam-exploded in 1986. It is regarded as the worst accident ever in the history of nuclear power. The core was so powerful that it blew up a concrete containment building specifically designed not to blow up under those circumstances, and so hot that it turned concrete to lava.
>
> To try to suppress the nuclear "fire" of the reactor, 10,000,000 pounds of mass—sand, lead, and boric acid—were dumped on the core in the first

---

38 The words of location here: around, above, beyond, within, outside of, etc., have no real meaning because when dealing with the psycan, we are beyond time and space as we know it. You can also consider that the NIR Masses are demodulations of the ESSENCE psycanic energy, rather than a shell blocking IT out.

> week. This did little to put the nuclear "fire" out; it just blocked and suppressed it enough to allow a massive, concrete containment shell to be built around the entire reactor building—what was left of it.
>
> The still highly radioactive core will be dangerously radioactive for about 10,000 years; the control buildings where people still needed to be to control the other 3 reactors were surrounded by concrete that is 650 feet thick. Imagine a 650 foot thick concrete wall. This is over two football fields—a serious mass. That is the measure of the power of a nuclear reactor—already suppressed with a mass of 10 million pounds of sand, lead, and boron. And they still have not contained it sufficiently: on top of all this, they have to build yet another confinement building around the reactor.

It takes a lot of mass to suppress and contain the power of a nuclear reactor. Not put it out, mind you, just block it out, hold it in, and keep it from showing up in the "outside" reality-experience.

I mention Chernobyl and its suppression mass because **this describes YOU**. You are God. Inside you is still all the power of God, more powerful than any nuclear reactor, more powerful than the sun, more powerful than all the suns ever created. It is not easy to hide or block that. It takes a lot of mass to do so. As a human being, you are like Chernobyl. The QUANTUM FIRE of Who You Are, not put out, but dumped on and buried under your Essence Suppressor Mass. Think of the 650 foot thick concrete block as your Essence Suppressor Mass; think of yourSelf encased in, buried under such mass, just as the Chernobyl core is. Your ESM is what is between you and your experience of BEing God again. It is what weighs and compresses you down from the INFINITE SPACE, AWARENESS and POWER of God, down to the level of BEing of a human being. (Now you know how you got to be so small.)

Not only have you created your AntiEssence Identity Mass, but **you are also maintaining it in existence by resisting it**. Resistance Causes Persistence. In fact, if you were not resisting it, you would have naturally and effortlessly discreated it long ago and you would already BE God again. You are so used to resisting it and your blocks to it that you do not even realize that you are doing so.

In the previous chapter, we showed your consciousness, subconsciousness and a few NIR Masses. In the following illustration 15-1, we are representing your complete AntiEssence Mass (ESM) as a shell. We are also representing your blocks as another shell inside of the ESM "protecting" your consciousness from your ESM.

As a human BEing, you are usually able to keep your NIR Masses blocked out of your perception. However, events can activate them, and they then "leak" through your blocks into your consciousness = experience. These leaks, activations of Self-AntiLove→NIRs = AntiEssence are the only known source of UPS in the cosmos. (On the other hand, I really don't know all that much about the rest of the cosmos.)

Illustration 15-1 shows the ESM successfully blocked out of your BE-FEEL= experience = consciousness; in others words, no activations. Illustration 15-2 shows a NIR Mass activated and therefore protruding through the blocks and into your perception = experience.

Remember that you FEEL such activations primarily as negative emotions, but the NIRs are always embedded within the emotion, and you can learn to BE-FEEL them once you know what to look for.

Illustration 15-1: You, your God Suppressor Mass, and your blocks.
No NIR mass activations within consciousness.

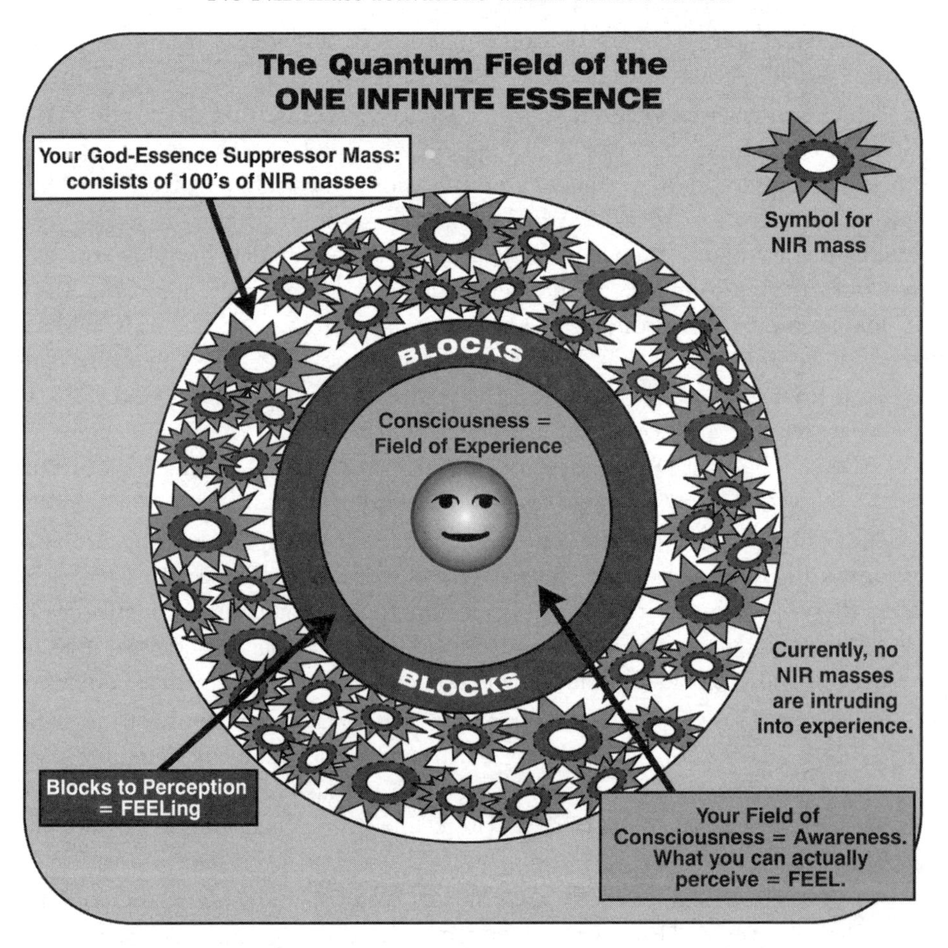

Activations of the God-Essence Suppressor Shell

As we have said, an activation is the triggering and movement of a NIR mass from out of perception to within perception and experience. **Your bouts of negative emotion—any and all negative feelings—are always the tips of NIR Masses protruding into your awareness = FEELing.**

This is shown in Illustration 15-2.

Illustration 15-2: Your God Suppressor Mass in Activation, "leaking" NIR mass into your experience.

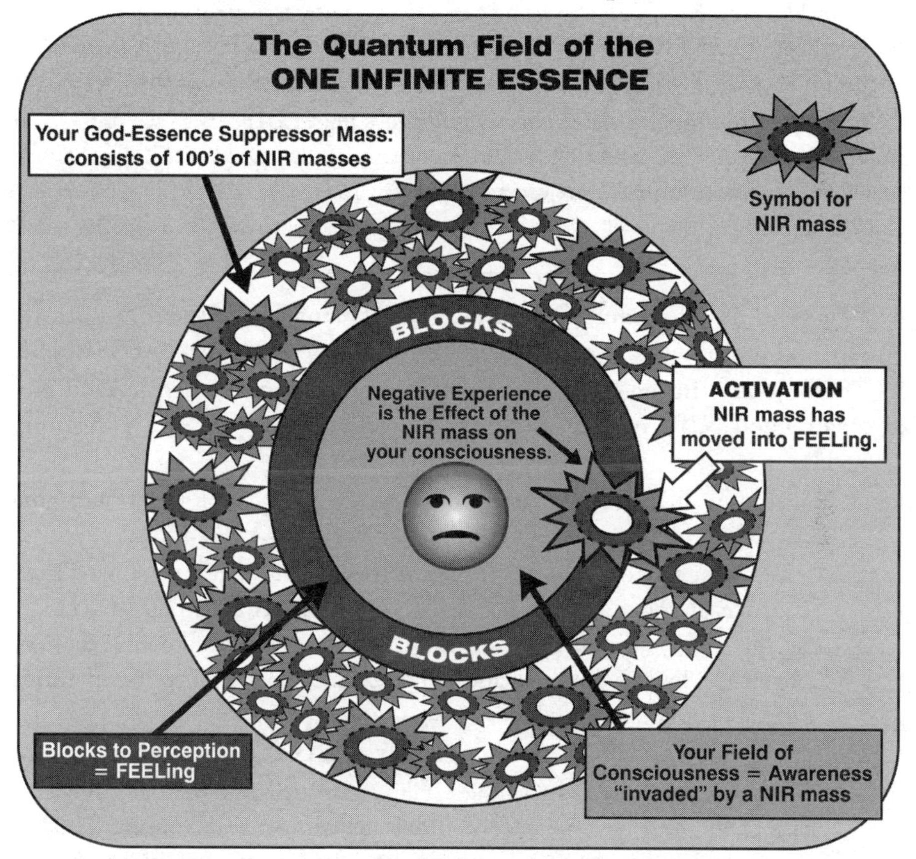

Your ESM is made of "tons" of AntiEssence = NIR Masses. Every time you experience any form of the AntiEssence IDentities, such as: I am ignorant; I am stupid, I can't learn; I am unable; I can't do it; I can't get it; I am weak; I am a failure; I am unworthy, I am undeserving; I am less than; I am not good enough; I am worthless; I am alone; nobody loves me; I am going to be rejected; I am ignored; I don't matter; I am unimportant; nobody respects me; I am BAD, etc, etc, etc.; you are experiencing sparks off of your AntiEssence mass.

Any time you FEEL any form of AntiLove including dissatisfaction, impatience, frustration, aversion, hostility, anger, rage, resentment, disgust, hate, loathing, anxiety, worry, stress, regret, guilt, fear, terror, panic, phobias, sadness, loneliness, sorrow, grief, mourning, desperation, depression, apathy, etc. you are experiencing charges and "leaks" of your AntiEssence Suppressor Mass.

Any time you are upset or worried or anxious, or have a problem and conflict with another person, you are experiencing the effects of your AntiEssence Mass. All your negative thoughts, programs and demands of life; all you addictions and negative behaviors are indirect effects of your AntiEssence Mass. All your negative THINK, RELATE, DO, and HAVE originate in your AntiEssence Mass. All your inability and frustration in manifesting what you want in life are effects of your AntiEssence Mass (God has no trouble getting what SHE wants.)

In fact, all that you are experiencing that is less than FULL WISDOM, TOTAL POWER, IMMENSE SELF ESTEEM (VALUE) AND INFINITE LOVE-ECSTASY is the result of your God Suppressor Mass. Your ESM is what makes you human instead of God.

What you do with each activation of a NIR mass is critical to both the quality and happiness of your human life, and to your Return to ESSENCE.

The objective in the Psycanics Technology for your Return to God is to discreate each NIR mass as it becomes available (comes into consciousness). This has great benefits:

1- This immediately ends that MoD (Moment of Dolor = Pain), that activation, and restores your happiness.

2- It liberates you of reliving over and over that NIR's negative Causal Sequence. It eliminates the negative THINK, RELATE, DO, and HAVE that that NIR is producing in your life. These include addictions, neurotic behaviors, bad habits, relationship conflicts, inability to manifest sufficient money, among others.

3- It increases your BEing, Wisdom, Power, and Love Joy as a human BEing.

4- Most importantly, it reduces the totality of your ESM by that amount of mass. Thus, you have taken one more step up on your journey HOME, back to BEing pure ESSENCE again. You BEcome that much more God-like with each NIR mass discreated.

In psycanics, you use all the negative things (BE-FEEL→THINK→ DO→HAVE) in your life to take you HOME. If something negative serves you, and does so powerfully, is it really negative?

Heaven's and Hell's Angels

If you are familiar with the Christian bible, you probably know the story of the battle in the "heavens" between the good angels and the bad angels, led by Lucifer[39]. The BAD angels lost and fell from the Kingdom of Heaven, supposedly to hell. They are since called the fallen angels, aka[40] "devils."

This story is not referring to some long ago, far away event, of little relevance to you. Nor is it a battle between two separate entities. **It is a story about you, right now!** It is the war that is waging in the Kingdom of Heaven *within you*, and ongoing every moment that you remain a human BEing. It is your internal battle between the "Good you" and the "BAD you;" between your ESSENCE and your AntiEssence, between your LIGHT and your dark. If you want to see those fallen angels, go look in the mirror.

You are BEing the "good angels" when you are robed in your PIR IDentities and are therefore God-like and Love. You are BEing the BAD angels when you are cloaked in your NIRs = AntiGod IDentities and AntiLove. The individual "bad angels" in this war are your NIR IDentities, which are you BEing AntiGod, the opposite of God. (Good) Angels are "like unto God;" and the fallen angels are "like unto devils," in Catholic mythology.

The BAD angels, your NIRs, have won so far and you have fallen from the heavens of your ESSENCE, to the hell of AntiEssence. Heaven and hell are not places, but states of BEing. You carry your heaven or your hell around with you all the time, determined by whether you are living in WPV+→LoveJoy, or WPV-→AntiLove = UPS. These last expressions are the mathematical formulas of "heaven" and "hell" (for the scientists among us).

Earth is where BAD angels "fell" to—and you are still here. The "hell" part you brought with you: **it, like the Kingdom of Heaven, is inside of you**—a matter of polarity again. But even as the BAD angels, you are still LIGHT: Lucifer means light bearer.

> All this understanding was given to me in a vision as clear as day while deep in meditation during one of my periods of isolation in my cabin in the mountains of remote southern Mexico where I went to practice mysticism. What bowled me over was the realization that someone, 2,000+ years before me, had seen this exact same thing—who we are and how we are made so by our NIR Masses—and was trying to report it to us. The only data that was omitted—or later left out—was 1- the fight between the angels is internal to us, not external between different BEings; and 2- we are those fallen angels.

[39] Revelations 12. However, you must go to an early copy of the Bible, even back to the original Greek, because in the later ones, this story has been changed and lost.
[40] aka: also known as.

By practicing CDT, you will learn to perceive your "fallen angels" as IDentity masses, convert them to charge, and then discharge them as energy to thereby discreate that reality mass. This discreates the darkness mass of your NIRs and lets your True ESSENCE LIGHT shine forth again. This is the process of your ascension from the "hell" of materiality and darkness (buried in NIR Masses) to the "heavens" of SPACE and LIGHT.

The ESM is called the "original sin" in Catholicism; and "karma" in Buddhism and Hinduism. In Catholicism, the "original sin" is what Adam and Eve did that expelled them from the Garden of Eden (aka the Kingdom of Heaven) into the world of struggle and tears. You, as their descendant, supposedly inherit that (apparently unforgivable) transgression against God so that it is still between you and God. (Supposedly, Jesus died to redeem you from the original sin and any others you may have picked up in the meantime.) The ESM is not a sin, but a creation, a mass of reality; however, it certainly is what separates you from God.

Karma is what you did in the past whose effects you are still carrying around and "paying" in the present. That certainly describes the ESM. You created it in the past to "descend" from the heavens to become a human being, and, if you are a human BEing, you are certainly still carrying it around with you and suffering its effects.

> I suspect that Jesus taught the discreation of NIR Masses, and that this has come down to us in Catholicism as the "confession of sins." Jesus taught SPace, which is the absence of BAD and the beginning of Love+ (as we shall see in a coming chapter). Without BAD, there is no sin, as sin is, by definition, BAD actions. Thus, Jesus never taught sin—that is a human distortion.
>
> However, all the Christian sects are purveyors of "BAD, evil, and sin:" it is their favorite polarity. I suspect that what was originally NIR Masses in the teachings of Jesus soon were painted with BAD and distorted into "sins." The priest, who now hears the confession of sins for their forgiveness, was originally supposed to serve as the CDT trainer that we use in psycanics to guide in the discreation of NIR Masses. The job of the CDT Trainer or "Pilot" is just to guide the discreator in the process of discreation until s/he learns how to do it hirself. Most people need this guidance before they can guide themselves.

Your current, fundamentally-ineffective weapons in this war against your NIRs = AntiGod are what we call the External Quest. The External Quest includes all effort to find happiness (remember that ESSENCE is the only happiness) outside of self, in the world. The concept of External Quest includes

- All forms of Ego, and all struggle for titles, honors, recognition, money, success, power, fame and fortune, to be happy.

- All efforts to avoid or suppress UPS (which you will remember is always NIR Mass activations) with substance abuse (food, tobacco, alcohol, mood medications, illegal drugs, etc.).
- All efforts to avoid, change or distract oneself from UPS with addictive activities, such as shopping, television, computer use, sex, gambling, constant cell phone use to avoid being alone, etc.
- All efforts to achieve happiness through relationships. The External Quest is the underlying cause of ALL relationships problems and conflicts, as is pinpointed in the psycanics Relationships Course.
- All neurosis (the inability to control one's behaviors in specific areas). All the AntiLove behaviors of humanity are caused within the External Quest for ESSENCE.

All of these behaviors are ineffective, some because they are forms of resistance (negation to experience). All are ineffective because they are a search outside of yourself while heaven is within. Nothing external to you, no amount of fame and fortune, can ever change or negate Who You Are, your NIRs. You must discreate them.

> Remember that the purpose of life is to re-create yourself anew in the next grandest version of the greatest vision you can conceive about Who You Are, **until you are finally ME again.** (4-6-114)

However, in one sense, you don't need much creation[41]. You already are God, the ONE—there isn't anything you need to create. All you have to do is uncover, dis-cover Who You Are. It is not primarily a process of creation; it is primarily a process of discreation. You have to eliminate what counter-creates, blocks, suppresses What You already Are. What you most need to do is discreate that which suppresses your experience and real-ization of Who You Are: your **Essence Suppressor Mass.**

To understand how this works, it helps to understand the nature of Created Reality (as opposed to Ultimate Reality = TRUTH = God). This is the subject of our next chapter.

41 However, in psycanics you will learn to do a LOT of creation. Creation is very effective in activating the counter-creations that you need to discreate, and the technology of Creation<>Counter Creation is a major tool. You will also learn how to create your physical life as you would have it.

Chapter 16

SPace

Enlightenment begins with acceptance, without judgment of "what is." (3-8-149)

Allow each soul to walk its path. (1-1-47) Everything is acceptable in the sight of God, for how can God not accept that which is? (1-2-61)

You cannot change that which you do not accept. (3—151)

Non-acceptance is Resistance, and Resistance Causes Persistence.

SPace is your original condition of BEing. Pure Consciousness with no content is pure SPace. God is the INFINITE SPACE in which all things exist. You, once upon a time, were God—and are trying to get back to IT, to BE SPace again.

SPace is nothing, no-thing. It is the formless. It is the absence of energy-matter. It is the absence of experience, and therefore of all realities. Where there is SPace, there is no energy-matter to change or move; hence SPace is static. It is, therefore, also Timelessness[42], which is not a long time, but the Eternal Present.

SPace–Density (of mass) is a polarity. The concept of Density, the opposite of SPace in psycanics, includes mass and resistance. Mass, matter, is resistance to the presence of another mass. It is a basic law of our universe that two masses cannot occupy the same space. In physics, space is that which separates matter and thus keeps everything from occupying the same space.

It may help you to get just how "spacey," how "mirage-out-of-nothing" is the hologram of physical reality, to consider this: If there were no space in the universe (at all scales from within the atom to between the galaxies), all the matter in the universe would be about the size of a pea.

As a human being, you are at the "south" end of the SPace<>Density Polarity. You are as material as a spirit can be. You are incarnated into matter, into a body;

---

[42] Time is change or movement of energy in space, be it the rotation of the earth, the sun, or the hands of your watch.

but more importantly, your spirit is trapped inside of the denseness and heaviness of your massive God Suppressor Shell. Another viewpoint on your Return to God is that it is a journey from Density to SPace, from Matter-iality to Spirit-uality.

When your mind = consciousness is empty of all thoughts and emotions, of all energy—particularly negative energy—you are in SPace. Of course, a totally empty mind is very difficult to achieve, usually requiring a lifetime of daily meditation. However, there is one level of mental Space that you can achieve quickly if you work at it: the absence of BAD.

Above all, **mental SPace is the absence of the creation of BAD**. It is the Creation of BAD that provokes you to create AntiLove and try to drive things out of your SPace of BEing, out of your presence, out of your experience, and often, out of existence.

When you are creating BAD, your consciousness is occupied by that creation and by the negative energies = resistances that it triggers. When you are creating BAD, you have no SPace: your SPace is occupied by the thought of BAD and all that that triggers of your Resistance = AntiLove. You are, therefore denying SPace to What Is to BE As It Is. Your SPace is filled with your negative energies, which are the only UPS that exist. Remember, when you create BAD, you are the first to suffer.

Thus, SPace is a state in which Good<>BAD Polarity does not exist—because you are not creating it. It is the place of neutrality, of neither Good nor BAD at the center point of the Good<>BAD Polarity.

I AM BAD as a mental creation (more exactly, an IDentity as a result of NIRs), is the trigger for all negative emotions. Therefore, mental SPace is the key to emotional space. The first level of SPace is to maintain your mind free of all your opinions = creations of BAD. This will help maintain your emotional SPace free of all resistance = negative EmoLoveJoy.

Emotionally, EmoLoveJoy-ingly, SPace is the resulting absence of negative energy, of AntiLove, of Resistance to anything. As the mental creation of BAD is what triggers negative ELJ, mental SPace to your NIRs leads to emotional SPace.

SPace is, therefore, the center point between Love and AntiLove on that polarity. It is therefore the end of AntiLove and the beginning of Love. As Love+/- is the only Happiness+/- there is, SPace is the end of UPS and the beginning of Happiness. We can see all this by looking at the polarity spectrum of EmoLoveJoy in the following illustration:

Illustration 16-1: SPace is the neutral point of no energy between positive and negative on psycanic polarity spectrums. BAD is the trigger for all <u>negative psycanic energy = AntiLove = Resistance</u>.

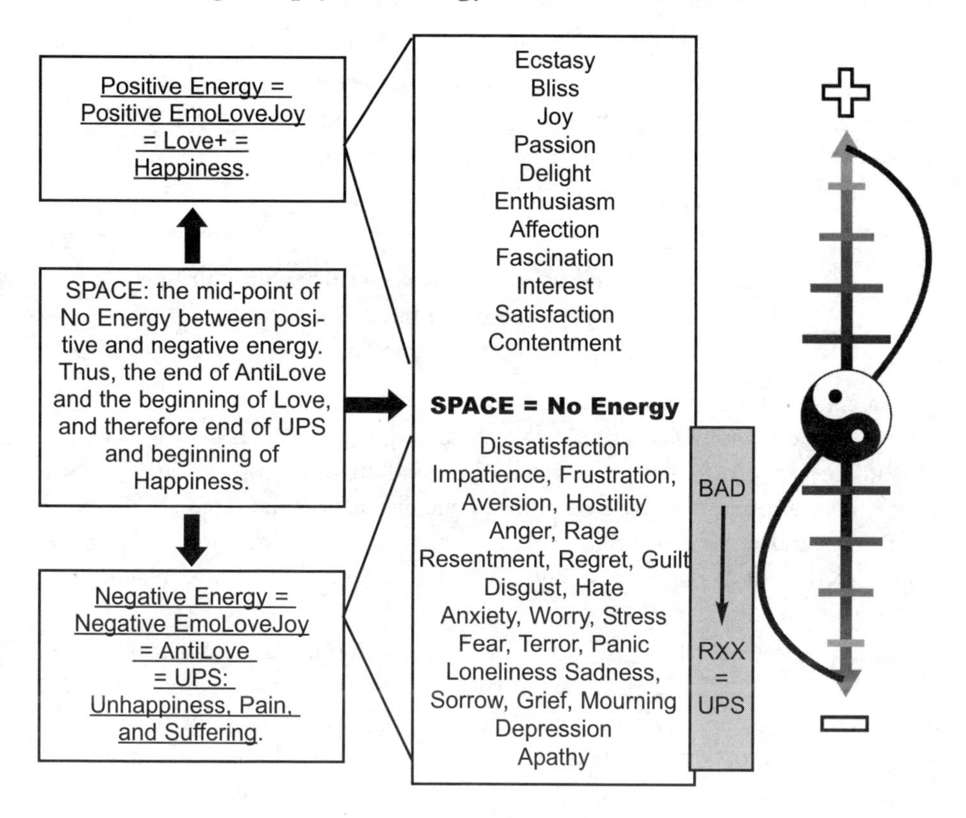

SPace, non-resistance, is the only solution to negative energy. The opposite of SPace, <u>resistance = negative energy</u>, only leads to more negative energy. When you throw negative energy against negative energy to resist it, all you get is more negative energy. Thus, SP is also Acceptance, Tolerance, and Patience.

Thus, to change anything, Self included, you must start with SPace, with acceptance of What Is. If you are creating BAD around what you want to change; you will be in Resistance→Persistence—and pain. NEVER forget that it is your own <u>resistance = AntiLove</u> that is the only source of UPS in life.

An example of SPace is Pardon and Forgiveness. To pardon or forgive yourself or others is to wipe out the <u>negative energy = AntiLove</u> that you are holding towards that person. While you are maintaining negative energy, you are not in SPace. To pardon is to restore yourself to a condition of SPace, of no negative energy towards that person. Thus, you forgive others not so much for them as for you; to restore you to SPace and LoveJoy.

Some of the Laws of Energy and SPace are:

Energy flows to Space.
Energy that Flows, Grows.
(Grow = goes up the polarity spectrum.)

Negative Energy = Resistance blocks the flow of Energy. This stops the discharge of negative energy that is the essence of discreation. Thus, Resistance Causes Persistence. SPace is the opposite of Resistance, and the first step in Discreation of your NIRs (and anything else in your life.)

Law:

You cannot create what you want by resisting what you have.
You must be in SPace to what you have (What Is) to stop
energizing= "persisting" it.

On another level, SPace is the condition of your consciousness when no NIR mass is activated: no mass, no matter, zero density, is SPace. It is likewise the state of your consciousness when you have discreated an activation (a triggered NIR mass). SPace is, therefore, the mid-point of the discreation and re-creation cycle in CDT. You are in SPace, nothing there, when you have eliminated the negative energy (NIR mass), but have not yet begun to create the positive realities you desire for your future.

On an even higher level, SPACE is the original and natural condition of your Spirit, of ESSENCE ITSELF. You BEcome SPACE again when you have discreated your entire Essence Suppressor Mass (ESM). Your ESM is the dense mass of energy, of realities, that counter-create your Godness. They make you "heavy" and "dark" as a being and "weigh," you down, bring you down, to the level of consciousness of a human being. When you discreate this mass, you return from being dense and localized to BEing the INFINITE SPACE and LIGHTNESS that is God.

SPACE is the State of God. God is the INFINITE SPACE in which everything exists, without resistance to it being as it is. As we said in the previous chapter; if the OMNIPOTENT ALMIGHTY thought that something "should not BE," which is to deny it SPace to BE; it would not BE; there would be no SPace for it. Therefore, if it is, then it has the SPACE of God to BE, and as GOD = SPACE is infinite; it exists within the SPace of God. As everything that can exist, does exist —Creation is INFINITE—everything possible is always in and has the SPACE of God.

Thus, Creation itself can be considered a polarity spectrum that runs from the INFINITE SPACE, LIGHTness and JOY; down to the grossest, darkest, densest, heaviest, most localized, most resistant energy-masses possible, of which the physical universe is one expression and the human being another.

Thus the process of BEcoming ONE again, of BEcoming God again, can be considered as a journey from Density to SPACE, from Materiality to Spirituality.

One of the most important forms of SPace that we seek as a human is to keep our <u>consciousness = experience</u> clear of NIR mass activations, by discreating them when they appear.

The final form of SPace that we seek, is elimination of our entire ESM that masses us down into a human being and is the wall that separates us from God. We want to return to our original state of SPACE, free from all counter-reality and God suppressor IDentity masses.

Table 16-1: The God<>Creation Polarity

God: The ONE, SPIRITuality INFINITE SPACE (Quantum Field) LIGHTness BLISS, ECSTASY CAUSE, CREATOR, POWER No Polarity
Polarity, The Many, Matter-iality, Mass, Density EFFECT of external causes Localized, Minimum Space Heaviness, Darkness Resistance, which is Painful to a Spirit

SPace is

- God. Everything that exists, the Many, exists within the SPACE of God.
- Nothingness, the STATIC. The Quantum Field everywhere-nowhere.
- Consciousness: the SPace in which all your experience occurs and exists.
- Clear Consciousness, Still Mind of no thoughts.
- The capacity to contain realities, including conflicting ones.
- Value Neutrality: the absence of BAD and of all polarization.
- The starting condition for discreation of anything.
- Absence of NIR Masses activations.
- Absence of <u>AntiLove = Rxx</u>→UPS and Perxx.
- The result of the discreation of NIR Masses to restore you to SPace.
- Serenity, Peace, Tranquility, Patience.

- Acceptance, Tolerance of What Is As It Is.
- The Beginning of Cause→Power (Resistance puts you into Effect).
- The Beginning of Love.
- For all of the above: the Beginning of Wisdom.

That is a lot of Juice out of No-thing!

The Opposites of SPace include:

- Energy-matter in any form.
- A Mind full of opinions, but especially of
  - any creation of BAD, which then triggers
  - invalidation and Rxx, which cause
  - UPS and persistence.
- Rejection of the realities and points of view of others.
- The presence of NIR Masses in the BEing (the ESM).
- The presence of NIR Masses in experience (activations).
- Reactivity.
- Negative EmoLoveJoy = AntiLove.

One way of understanding your Return to the ONE is that it is a path to

Return to and BE SPACE.

This includes:

- Having no opinions, no judgments, no creations of Good<>BAD.
- Having no Resistance, no AntiLove, to anyone or anything.
- Discreating your NIR Masses, your individual Nuclear IDentities that counter-create the God in you, thus transforming mass to SPace in your BEing.
- Discreating your entire Essence Suppressor Mass (which is the sum total of your NIR Masses) to return you to the FULL and INFINITE BEING of SPACE that you are.
- Expanding the SPace of your BEing to re-incorporate, to include everything that exists. This you do by
  - having **zero resistance**, the condition of SPace, to everything around you and to all that exists. This zero resistance includes to your NIRs, and is the beginning of the process of discreation of them. And
  - perceiving life as a parade of events in which none are good or BAD, and which you have no grasping and clinging, or aversion and resistance, to any event whatsoever. This is to give SPace to life to unfold as it should.

Above all—and what is most important to us now as we go into how to discreate your NIR Masses and ESM—**you need a relationship of, a state of, SPace to be able to discreate them**. Thus, SPace is both the goal and the means. As SPace is the beginning of Love, this is to say that Love is both the goal and the means to Return to God. The State of SPace is the State of Grace.

If you are in resistance to your NIRs, you are AntiLoving them and you are persisting them. It is your SPace = Love that discreates your NIRs. The Law is:

Love is the Universal Solvent: **Love dissolves AntiLove**.

Your Love begins with your SPace, and that SPace must begin with your SPace to yourSelf. Where you most need your SPace is where you are most denying it to yourSelf: in your creations of yourSelf as NIRs. You are denying yourSelf that SPace by your creations of BAD to your NIRs and with the negative energy of your AntiLove = negative emotions = UPS.

You return to SPace by discreating your creations of BAD, which automatically dissipates your resistances and negative emotions. This clears your path of re-integration and BE-FEELing = Love-ing of your NIRs, which is what discreates them.

Love starts with
giving yourself and others the SPACE to BE
as they are, and to not BE as they are not.

SPace is the beginning of Love and therefore of Happiness.
That which most needs your SPace is you.

You can only give Space to others
to the degree that you give Space to yourself.
You can only Love others to the degree that you Love yourself.

Your path of return to God is one of SPace
to re-BEcome SPACE.

SPACE is the goal and SPace is the means.

The State of Grace is the
State of SPace in the Kingdom of Heaven.

Chapter 17

Introduction to the Theory of Discreation

> You have placed yourself in a perception shell that blocks out the Total Reality. (3-5-52)

We are now going to go deeper into the nature of your God Suppressor Mass, into the mechanics, the psycanics, and the science of it. We are going to introduce some sophisticated concepts of advanced psycanics about the nature of reality and experience, concepts that are important to understand Creation and Discreation, which abilities are our goal with CDT. We want to discreate our NIR Masses, and thereby eventually, our God Suppressor Mass. We also want to take control of our life and be able to create all that we wish to experience.

Existence is a polarity spectrum of energy formed into realities that runs between two poles of the **Causal SPacial Static No-Thingness** of the TAO = the Quantum Field, down to the **Effected, Material, and Denseness** of the lower end of **Created Reality**, which is the physical universe[43]. We can call these two poles **SPIRIT-uality** and **MATTER-iality**, as shown in the figure to the right.

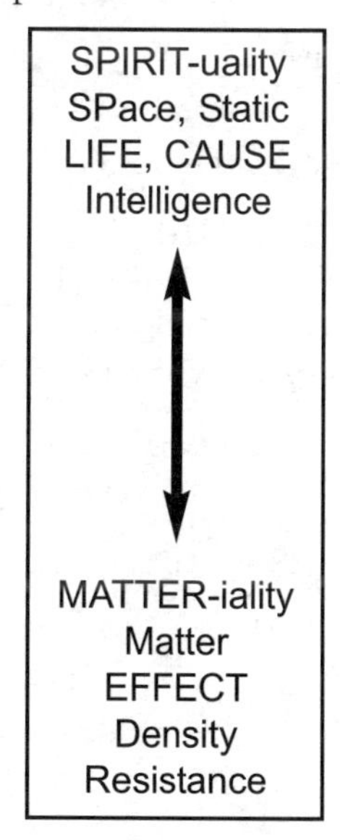

Created Reality is formed by the ULTIMATE REALITY out of ITSELF, for there is nothing else from which to form anything. The purpose of the formation of created realities is **experience**. The universe is God forming HERSELF into all HER infinite possibilities of realities→ experience for the purpose of experiencing HERSELF in all those infinite possibilities of BEing, FEELing, THINKing, DOing, and HAVEing.

---

43 I understand that there is at least one realm of Created Reality lower than the physical universe we know.

We want to examine the nature of created realities, and for a good reason. **Our God Suppressor Mass is a mass of created realities**, and all of the Laws of Reality and Experience apply. By applying those laws, we can discreate it and so Return to BEing the ONE.

Reality, Experience, Real and Not-Real

> Foreword on "Reality versus Truth." We are going to introduce the psycanics concepts of Reality, Experience, and Real. Do not confuse Truth with reality. Truth is the degree of verifiable correspondence between a reality and a statement about that reality. Truth is a report of What Is, of nature of a reality, although it must be verifiable to establish that It Is.
>
> Reality (other than ULTIMATE REALITY) is always a creation, and what is created can be discreated. TRUTH in all capital letters is another name for LIFE = God.
>
> One of the problems that people have in discreation is that the confuse Truth with reality. This blocks discreation because you can't discreate Truth, only realities. Your NIRs are always realities; they are never Truth.

"**Experience**" is a major concept in psycanics. Your experience is everything that you can perceive in any way or form. You have psycanic experience[44]: of Self, emotions, thoughts, etc; and you have physical experiences of the body, and through the body, of the physical universe. Here, we are only interested in your psycanic experience.

A **reality** is any mass or form of energy, therefore, any *thing*. Anything that exists is a reality. All realities are creations. An **experience** is your perception of any reality. These two, reality and experience, are Cause<>Effect.

All energy, and therefore all experience, is legal: it obeys exact laws. There a number of Laws of Reality-Experience that describe how it all works[45]. Here are some examples of them:

The Purpose of ALL the Creation is Experience (God knowing HERSELF).
The Purpose of the Creation of any Reality is Experience.

Realities Cause Experience. Experience is the Effect of a Reality (on consciousness).

The Cycle of Existence of a Reality→Experience is:
Creation→Experience→Discreation.

A Reality persists until it completes its
Purpose of Existence = its Cycle of Existence: i.e. until it is fully experienced.

44 We are including mental experience with psycanic experience for simplicity.
45 These Laws are explained in depth in other psycanics materials.

Ergo: Experienced Experience Disappears.

Resistance to a reality is the refusal to experience it.
Ergo: Resistance Causes Persistence
(by not allowing the reality to complete its Cycle of Existence).

You discreate realities by completing their Cycle of Existence = experiencing them fully.

You create ALL your experience: your thoughts, your emotions, your IDentities and your identities (human roles). You do this by molding and injecting energy into masses, which are "realities"—any energy form, any "thing." You eliminate unwanted experiences by discreating the reality causing them. You do this by applying the Laws of Reality-Experience introduced above. Basically, you reverse the process of creation by flowing energy out of the reality-mass, where in creation you flow it into it. You control, alter and eliminate unwanted experiences by discreating those realities, which is a process of releasing from that form = reality the modulated energy of which they are made. You do this by "experiencing them out." Will creates; Consciousness (experience) discreates.

Real: Be careful of the word "real," because it has a specific and special definition in psycanics. A reality is real when you are experiencing it, and not-real when you are not. "Reality" is anything that exists. **Real means that a given reality is being experienced in present time.** Therefore, you can have realities that exist but that are not-real at the moment (and possibly never for you). For example, everything in your subconscious (memories, knowledge, plans, etc.) is a not-real reality, until you call it forth into consciousness and so re-experience (remember) it, at which time it becomes real. So do not confuse "reality" and "real;" they are very different concepts in psycanics.

Understand this about realities and real: **The only thing you try to do in life is make realities that you want to experience real; and to make realities that you do not want to experience, not-real.** You want to make a new car real (notice that it already is a reality—at the dealer) by manifesting it into your possession = full experience of it. You make an old car you no longer want not-real by selling it or gi. It is still a reality, but no longer real for you. This is the only thing you do in life: try to control your realities—to control your experience. You want to make illness not-real, and good health real. You want to make poverty not-real, and wealth real. (Of course, the Existential Imperative is that the reality you *really* want to make real is your ESSENCE.)

- You have made your God ESSENCE **not-real**. It is still a reality (IT is ULTIMATE REALITY), and it is TRUTH, **but it is not-real**. Remember that not-real means that it is out of your perception = experience at the moment, not that it does not exist.

- How did you make REALITY not-real? You have made your TRUE BEING not-real by counter-creating and blocking it with other realities. These are created realities: your Essence Suppressor Mass which is consists of all your NIR Masses. As they are created realities versus ULTIMATE REALITY they are illusions, but no *less* **real** (*causing of experience*) for that.
- The Existential Imperative is to make your ESSENCE (WPVLJ) *real* again. This is the Game of Life in which you are engaged: Return, Re-Integration, to the ONE.
- To do this, you must make your AntiEssence = ESM = all your NIR Masses not-real. You are trying to do this, make your AntiEssence Mass not-real, and your ESSENCE real at all times.

Here is where the matter is delicate:

- When you do not understand Energy, Reality, Experience, Real, Resistance, and Discreation, you will try to make it not-real in ways that do not work. These erroneous ways include resistance and all the forms of the External Quest.

Making something Not-Real: Discreation versus Resistance

There are various ways to *try* to make a reality not-real.

1. The first includes all forms of resistance as "negation to experience." You can try to get away from it, get out of perception range. In the physical universe, you can run away from a reality (such as the snake). But you cannot run away from your psycanic realities, particularly NIR Masses. They are in your psycanic universe and accompany you wherever you go.
2. A second way is to try to make psycanics realities (NIR Masses, specifically) not-real, to block or suppress your experience of them. You can suppress your emotions (NIR activations FELT as anger, fear, or grief, etc.) by tensing your body or holding your breath, among other things.
3. A third way is to divert your consciousness, which is your ability to experience, into some competing experience. You can try to distract yourself from FEELing depressed, for example, by going to a movie or watching television, or going shopping. Many people avoid loneliness by constantly calling others on the phone.
4. A fourth way is to try to reduce or turn off your consciousness to not feel your emotional realities with chemical substances, including tobacco, alcohol, mood medications, illegal drugs, etc. This is the cause of all addictions. The force of your addictions over you is always the force of your Existential Imperative to avoid negative EmoLoveJoy.
5. Another way is to attack the reality with negative energy to change or destroy it. You can attack the snake to kill it. You can attack others with

anger to stop or change what they do that disturbs you. However, attacking your NIR Masses with negative emotions is a resistance energization that only persists and grows them. Not a workable strategy for making them not-real.

6. Yet another way is to counter-create the reality with another reality that is bigger or closer so that it blocks out the first negative reality that you wish to avoid experiencing, thus making it not-real. You then experience the counter-reality instead of the now-blocked REALITY. God says as much in *CWG*: Your thoughts about God do not create God, but they do create your experience of God. You then experience those thoughts instead of the Truth.

Notice that in all of these cases, the original, negative reality continues to exist. None of the above techniques make a reality not-real by discreating it. Thus, all of these forms are forms of resistance to the reality, and as you well know by now: Rxx→Perxx[46]—not to mention UPS. It always requires effort and energy, including negative EmoLoveJoy = negative emotion = UPS, to maintain your resistance to experience; that is tiring and AntiHappiness.

Furthermore, as you are not discreating the reality, there is always the possibility that it slips through your Resistances so that you end up experiencing it partially or fully anyway. This is exactly what happens with your NIR Mass activations.

The best way to make a reality not-real is to simply discreate it. When it is discreated, it no longer exists and therefore **can no longer cause experience**. Discreation is done by releasing or discharging the modulation of its reality-mass back into free, unmodulated energy[47]. The reality then no longer exists as such, and so can no longer cause experience. Furthermore, there is no longer anything there to resist, so you do not fall into the trap of resistance later. **Discreation**—not resistance, blockage, counter-creator, distraction, suppression, or ignorance—**is the best way to make a reality not-real, the only way that "really" works**.

On discreation, the reality is gone forever. You have nothing to resist; you have nothing to counter-create: you are free of it altogether. The total absence of that reality puts you into the condition of SPace that we studied in the previous chapter. This also means that you need only the lightest creation, the lightest amount of a positive reality, lightest touch of reality, to cause you the positive experience you desire. Life becomes light and easy, as opposed to heavy and dense as it is when you are trying to resist and counter-create your negative realities.

---

46 Resistance Causes Persistence.

47 It is not a discreation of the energy itself, but the demodulation of it. Modulation means the frequency, form, density, flavor, and any other characteristic that makes a thing, an energy-form unique and a uniquely causing its experience.

Therefore, we always want to discreate any opposing realities before we create the positive ones. We want to move from a condition of negative reality→negative experience, to zero reality→zero experience, which is the condition of SPace. From the condition of SPace, we only need a quick and easy creation of positive reality to give us the positive experience we desire for the future.

Real and Not-Real as Regards Your BEing God

As a normal human being, it is not-real to you that you are God, which is to say that your experience is that you are Not-God. Your purpose in life, the Existential Imperative, is to **make real (experiential)** again that you are God. That is not just a (created) reality; it is REALITY and TRUTH. You are God, but it is not-real at the moment. As this REALITY = TRUTH already exists, **you do not need to create being God**. But obviously, you need to do something to make God real again. This is where we are going.

The TRUTH already exists. IT is infinite in size, omnipresent and your own TRUE NATURE and ESSENCE. There isn't anywhere you can go to escape being God. You are always at the exact center of God Who is a sphere of BEing, infinite in all directions. There is no place you can go to make IT not-real by getting away from IT, by getting out of perception range of IT. IT is always all around you and inside you. IT permeates you. You are made of IT.

This brings us again to the Two Great Questions: How did you make the biggest "THING" in the cosmos, OMNIPRESENT ALMIGHTY GOD HIMSELF, not-real?

We mentioned before how magicians have created illusions to disappear (make not-real) big things like an elephant and even the Statue of Liberty. But that is nothing compared to what you have done.

You have disappeared the ENTIRE KINGDOM of HEAVEN,

God and All—including the entire host of the "Good" Angels!

Not only that, but **you disappeared IT ALL INSIDE of YOU!**

The Kingdom of Heaven is nothing if it is not the residence of God. Buddha taught God is within; Krishna taught that; all the Great Teachers and all the mystics have taught that. Many schools teach meditation. Jesus said it 2,000 years ago: "The Kingdom of Heaven is Within." God confirms it in *CWG*, and also stresses meditation, to seek and be with HIM within.

So, within you is the entire Kingdom of Heaven, God. Within you is the CREATOR HIMSELF[48]. And IT is totally **not-real, not experienced, not perceived,**

[48] Within you is the CREATOR and all of the Creation. I know the world appears "out-there," but it is really inside of YOU as the INFINITE GOD-SPACE in which everything exists.

by you as a human being. Totally NOT-REAL! Like it's not even there. **How did you do that??? How have you hidden, disappeared, vanished, made not-real, the entire Kingdom of Heaven???**

Inside of you is THE ALL THAT IS, the Beginning and the End, the Alpha and the Omega, and the Everything In Between. The CREATOR and therefore all of CREATION as there is no distinction. Where is IT? Where did you put IT? How did you make ALL THAT not-real? And you are still doing it; doing it right now as you read this.

> Notice that all of this is a question of **Reality**, **Real**, and **Experience**. These operate by exact laws, laws that are precisely codified in psycanics.

Is that not an incredible feat? Is not "How do you do that?" a tremendous question? Can there be any question more important—other than the Second Great Question:

"How do I make <u>IT = God</u> appear again?"

This question, scientifically phrased is: How do I make that which is not-real, real again?

Are not these the questions that should have most occupied humanity since we first learned that the Kingdom is there, within us? Is this not where all our philosophy, science, investigation and research should be most focused?

NOTE FROM THE AUTHOR:

These are the questions I have spent my life investigating and which I am answering in this book. That is why this book and all of psycanics is the perfect complement, a technology, for *Conversations with God.* Psycanics is an extremely powerful, fast technology for uncovering the Kingdom of Heaven within you. It can take you to a continual experience of the LOVEJOY within a few years.

That psycanics is coming forth is no accident. There are no accidents, no coincidences, and no randomness. It is all part of the great plan for the Transformation of Consciousness for humanity. Given the effects of untransformed, AntiEssence-AntiLove, human consciousness on the planet—destruction—Transformation is urgent: It is Transform or Perish.

How You Block and Counter-Create the Truth and Reality of Who You Are

You can't discreate the TRUTH of Who You Are, but you have certainly made IT not-real. How have you done so? You are using **all** of the forms of resistance we mentioned before to make IT not-real. However, the primary one is Counter-Creation.

You have created the reality = experience of not-BEing God by creating an enormous mass of realities→experience[49] that you are Not-God. These are your AntiEssence IDentities, which are the core of your NIR Masses, which in totality form your ESM. Remember that realities and experience are the two sides of the same coin. As a human being, it is your reality→your experience that you are Not-God. It is your creation of certain realities that cause you the experience of not-BEing God. To cite God again:

> Your thought about God does not create God. It merely creates your experience of God. (4-12-249) **You then experience those thought realities instead of the Truth.**

Obviously, such realities must be about you, and any creation = reality about you, any I AM this or that, or I AM NOT this or that, is an IDentity. These creations = realities = identities of AntiGod we have already seen. They are the ones that you have created to cause you the (albeit illusory) reality-experience of not-BEing God. They are your AntiEssence or Negative Psycanic IDentities. You will remember that there are three basic flavors: AntiWisdom, AntiPower, AntiValue, around which you generate AntiLove.

You as a human being are existing inside a huge, thick shell of AntiEssence, of counter-creation of yourSelf as God; of creation of yourSelf as Not-God, Not-Essence = AntiEssence. We can call that shell your **Essence Counter-Creation Mass**, your **Essence Suppressor Mass**, or your **AntiEssence Reality Mass**, or your **AntiEssence IDentity Mass**. All of these are good labels for it. For short, we can also call it the "Shell." You are the sole and soul creator of your Shell.

To Return to the ONE, you must make not-real that which blocks and suppresses you from BEing God, your Essence Suppressor Mass. **This you must do by discreating it—not by resisting it, which is what you have been doing, and which only causes it to persist.**

This is all that you have to do to let the Truth and reality of **Who You Are = God** become real = your experience again. You only need to discreate your created realities = identities that are causing you the experience of not-BEing God.

49 "Realities→experience" means "realities causing experience." Remember that realities and experience are the two sides of the same coin. It is your reality and your experience that you are Not-God. Your creation.

This IDentity mass we call the Essence Suppressor Mass. You will assist the process by also creating—affirming is a better word as you do not need to create what already is—your Godliness; but discreation is a most powerful path of Return to ESSENCE.

I repeat, because it is a key concept: Your Essence Suppressor Mass is the totality of your NIR Masses. You cannot directly discreate your Essence Suppressor Mass, it is far too big. But you can easily discreate it one NIR Mass at a time. Furthermore, life itself will serve them up to you, one or a few at a time, in the form of your activations of negative emotions.

The ESM is a mass of modulated energy, a mass of realities that counter-create for you the Reality = experience of BEing God. We have already seen these counter-creations: Your AntiEssence IDentities. (God, remember, is WPVLJ: Wisdom, Power, Value, LoveJoy.) To counter-create your reality = experience of BEing WPVLJ, All Wise, All Power, All Valuable, All Love, and totally Blissful; you had to create yourSelf as the opposite polarity. You did so by creating your Negative Nuclear IDentities that trigger your Self-AntiLove, which is the only Unhappines, Pain and Suffering that exist. You did a marvelous job: here you are BEing a human being instead of God.

Your ESM is made up of about 20,000 CDT watt-hours of AntiEssence Mass.

Between you and your ESM, you have created a shell of **blocks to perception**, to FEELing, to knowing, to remembering: in other words, to your Consciousness, to the ESSENCE ability of Wisdom. (Actually, you have reduced Consciousness, but the net result is as if you had created blocks.) These blocks keep the entire ESM from coming in on you, which would be extremely painful, beyond the ability of a human to bear. It would be, literally, hell. You have to confront the ESM and discreate it little by little, thereby re-increasing your Essence to eventually be able to handle and discreate ever-larger chunks of the ESM.

Your ESM bears down on your Consciousness = experience to counter-create your perception = BE-FEEL of ESSENCE. The combination of your ESM and your blocks creates your every day, non-activated, experience of being a human being. This is your chronic level of Essence<>AntiEssence experience, as opposed to your acute activations of AntiEssence that are your NIR Mass activations. These you can think of as stimulation "leaks" of AntiEssence→ AntiLove into your internal SPace of awareness = perception = FEELing. For example, when you are sad, depressed, or lonely, you have some ESM leaking in on you. On top of these mild leaks, there are also acute activations of your NIR Masses, where these components of your ESM move in on your FEELing.

In the following illustration 17-1, we show the ESM as a band of reality-experience mass around you-psycan, without indicating the individual NIR Masses as we did in the previous chapter.

Illustration 17-1

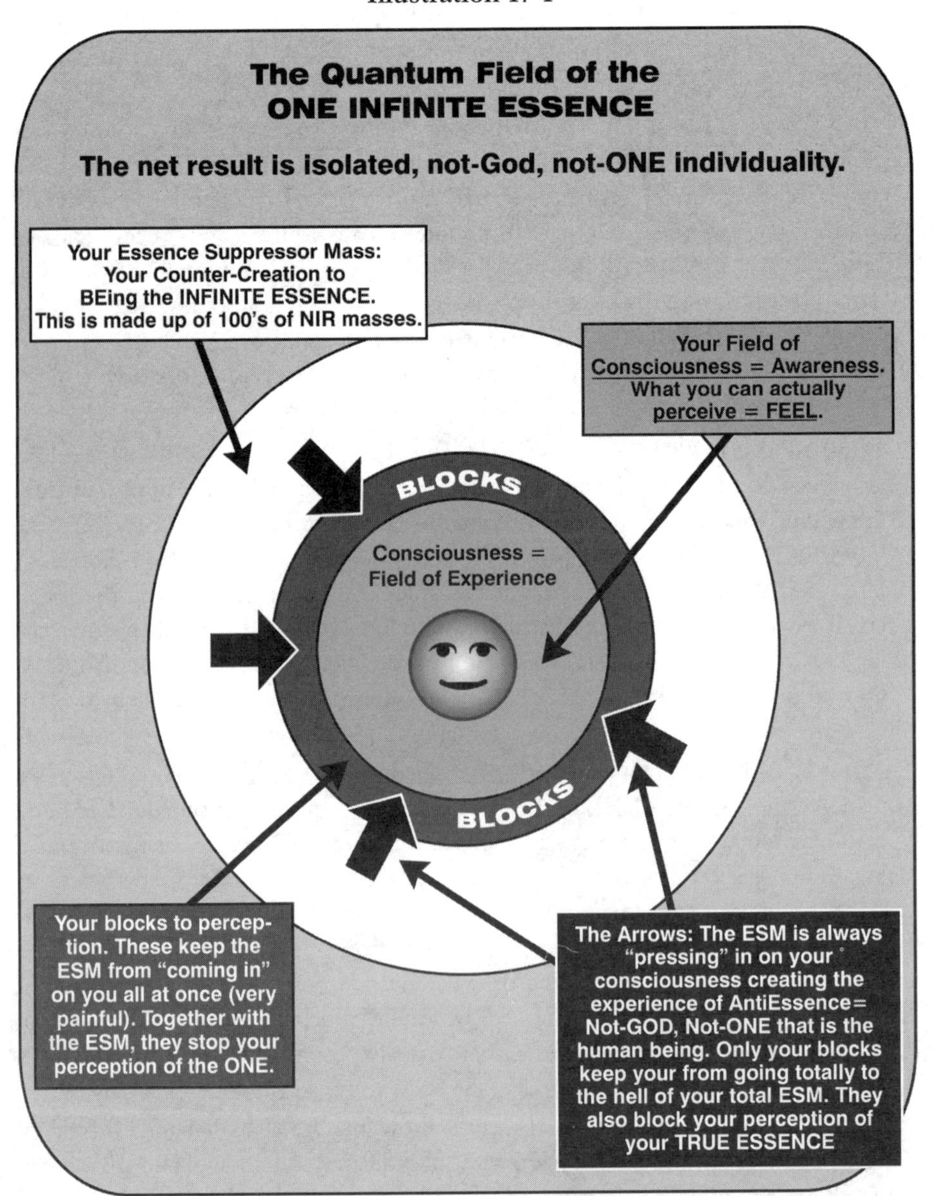

Chapter 18

Creation

God speaks of creation quite a bit in *CWG* and it is indeed a most powerful tool on your return to God. You do not need to create that you are God, but the constant creation of PIRs is a very powerful tool to remind you Who You Are and help you to remain in that awareness.

However:

Without discreation, you will not be able to do truly powerful creation.

By truly powerful creation, I mean where you are generating and moving totally sensible flows and masses of energy. You can feel the energy running through your body, tingling your entire nervous system and shivering your body. I am speaking of generating levels of creation of IDentities (PIRs) where the resulting LoveJoy approaches that of a sexual orgasm.

To restore yourself to these levels of positive energy, you must be totally comfortable with and capable of handling similar quantities of negative energy, because negative energy is what you must remove for the positive energy to flow again. Positive energy activates negative energy. Love activates AntiLove.

One of the Laws of Realities is:

The intent to create a reality can activate the counter-realities previously created and still with the BEing.

This is polarity at work. Let's say you want to make more real your "Power" and you start to create (intend, energize, and love) the IDentity, "I AM POWERFUL;" I AM THE CREATOR of everything in my experience." However, as a human being you are inside a mass of NIRs = ESM that consists of the opposite realities: "I AM NOT POWERFUL. I AM NOT even RESPONSE-ABLE for what I experience, much less the creator. I CAN'T CREATE what I want." etc.

These realities-IDentities are masses of modulated energy in the God Suppressor Shell around you. You are their creator (long ago when you became human), and now you are at the effect of your creations such that they act on you to cause you their negative experiences of self (NIRs).

Your efforts to counter-create these NIRs (which themselves are counter-creations to your Godness) with PIRs will cause the new creations of PIRs to "bump up" against the old creations of the NIRs. You might say that there is no space in your BEing for the PIRs because your SPace of BEing is already packed with the NIR Masses. **Trying to create PIRs activates the NIRs**, which is to say it "knocks" them loose from the ESM and "down"into your consciousness = experience, where you can discreate them.

In other words, the effort to create one side of a psycanic energy polarity will activate into your FEELing the other side of the polarity if it is already there.

The effort to create PIRs→ELJ will usually activate NIRs→UPS.

This activation is marvelous—**IF YOU KNOW HOW TO DISCREATE the NIRs**. In fact, this technique of using positive creations to activate negative ones so that you can discreate the negative ones, thereby creating SPace in your BEing into which you can then place the positive creations with minimal creative effort, is one of the most powerful tools in CDT.

For one thing, it frees you from having to wait for external triggers to activate you to have NIR Mass available for discreation to so free and expand your BEing. **You can now activate yourself whenever you want.**

Furthermore, you activate yourself exactly where you want to be activated to transform yourself to exactly Who You want to BE next. You can now activate the precise limitations to achieving exactly what you want to achieve in your BEing and in your human life. **You are thus able to work on your BEing with total precision to make the exact changes you want when you want them.**

This precision control of creation and discreation is important not only for your mystical Return to the ONE, but especially so for controlling your human life, emotions, behaviors, relationships and your power to manifest in the world. Never forget that Life is a Causal Sequence. Your control of your BE-FEEL is your vertical progress back to God and it is also the secret to controlling all your behaviors, relationships, happiness, and material results in your human life. (The subject of how to control your human life is too large for this book and is found in the companion volume of *You Are The Creator Of Your Life*.)

**The effort to create PIRs→ELJ will usually activate NIRs→UPS.
It will always activate them if you put enough creative energy
into the PIR.**

The way to be truly powerful as a creator is to be equally at home with both positive and negative energy. The way to be a truly powerful Creator starts in being a truly powerful discreator.

When you do not know how to handle the negative realities and energies, you will subconsciously not dare to energize your positive creations to the point that they will activate the negative ones. You will subconsciously avoid doing anything that will activate NIR experience—that is the Existential Imperative at work. And if you do activate NIRs, you will have the experience that the positive ones are just not real, not the truth, that you are just not that way (PIRs). Thus, you subconsciously self-limit your Creator Power for positive to avoid activating negative.

Without understanding this and being able to discharge negative energy and discreate the NIRs, you efforts at creation will be very feeble compared to what you are capable of as a CREATOR of Reality, especially with your all-important Reality of Self, your IDentities. Think of energy as alternating current: you must be able to handle both sides, both polarities, with equal aplomb.

To learn to create powerfully, you must first learn to discreate powerfully.

Chapter 19

How to Discreate your AntiEssence

When you first start seeking the Kingdom of Heaven within, what you will mostly encounter is just the opposite: hell. By hell, I mean negative energies: unpleasant, painful, ugly energies, both emotions and IDentities (NIRs): in other words, you will encounter your AntiGod Mass. You will find all flavors of the AntiEssence IDentities, and in the deeper levels within, tremendous amounts of Self-AntiLove = negative EmoLoveJoy.

Heaven lies on the other side of hell. Both polarities are within you. You must go through and love hell—and that will spring you into heaven.

You cannot get to the positive polarity (heaven), by resisting the negative polarity (hell)—which is exactly what you are doing as a human being. Resistance is how you are maintaining in existence your God Suppressor Mass (Rxx→Perxx). As a human being, you are in a total resistance to the "hell" within you, and that locks you out of heaven = BEing God again.

> Be sure to understand that I am speaking here of heaven and hell metaphorically. There are no such places (or BEings) in reality. The only heaven that exists is the BE-FEEL of the Infinite Wisdom, Power, Value, and LoveJoy-Ecstasy that you are. The only hell that exists is the experience of the opposite polarity of that, which is your AntiGod Mass, and which you are in resistance to experiencing as a human being. It is that resistance, that negation to experience your AntiGodness, that causes its persistence and keeps you here in hell = trapped in your Essence Suppressor Mass.

To avoid "all the hell" within us is exactly why we don't go within. Most people avoid going within, consciously or unconsciously. One of the ways we do so is by thinking all the time. We are constantly lost in our minds (the parent of Time) instead of focused in our experience in the Here and Now.

This is also why so few people meditate. This is why, if you do meditate, meditation is so difficult. When you try to meditate, you will, a thousand times, bounce into mind, into THINKing. **Fleeing to mind = THINKing is one of**

the ways we avoid FEELing what is within. (Meditation is a process of not THINKing to transcend the mind. The QUANTUM FIELD lies on the other side of your mind.)

Here is a process for you to try: Turn off your mind and open your FEELing. (Just tell your BEing to do this; it knows how.) Stay focused in your present time experience and just feel what you feel. Above all, focus on feeling the truth of how you feel about Self and about life. Keep doing this until you are truly without thought and truly feeling your Self. If you do this correctly, you will soon feel uncomfortable and unhappy. That is smoke coming off your ESM. Most people, however, cannot do this because their mind will kick in to "save" them from that "uncomfortableness" that is the beginning of pain.

What you need to open the gates to heaven is know-how; the technology of how to go to "hell," and not only survive there, but thrive there. You need the technology of how to handle negative energies; above all, of how to eliminate them and free your BEing of them completely. This technology we call CDT: Creation and Discreation Technology. It is a very precise set of steps that enable you to handle and create or discreate anything in your universes, internal or external.

Discreation is very simple in theory. In fact, we can sum it up in one law and one instruction. The law is: **Love Dissolves AntiLove**. The instruction is: **Love Thyself**. This, of course, is something we have been hearing for thousands of years.

The first problem with loving yourself is that people do not know what Love really is, and the ideas that they have about it now are mostly wrong. (This is also why people have so many problems in their relationships: ignorance of what Love is.) You were never taught what Love is, nor *how* to love yourSelf

The second problem is that, although the theory is simple; when you start to discreate, you will probably need to be guided through it several times until you get the hang of it.

There can be a third problem. For those people who are already FEELers, opening up to let your NIR Masses in to discreate them, can open the gates to many NIR Masses coming in and to your being overwhelmed. Thus, you may need an external control and guide element until you learn how to handle so much energy.

How to Love Yourself and Discreate Who You No Longer Wish to BE

First, we need to see what Love is. Table 19-1 presents some of the polarity spectrums of Love+/-. The top half is positive Love, the bottom half is AntiLove. (As Love is really all one thing, you will find a lot of overlap between one concept and the next.)

Now look at that table and plot where you have been operating in regards to your NIRs.

Table 19-1: Characteristics of Love and AntiLove

Movement	Distance	SPace	Union Integration	Experience BE-FEEL	Energy
			LOVE		
Movement TOWARD that which is loved. To draw nearer.	To move closer, approach. **Decrease Distance** between Lover and Beloved.	**To be in and share same SPace.** **To give SPace to BE** as is. **OPEN TO**	To seek integration and union. **To BEcome ONE.** (Marriage, Sex)	To experience and enjoy the beloved as much as possible. To make as real as possible.	To give positive energy to. To help, support, build, grow, and increase that which is loved.
			SPACE - NEUTRAL		
Movement AWAY FROM that which is AntiLoved.	**Increase Distance** between AntiLover and the AntiLoved. Move away, separate.	**CLOSED TO** **To avoid being in the same SPace.** **To deny to others SPace to BE** with one, or to BE at all.	To avoid union and get away from. **Many, divided.** **To divide, separate, segregate.** (Divorce)	To avoid experiencing that which is AntiLoved as much as possible. Have it be not-real.	To give negative energy to, to obstruct, diminish, harm, punish, destroy.
			ANTILOVE		

- Have you been **moving towards** your NIRs, or away from them; trying to increase or decrease the distance between you and them?
- Have you been giving them **SPace** to BE as they are; which is to give you SPace to BE as you are (NIRs); or have you been denying them SPace to BE, trying to attack and change them?
- Have you been seeking **integration** and **union** with your NIRs, or have you been trying to separate, get away from them and avoid them?
- Have you been openly and **fully experiencing** your NIRs, BE-FEELing them; or have you been trying to not BE-FEEL them?
- Have you been giving positive **energy** to your NIRs, appreciating and celebrating them; or have you been generating negative energy towards them: anger, fear, sadness, depression, etc., trying to stop, change or destroy them?

Obviously—because of ignorance—you have been relating to yourself in the form of your NIRs in the negative polarity of Love, as shown in table 19-1. **You have been AntiLoving your NIRs**, which is to **AntiLove yourSelf** as you yourself have created you.

> The first step in being fully loving is to fully love your Self. (4-15-311)

Full, unconditional love for yourSelf, for your NIRs, is exactly what you must learn to discreate your NIRs. Your AntiEssence Identities persist because you are AntiLoving them, AntiLoving yourself as you yourself have created yourSelf Your AntiLove is resistance. And Resistance Causes. . . what?

Yes: Resistance Causes Pain and Persistence.

Your NIRs are still with you and you are still living with lots of UPS. So note that your resistance is functioning perfectly to persist exactly what you don't want.

To discreate your NIRs, all you have to do is love them. How? Just start treating them as shown in the upper half of the Table of Love<>AntiLove. Stop Resisting (by discreating BAD). Move into them, open to them, give them SPace to BE as they are = you to BE as you are; integrate and unite with them, experience them fully. BE-FEEL them: BE and FEEL how it FEELs to BE your NIRs.

Do this on each NIR as it appears and keep doing it until the NIR experience is gone.

> An analogy: You discreate your negative realities by "eating" them. By "eating" them, we mean you must fully "taste" = experience them. You must BE-FEEL them, integrate with, and let yourself fully BE as you have created yourself: your NIRs. You must "absorb" them, which paradoxically does not leave you with them, but discreates them. All this is to love yourSelf, and you do so by experiencing yourSelf, especially those parts that you have been most AntiLoving: your NIRs.

Another analogy that can help you understand how to discreate is that of a balloon. Imagine the balloon filled with ugly, smelly air that represents your NIR Masses. The balloon is to one side of your face. You don't want to smell the nasty, painful NIR air, so you are constantly resisting letting the air out of the balloon onto your face (which represents your consciousness, your FEELing). The way you resist air coming out of the balloon is by "counter"-blowing air back into the balloon. This not only keeps most of the air from coming out of the balloon, but also puts even more air into the balloon: thus, Resistance Causes Persistence and an increase of that which is resisted.

What you have to do is stop resisting and let the air out of the balloon onto your face. While it is discharging, you are going to experience, smelling, that ugly air. But eventually, the balloon will empty of air and the smell = experience of the NIR is gone forever.

A third analogy: Think of a plate of food that you do not like, but must eat. As long as you resist it, it remains in front of you where you have to see and smell it. The only way you can get rid of the food is to eat it, which will require you to taste and experience it. But once you have done so, it is gone forever. The more you "eat" your negative energies; the fewer there are of them left, and the stronger you get to better "eat" even more of them and faster and faster.

The only thing that can stop you from "eating" your NIRs, BE-FEELing them, is your resistances to them. You resist them because you have created that they are BAD, that it is BAD to BE that way. You discreate your BAD→Rxx by taking responsability for being the creator of the BAD→Rxx and then just experiencing out your BAD or Rxx until it is gone.

Your negative emotion is your AntiLove resistance to Self as NIRs. Your negative emotion = Self-AntiEmoLoveJoy is ALWAYS proportional to the BAD. The more BAD that you have created, the more emotional charge you will have. If there is much charge, so much that it interferes with either finding the NIR or with focusing on it to discreate it, then discreate BAD to lower the charge.

However, keep in mind, if you totally discreate the BAD, all emotion will disappear and you will appear to be in SPace. However, this emotional space is not the end of the process. YOU MUST STILL DISCREATE the NIR[50].

Once you have discreated the NIR, you should recover your determinations (decisions about life) and change any negative ones.

---

50 The process of discreation is explained in greater detail in the book *Emotions, Love, and Happiness*. You may obtain a free download of that chapter of ELH from www.psycanics.org

Next you should decide Who You Want to BE in the future, both in relation to that trigger and in general, and energize that. Impregnate yourself with that reality, that energy. Then create the positive Causal Sequence that you desire to live in the future.

> A Master can disappear the most grievous pain. In this way a Master heals. (1-1-37)

I want to give you an example of the power of CDT to heal. We had a case where a mother in her mid-twenties lay down to sleep with her second child of only three months in her bosom. She awoke hours later to find the baby dead still in her embrace: she realized she had smothered him.

Can you imagine the pain of that? Is there any pain in life more severe than that of losing a child—except that of having killed it yourself, by your own negligence?

(If you can think of one, please email me, because I would like to know what it is.) A truly loving parent would rather die hirself than lose a child, much less than by hir own hand.

A member of the mother's family knew about psycanics and contacted a CDT Trainer in San Diego. He applied CDT to guide the mother for eight hours to totally discreate the IDentities and therefore all emotional charge connected to the incident (including guilt). (Eight hours to discreate a NIR Mass is much longer than normal, but on the other hand this was a BIG charge, and fresh—this was within a couple of days of the incident, not years later.)[51]

I know the charge was totally discreated because I was in San Diego about a month later to give a seminar and the mother attended. I had the chance to talk to her about the incident and she was able to tell me everything in serenity[52].

Contrast this with how people carry charges from their past, including from childhood, for years (if not all their lives) of not only serious traumatic incidents (abuse, violence, rape, PTSD, failure, etc.), but also "lighter" charges of anger, resentments, hate, fear, guilt, shame, etc. All of this—in fact ANY EXPERIENCE whatsoever—can be discreated and quickly.

> A Master knows that we are immortal BEings and ONE. Therefore, s/he experiences the death of anyone, including hir own, with total SPace.

CDT will take you to that place of mastery. As you discreate every NIR Mass as it appears in your SPace, you no longer become reactive to any event. You eventually BEcome TOTAL SPACE again.

---

51 I have the mother's and the CDT Trainer's written testimonials on file, as well as many others.

52 The coroner's autopsy later showed that the baby had died of natural causes—crib death (SIDS)—but the mother did not know that at the time of the CDT and firmly believed she had killed her baby.

Once you have the technology of handling and discreating negative energy, you are armed to face anything the external world can throw at you. You can discreate any activation, any pain. You are also then prepared to go within and discreate your way through hell to heaven.

As you discreate your Essence Suppressor Mass, your sense of ESSENCE and ONEness increases, and all not-Godness, pain and disappointment vanish from your life.

Chapter 20

The External Quest

The Ultimate Motivation, the Existential Imperative, of all human behavior, from tyranny and terrorism, through all relationship conflicts, all substance addictions and suicide, to patriotism and heroism, is to BE the ONE God again. There are no exceptions to this compulsion to Return to the ONE.

The Existential Imperative has a sequence of elements to it, which we covered before and I will repeat here briefly (take a deep breath):

> The motivation of all human beings is to control experience; which is to avoid pain and be happy; which happiness is purely emotional; which emotions are the Love Energy Polarity, which is not just Love; but Self-Love; which springs automatically from BEing love-able; which comes from BEing the LIFE energies that are Wisdom, Power, Value, LoveJoy; which is to BE-FEEL your ESSENCE; whose maximum experience is to BE-FEEL Self as GOD, which is to Return to the Kingdom of Heaven whence you come.
>
> Thus, we can speak of the Existential Imperative at many levels of experience and motivation; but the ultimate goal is BE the ONE GOD again.

You obey the Existential Imperative; you have no choice in the matter; it is programmed into your spirit at the highest level of your individuality itself. However, your efforts to obey, to return to ESSENCE, can take either of two directions: the Internal or the External Quest.

The Internal Quest: You can seek the God-Heaven within, as recommended by Jesus and God in *CWG*. The Internal Quest is all your efforts to work on yourself to dis-cover who you are. It includes such activities as reading, courses and seminars, yoga, diet, breathing exercises, meditation, and above all, CDT. The most powerful tool is **meditation combined with CDT; these two reinforce each other**. We will come back to the Internal Quest in the next chapter.

The External Quest: When you do not understand all that we are saying in the book you will try to obey the Imperative, to seek Happiness (ESSENCE) **without**, in the external world, in the physical universe—*where it does not exist.*

The efforts of a person in the External Quest to fulfill the Existential Imperative (be happy) have three principal directions:

1- Try to stop all the negative events that seem to be causing one's UPS. (Attack or manipulate externals to control the world to stop BAD things.)

2- Use substances or activities (chemicals, food, shopping, television, alcohol, sex, gambling, etc.) to suppress negative experience and, where possible to cause Self positive feelings.

3- Try to accumulate and hoard those things that appear to cause happiness: money, relationships, material things, power, fame, etc. This, as we saw before, only causes MoPs: Moments of Pleasure, as the result of externally triggered, fleeting Moments of PIRs.

Such efforts do sometimes momentarily succeed in stopping negative events to stop UPS; and in triggering MoPs. Thus, changing the externals seems to confirm work-ableness of the External Quest. This is unfortunate, because it contributes to the illusion that external things control our experience.

However, "all roads lead to Rome," and even the External Quest will eventually take you home. But it does so by using pain to eventually force you to go within to seek the answers, anyway. Thus, it is the long and painful way around and back to the ONE. Thus, although no one is ever lost and we all find our way back HOME eventually, we will call the External Quest the "impossible dream."

The faster you get yourself out of the External Quest, and into the Internal Quest, the faster you will stop suffering, begin to have your life work naturally and effortlessly, and begin to make serious progress on the road HOME. So for our purposes, we divide life into two parts: one that works (for going back to God): the Internal Quest; and one that doesn't work and keeps you in constant UPS: the External Quest.

The **External Quest** is all efforts to find happiness in the world (never forgetting that the only true happiness is ESSENCE). The External Quest is all efforts to make the Causal Sequence work in reverse. The External Quest is THINK→DO→HAVE→(BE)→FEEL. (I put the BE in parenthesis because the person is not always aware of the effort to BE and may think s/he is only trying to FEEL good = happy.)

It is all THINKing→DOing→HAVEing in order to FEEL good and BEcome "someone" in the world: **smart**, **successful**, **powerful**, **beautiful**, **important**, etc.— and usually "more and better so" than others, which is Ego. Notice here the search for identity (the words in bold just above) in the external world as part of the External Quest. We are always seeking BE→FEEL, even when it is externally sought.

The Fatal Identity and Paradigm: Root of the External Quest

Under the Existential Imperative, all BEings must seek Ultimate Happiness, the INFINITE LOVE, the ONE, to BE God again. You have no choice in the matter. When you don't know that ESSENCE is within, you can only think to seek it without, in the External Quest. Let us look at more of the mechanism involved:

The Fatal Identity is that "**I AM NOT the Creator of my experience**." People create this IDentity because they see their lives, the negative IDentities, negative emotions, relationships conflicts, failures, pain and suffering, etc., and label them BAD. If they were the Creator of all that failure and BAD stuff in their lives, then *they* would be a failure and BAD. People try to escape these AntiEssence IDentities by denying Response-ability for their creations and experience, which they do by Assigning Cause to external agents. This, of course, creates the Victim. (We covered this in a previous chapter.)

One of the consequences of the Fatal Identity is the Fatal Paradigm. The Fatal Paradigm is the THINK = belief that, given that "I AM NOT the Creator" of what I experience; then other people and external events must be (the external agents of Cause). This reinforces Victim: "They are doing BAD things to me, hurting me: I am their Victim."

The Causal Sequence includes THINK→DO. The mirage of the Fatal Paradigm (THINK) then sends the person on the External Quest (DO) to control hir experience by controlling externals, whether these externals are other people (RELATE) or things (HAVE). However, it is impossible to ever have much control over externals. Nobody has all that much control over what others do and say, or what happens in our lives. This means that the External Quest is impossible of success; the real "impossible dream." For most people, it is impossible to get everything they want and think they need to be happy. And for those few who do get "it all" in life; they can only discover that it still is not enough, and that they still want and need "something more."

The Fatal Identity-Paradigm Complex blocks Power because it negates to the person the consciousness of and ability to control hir experience (BE-FEEL) directly. It sends hir on the impossible dream-quest of trying to control externals to control hir BE-FEEL. Thus, the External Quest puts the person into a lot of failure (to control externals, and to control hir experience and be happy). All that failure tends to keep the AntiPower and AntiValue IDentities activated, which is constant UPS. Most of humanity lives in this mechanism of unhappiness.

To create a Transformation of Consciousness on the planet, a 180 degree change of direction from the External to the Internal Quest, it is essential that people learn the psycanics (the spiritual mechanics) of their BEing and experience.

There are a myriad of forms of the External Quest and I do not pretend to catalog all of them. The more common ones include:

1. **Greed:** All greed (aka avarice) is part of the External Quest. Greed is the excessive and insatiable desire to get, accumulate and hoard anything and far beyond one's needs, usually at any cost to self, family, others, and the environment.
2. **Ego:** Ego is all effort to make one appear greater and better than others: wiser, more powerful, more successful, more value-able, and more love-able, than others. It is the effort to steal ESSENCE from others by belittling their BEing to make oneself appear greater. Most ambition is a combination of Greed and Ego. Ego and Greed can be involved in all of the following types of External Quest:
3. **Relationships:** (Couple, parent, child, extended family, friends, etc.) ALL relationship problems and conflicts are due to the External Quest to control others to make ourselves happy. Look at the anger, invalidation, attacks, blame, sabotage, control intents, blackmail, victim, covert manipulation, punishment, withdrawal—any and all AntiLove behaviors in your relationships, and you are looking at the External Quest in operation.
4. **Money:** Effort to accumulate money can be attempts to create the experiences of security, freedom, power, success, ego (better-than-thou), among others. Notice that these are all ESSENCE experiences. If you want to see your External Quest around money, imagine that you lose job, savings, investments, house and everything and are on the streets tomorrow, homeless and penniless. See how much fear and anxiety activates. (The quest for money can also be a quest for power.)
5. **Hoarding Material Things** and "toys." This includes accumulating property beyond one's needs, jewelry, expensive shoes and clothing, always sporting the latest model car, and all ostentation to be "more or better than" others. The entire advertising industry preys off people's NIRs by selling them "solutions" to appear as Wiser, more Powerful, more Value-able, more important, more successful, more Love-able, so that finally they will be happier. The gist of advertising is, "You will be special, love-able, wonderful and happy when you have (whatever product)." In effect, they say. "You will be PIRs instead of NIRs when you buy my product."
6. **Success:** Including job or career success. How many people sell out their lives to achieving "success" (however they define it) at all costs? The only true success that exists is your daily experience of Joy, and that is the measure of your ESSENCE. To paraphrase one of God's statements in *CWG*, "On your deathbed, you will never look back at your life and say, 'I wish I had spent more time at the office.'"
7. **Fame:** Seeking recognition and acclaim by others: trying to achieve reputation, prestige, fame and often influence, which is a form of power. (For some, this is a measure of success.) The artistic, sport, political,

religious, and academic worlds are rife with the search for recognition and fame. For an example of the AntiWisdom NIRs at work, the academic world is famous for people vying for recognition, honors and titles: "Publish or Perish."

8. **Power:** Control through force or wile of people, places, and resources. The quest for power includes getting to the top (or as high as possible) in organizations: business, politics, governments, military, religions, etc. The quest for power can be seen behind all dictators and tyrants and almost all politicians, for that matter. (And the American politicians are not any better than others. If not controlled by checks and balances, they would be tyrants also. Megalomania respects no nationality or political systems.)
9. **Attachments:** Holding on to anything to avoid the activation of NIR masses. Almost every human being has many attachments. If the loss or absence of any person or thing from your life would cause you pain (spouse, child, parent, pet, house, money, job, etc.), you have an attachment. To see your attachments, imagine the death of the person you most love. If you would feel negative emotions = self-AntiLove, you have an attachment. You are using that person or thing as an external security blanket to avoid FEELing UPS. This is yet another face of the External Quest.
10. **Addictions:** The use of substances to enhance or suppress the mind and the emotions. These include: tobacco, alcohol, mood medications, illegal drugs, and food. It also includes activities such as television, shopping, talking on the phone all the time (not able to be alone), partying, gambling, showing off, sex, etc., when these are used like addictions to change or distract from our feelings.
11. **Ostentation and Glamour:** Exhibiting or parading one's symbols of success (money, property, titles, etc.), of "more and better" than others. A classic example of this behavior is common with the *noveau riche*, but it can also be seen in royalty, Hollywood, the music and sports stars worlds. It is a form of Ego, and can also be found in relation to all of the above forms of the External Quest, even Addictions.

The human experience of insufficiency is the root cause of all worry, all pressure, all competition, all jealousy, all anger, all conflict, and ultimately, of all killing on your planet. (3-19-312)

"Need" occurs when you imagine that there is something outside of yourself that you do not now have and that you require to be happy. (4-7-161)

First, it is an illusion that there is anything outside of you. Secondly, even allowing that illusion, there is nothing outside of you that can ever make you happy. Only ESSENCE is true, lasting, impregnable Happiness, and that is within.

The experiences of ignorance, insufficiency of power and of love = joy are caused by our experience of the AntiEssence IDentities. The only thing we really "need," and feel lack and insufficiency about, is ESSENCE. If you are living in the experience of BEing the ONE-EVERYTHING, in your immortality, and in ecstasy that is the natural result of WHO YOU ARE, how can you need anything?

However, few people understand that the cause of our experience of not enough, of emptiness, of lacking love, of loneliness and sorrow, is the absence of our ESSENCE as caused by our AntiEssence IDentity Mass. We don't understand that the real solution is within. But seek ESSENCE we must; it is the Existential Imperative. Therefore, we embark on the External Quest. The External Quest is the search for fulfillment and satisfaction outside of us, in the world. It is impossible. The only thing that will ever fill our internal void and quell the quest is finding our ESSENCE, and that is within.

The External Quest is the predominant human behavior on the planet and is now close to destroying civilization and perhaps much of life on the planet. The rapacious greed of the External Quest to accumulate power, fame and fortune no matter the cost to others and Nature, has led us to a most critical point in the history of the planet. We are depleting, exhausting, trashing, polluting and poisoning the oceans, the air, the soil, the forests, the wildlife, and all resources, such that we are on the brink of triggering major and irreversible environmental changes. In fact, these are already appearing. No matter what anybody argues about any specific area, or when things will come to a head; human civilization as it is now is not sustainable: not in energy, not in environment and ecology (both as to the preservation of other life forms and as to pollution), not in the extraction of mineral resources.

> You cannot use advanced technologies beneficially without advanced thinking. Advanced technology without advanced thinking creates not advancement but demise. (3-15-269)

Law of psycanics: **Power without Wisdom and Love always destroys.**

As if the environmental perils were not enough, we also have the diversion of a major part of the wealth of the planet into armies and instruments of war, destruction, and death. These serve only the External Quest for power and wealth of a few. Instead of adding to the wealth and well-being of humanity—or at least being neutral to it—these bring only more destruction, maiming, death, poisoning and pollution any time they are used. How unwise is it to use wealth to destroy even more wealth?

As God notes in *CWG*, humanity is at a cusp, a critical intersection of forces and so of history. S/HE notes that humanity reached this point once before—and destroyed civilization (the legends of Atlantis and Mu). We are at that same point again, in the same clear and present danger. Can we stop the External Quest and refocus on the Internal Quest before we trigger entropic forces of nature totally beyond our control? Can enough people understand what life is about, who they are, what ESSENCE is, and how to go within to discover it, before we destroy ourselves?

The External Quest is a compulsive behavior, the greed addiction to ego, money, things, power, and fame that destroys everything eventually, including the person. The External Quest is the result of the Existential Imperative wrongly focused, externally. IT CAN ONLY BE STOPPED THROUGH THE DISCREATION OF NIRS.

I see many campaigns around the planet for many things: peace, end of poverty, protection of the earth. All these are well and good, but THERE WILL BE NO SUBSTANTIAL CHANGE IN THE CAVEMAN BEHAVIORS OF HUMANITY UNTIL NIRS ARE DISCREATED.

To both want to and to be able to refocus your life, you must understand what is really happening within, the nature of ESSENCE and AntiEssence. You must understand that between you and external events are always your IDentities, and that your IDs are both your only real Point of Power, and the only thing that you really need to control.

You must understand that there are two entirely unrelated universes of experience: your physical universe and your psycanic universe. Your physical universe is never the cause of your psycanic experience. You must handle each experience in its own universe, separately. The External Quest is trying to use the physical universe to control your psycanic universe. This is impossible.

You must also have a technology that gives you the power to control your IDentities and therefore your experience. Knowing without the ability to do only leads to frustration.

Only with these understandings is it really practical for most people to make the transition from External Quest to Internal Quest. We have known about the Internal Quest for 3,500 years through the Vedas, Hinduism, and Buddha. Jesus stated it clearly 2,000 years ago, in case you missed it from Buddha. But it has made no difference on the planet. Humankind has not evolved in its most basic instincts much beyond the caveman era. (2-9-125)

With *CWG* and Psycanics, we now have the exact knowledge and precise technology to understand what it means that the Kingdom of Heaven is Within, and how to reach it.

The question now is: Can we get the knowledge out there to enough people in time to soften, avert, or change the direction of civilization in time?

Chapter 21

The Internal Quest

> There comes a time in the evolution of every soul when the chief concern is no longer the survival of the physical body but the growth of the spirit; no longer the attainment of worldly success, but the realization of Self. (1-12-180)
>
> What differentiates societies, and individuals within a society, is what they define as pleasurable. Advanced societies are structured around the pleasures of their spirituality. What characterizes the earth as a primitive society is that you structure your lives mainly around pleasures of the body, as opposed to around the joys of your soul. (3-8-149)
>
> ***Let the outer world be as it is. Concentrate on creating your inner world as you would have it be.*** (4-16-321)

The Internal Quest is the journey of each psycan (soul) back to the ONE, to BEing God again. Paradoxically, it is not an externally-focused expansion to encompass the physical universe, but a going within to discover, un-cover that the physical universe and everything else ever created is within you. You are the INFINITE SPACE in which all exists, and the INFINITE QUANTUM FIELD of which all is made; and the INFINITE CREATOR who fabricates it all. And you now have IT ALL hidden inside YOU.

> God plays a game with HIRSELF. The game is to see if S/HE can create something so far from God that S/HE cannot bring it back. You, the human being, are the ball in that game; and it is a game you are playing with yourSelf. Have you gone so far from God that you cannot get back? Do you feel lost and far away from LOVE? Does it seem hard to get back?

We have gone to the far opposite polarity of God, as far from ONE and ESSENCE as possible. We have gone far into the Many and into separated and isolated individuality. We have reduced our infinite Wisdom to the total ignorance of an caveman. We have reduced our infinite Power to where we can actually starve to a physical death. We have reduced our sense of infinite Value (self-esteem) to the depths of sinner and unworthiness. We have descended into AntiLove such that life shows up as a valley of tears and darkness. We have gone as far from ESSENCE as it is possible to go and still retain a spark of Conscious Creator. (The next step down is animal and they are not conscious creators.)

The Internal Quest is your Ascension back up the Polarity Spectrum of Essence to BE IT ALL again.

The Internal Quest is the penetration of yourSelf to discover Who You Are.

It is the Seeking of the Kingdom Within.

The most powerful way to do this is to discreate your God Suppressor Mass, that reality that counter-creates the God of you; creates for you the illusion of not BEing Who You Are.

Meditation and CDT

> Begin by being still. Quiet the outer world, so that the inner world might bring you sight. This in-sight is what you seek, yet you cannot have it while you are so deeply concerned with your outer reality. See, there, to go within as much as possible. If you do not go within, you go without. (1-1-44)

To combine traditional, mystical meditation[53] with Psycanics CDT is the most powerful combination of path that I know of. They both work together to reinforce the power of each other.

CDT empowers meditation by sweeping away all that the meditation will activate. Meditation empowers CDT by increasing your ability to focus into and activate your God Suppressor Mass, and to confront all the negative energy that will arise from within. You then discreate the negative energy with CDT. They work hand in glove.

Your overall challenge and adventure is your journey of dis-cover-ry of Who You Are to BE IT ALL again. In your Internal Quest, the external world serves you as a mirror in which you can see Who You Are. The most obvious and powerful example of this is when externals trigger your activations. Remember that behind *every* negative emotion, every moment of pain, are your negative IDentities. Thus, the external world is putting your AntiEssence BEing in your face every time you are activated. That is the opportunity to discreate that amount of your AntiEssence.

Your external world is also the creative result of Who You Are, your BEing. This is your HAVE in the Causal Sequence: BE-FEEL→THINK→DO→HAVE.

---

53 There are many things being taught and called "meditation" that do not qualify as true meditation. Meditation seeks to go behind mind, which is creator of universes, into the Quantum Field. Anything that involves THINKing or focusing on anything other than your own consciousness, is not mystical meditation.

Your HAVE is a natural emanation of your BE. When your BE is really BIG, such as that of Jesus, you can create→HAVE anything instantly. At our human levels of BE, there are other factors that affect our ability to manifest (HAVE); one of which is what is necessary at the moment for our Return. Our lives are being guided at higher levels of our Self to give us the experiences we need to awaken and Re-Integrate to the ONE.

The important thing here is to treasure those moments of activation and use them to discreate the NIRs. This has three great benefits:

1- Discreation of the NIR and therefore its negative ELJ mass = UPS stops our pain of the moment;
2- Discreation of that NIR mass reduces our reactivity to that trigger. It reduces the frequency and severity of our activations for that trigger. With a few hours of CDT, you can become totally non-reactive to a given trigger.
3- It moves us that much closer to the discreation of our entire God Suppressor Mass and therefore that much closer to BEing God again.

Thus the external world = triggers→activations is an extremely useful aid for our Return to the ONE.

The Internal Quest is simple: Combine Meditation with CDT. Discreate every NIR mass when it activates. Use the technique of Creation<>Counter Creation to activate even more NIR mass so that you eventually get it all.

How to Handle the Exterior World When You are in the Interior Quest

> There is nothing that you need to be perfectly happy. Your deepest, most perfect happiness will be found within. Nothing exterior to your Self can match IT, nor can anything destroy IT. (4-1-163)

The next question to consider is that, once embarked on your Internal Quest as your first priority your life, what is your relationship to and how do you handle the physical universe?

First of all, your life consists of your Causal Sequences. Just applying the Causal Sequence to every activation to find and discreate the NIR and then affirming your PIRs will change your human life. On changing to the PIR, the entire Causal Sequence changes. Your FEELings change, your THINKing changes, your actions and behaviors change, and therefore your results, your relationships and your material things, change.

The Causal Sequence handles both your human life and your Return to the ONE.

Life is a series of events. There are no accidents, coincidences, randomness or chance in the events, in the parade. Everything is a creation at one level or another of your entire Spectrum of BEing

> You are a multi-level, BEing; you might say "vertically integrated." You are part of a bigger BEing who is part of a Bigger BEing who is part of an even bigger BEing, all the way back to the ONE. (The "parts" of you on different levels include subconscious, conscious, superconscious, Higher Self, over-Higher Self, etc., back up to the ONE.)

> All of life's events present themselves as opportunities for you to decide and be Who You Are. (1-1-32) Nothing happens by accident or coincidence. (1-1-46)

Every event always has multiple purposes, the highest of which is whatever experience will help your Return to the ONE. When you understand this, you can begin to trust the Flow, the TAO, and let Life be. Most people fill their lives with struggle and effort to control externals (because of trying to fulfill the Existential Imperative through the External Quest). As we saw, this is impossible and just activates the AntiPower Identities even more. When you are in the Internal Quest, you totally relax from trying to control the external world.

As I describe in the book *The Psycanics of the Mind*, people create all kinds of mental realities about events. They distort them, add meanings and interpretations to them, leave out parts, make themselves the Victim, and so on. All these are mental hallucinations. No event means anything, has any significance, until you create and assign to it a meaning—which is always your creation, your interpretation of things. It is always something made up, because you do not have the consciousness to see the incredibly complex web of the God-purposes of events.

Your creations that most cause your problems in life are "BAD" (event, thing or person). As we have seen, this triggers you into resistance. Life is simply a smorgasbord of events. There are no good or BAD events, **except as you create them so—and that is the problem!** You create them Good or BAD according to how they affect your IDentities, because you are not home controlling your IDentities as you should be.

According to whether you have labeled the event Good or BAD, you cling to it, or you resist it. Thus do you grasp at or resist the Flow, the TAO, of life. By creating the slightest preference you "set heaven and earth infinitely apart." You expel yourself from the Garden of Paradise, from the Kingdom of Heaven.

There are just events. All events have purposes on many levels, which you can never understand fully at the human level. You only try cling to or resist events as an attempt to control your BE-FEEL (the External Quest again). Stop this! Learn to control your BE-FEEL internally, directly. This is the purpose of life, of the external universe: to let you see and so be able to "grow" your BEing. Learn to use the external universe to see who you are so that you can change that to your next step up in ESSENCE.

You are operating in one of two modes: You live deciding Who You Are in relation to each event, or you live letting events decide who you are (activating your PIRs or NIRs). If you are in the second mode, the External Quest, you live trying to control events to stop or avoid the BAD ones to stop your NIR activations→UPS; to cause "good" events to give yourself MoPs.

Your objective is to become totally free of the world. You do not need anything in the world to control your experience, either to make you happy or to stop your UPS. This is to say that you do not need anything in the world to control your IDentities. You do not seek things to trigger PIRs→MoPs as the mirage of happiness. You do not need to control the world to stop it from triggering your NIRs→UPs. You do not need the world for anything. You are free.

You already are the grandest thing possible: God. What you most need to do is uncover, dis-cover, re-integrate to THAT. What you most need to do is discreate that which suppresses your experience and realization of Who You Are: your God Suppressor Mass. That is the Internal Quest.

Let the outer world be as it is.
Concentrate on creating your inner world as you would have it be.
(4-16-321)

Life is a parade of events.

Relax and trust the Flow; enjoy the show!

Follow the TAO; IT will take you HOME.

Events are only Good<>BAD by your opinion and
from your very limited human point of view.

Set not heaven and earth apart with your opinions.

Do not cling to or resist any element of the parade.

The wise person resists and laments not any event,
but always appreciates[54] them all.

Enjoy the show that is Created Reality.

54 Appreciation is a very powerful flow of energy, of love and admiration.

Everything on this planet, including your individuality, is an illusion. It is the Divine Matrix, the Quantum Field forming ITSELF into the holograms. Your purpose within the illusion is to wake up to Who You Are and remember that it is an illusion. Once you truly get all this, you can live within the illusion or outside of it, at will. No drama necessary.

As we said above, one of the purposes of the events of your life is to give you opportunities to see Who You Are, as these are very useful for changing to Who You Want to BE. Like using a map, it is helpful to know where you are to be able get to where you want to be.

This is especially true and useful when the events trigger your Self-AntiLove = UPS. Trigger events put your NIRs→AntiLove "in your face" so that you can discreate these masses. The constant discreation of your NIR masses gradually dissipates the Essence Suppressor Mass, which is what separates you from BEing the ONE again. Thus, the parade of events that is life will take you back to God; and the negative events (those that trigger you) are especially useful. Negative events are like the highway. You only have know how to use them—which starts with ceasing to resist them, and finishes with discreating the activated NIR mass.

If something negative serves you, is it really negative?

> When you find Inner Peace, neither the presence nor the absence of any person, place or thing, condition, circumstance or situation can be the Creator of your state of mind or the cause of your experience of BEing. (2-11-152)
>
> This one simple change—seeking and finding peace within—could end all wars, eliminate conflict, prevent injustice, and bring the world to everlasting peace. There is no other formula necessary or possible. (2-11-152)

There are two points to note about the illusion of Created Reality. First, it is an illusion that there is anything outside of you; you are the ONE. Therefore, as you look about the universe, you are always looking at one of the Faces of God, at one of YOUR faces.

Secondly, within that illusion, within Created Reality, there is nothing that can ever fulfill your Existential Imperative and make you happy. The only happiness that exists is BEing ESSENCE again, and that is within you, and "behind" or "underneath" Created Reality. Again, to uncover or dis-cover THAT, all you need to do is discreate that part of Created Reality which blinds you to your SELF: your God Suppressor Mass.

How to Control Externals

Your ability to control the physical universe depends on your level of BEing or Consciousness, your Life Script, and on how you control your mental energy, what you focus on.

There is nothing accidental or random in your life. At the Higher Self level, you have a plan for your Return to the ONE, and as part of that plan, you have a plan for each incarnation. You incarnate into each lifetime with a "Life Script" of what you are going to do and achieve, both your legacy to this world, and for your BEing and Return to the ONE. Think of life as a movie where spirits come to act out their chosen dramas for the fun of it. Before you can create a movie, you must have a script. In the same way, before you incarnate, you have a plan for this lifetime.

Like the director of a movie, your Higher Self controls all that is necessary for your Life Script to unfold as planned in physical realities. This has two sides:

1- Everything that you need for your script will arrive without creator effort on your part, JIT[55].

2- Similarly, you will not be able to manifest anything that would interfere with your script.

Within the limitation of #2, you can create what you want here on earth to decorate your path. How to do that is somewhat involved and beyond the scope of this book. What we do want to cover here is the effect of your God Suppressor Mass on your power to create and manifest.

Basically, it is simple. God is the Creator and the Power. Your God-Suppressor Mass is the Anti-Identity of Creator and Power. As AntiEssence you are going to be dramatizing the opposite of Creator and Power, which are Victim and No-Power; i.e. the inability to manifest what you want. How much AntiPower, not getting what you want, have you experienced in life?

Your AntiEssence IDentities not only block your Creator Power, they also block your opening of BEing and personal universe to receive. In fact, more creations are "lost" by failure to open to receive, than are "lost" by failure to communicate to the ENERGY what you want.

Your AntiEssence IDs block your creations from arriving into your universe (experience). **The UNIVERSAL CREATOR ENERGY obeys your (creations of) IDentities and will not send you anything that contradicts Who You Are BEing** (be this conscious, or unconscious). You can visualize and energize whatever you want to manifest, **but as long as your ID is not appropriate to that thing**, it will not come into and stay in your life.

For example: if you have the NIR: I AM not worthy; or I AM not good enough; then two things happen.

1- To the degree that you are in the External Quest, you will buy things and try to manifest things to show that you are "worthy" and "good enough:" the latest fashions, fancy cars, etc. You will be using HAVE to try to counteract your NIRs—but the best you can do is MoP yourself.

---

55 JIT: Just In Time.

However, you will often not even be able to produce a MoP:

2- **The universe cannot violate your IDentities. It must obey I AM UNWORTHY, and I AM NOT GOOD ENOUGH. Thus, IT cannot put into your SPace of BEing (your world) any thing that would contradict "unworthy," and "not good enough;"** a new car, for example. You are unworthy of it, by you own declaration of IDentity and therefore it cannot appear in your life by you own decree.

Due to #1 above, such things to counteract your NIRs will be exactly what you most want and are trying to manifest, at the same time they are what is most blocked.

Manifestation of a desired HAVE is more blocked by problems of IDentity, and therefore openness of BEing to receive, than by lack of visualization and energization.

Obviously, all this creates huge amounts of frustration and activation of the AntiPower NIRs.

The person in the Internal Quest, first of all, knows that life is a perfect parade of events; and that it is being controlled by INTELLIGENCE and POWER far beyond hir human level; that is, by hir Higher Self. S/He knows that s/he does not know what needs to happen to have life work for everybody (the ONE) all the time, or even for hirself.

Thus, s/he does not label any event BAD<>Good, and so does not resist or cling to any event. Thus, s/he lives in the Flow and in the Present Time Moment, the Here and Now. S/He stays out of hir mind, as s/he understands how it drags hir into the past or the future, and therefore into UPS. S/He concentrates on savoring each moment as a unique event and experience.

S/He is able to sense hir Life Script intuitively and so lives always aligned with it, in the certainty that each event is moving hir towards fulfilling all hir purposes. S/He takes 100% responsability for everything that shows up in hir life as hir creation *at some level of hir BEing.*

S/He applies the technology of creation and manifestation for every aspect of hir life. S/He consciously and deliberately creates everything that s/he would like to experience. But s/he completely releases the results, knowing that whatever shows up is perfect.

Need nothing. Desire and create everything. Enjoy what shows up.

Above all, s/he knows that what is important in not the external events of hir life, but hir internal universe. There, s/he knows s/he has full power to create the non-physical experiences s/he would like to live, of which hir ESSENCE, Wisdom, Power, Appreciation, and LoveJoy, is the most important one. Furthermore, s/he understands that s/he does not have to create that ESSENCE, only discreate hir suppressor mass that blocks hir perception of ULTIMATE REALITY.

S/He understands the words of Jesus:

Seek First the Kingdom of Heaven, and all else will be added unto you.
The Kingdom of Heaven is Within.

Live free of expectations and unattached to results.
There is nothing scary or difficult about life if you are
not attached to results.

Desire Everything, Need Nothing. Enjoy what shows up. (2-11-153)

Words of Wisdom

The universe is friendly to you.
There is a virtually infinite supply of everything you need.
There is always enough money, customers, time, love, friends, etc.,
so that no situation can leave you without those things for long.
You do not absolutely need "that one;"
you can move on to the next.

It is not your action that makes things happen,
it is your intent.

Make your decisions based on what you *intend to experience*,
not on what you think you can afford.

You can reduce the need for action to a very minimum by
allowing yourself to focus on what you desire until you feel
the *positive, creator, entheos energy* begin to move within you.
This *energy* is the opposite of doubt, fear, anxiety, worry or need.

Focus on what you want instead of what you don't want
or on the obstacles and difficulties to what you want.
You cannot create what you want resisting what you have.

You will know when it is time to take action.
Doors open and the entire universe will conspire to assist you.
You action and your results will be effortless.

A person of power sees everything as an
opportunity and a privilege to adventure and grow.
A person of power embraces challenges in complete gratitude.
No matter the situation life may bring,
discontent is never justified.
A Master is NEVER unhappy.

(Sections pharaphrased from James Arthur Ray)

Chapter 22

Your Return to the ONE

Your return is the ONLY purpose of your soul. It knows there is nothing on earth, not even the highest drug or sexual ecstasy that can compare with INFINITE ESSENCE.

However, your human identity thinks what you DO and HAVE in the physical universe is important and will send you on the wild goose chase of the External Quest.

The question, then, is: Who rules your life?

Your Return requires that your whole mind, body and spirit be dedicated to the process of realizing yourSelf as God, all the time, moment to moment, day after day. The instruction was: Seek FIRST the Kingdom of Heaven. "FIRST" is a key word here. That means **before all else; first in your priorities**.

As long as you are putting relationships, money, success, (whatever) first, as more important that your Self-Realization, you are putting "false gods before ME." You are laying up your treasure on earth where shall your heart—and soul—remain. What does it serve a person to gain the whole world, but lose hir soul?

On the other hand: **Your RETURN is certain.**

Even if you do not consciously work on your Return, your Re-Integration to the ONE; it is assured.

- You never left. You are still THERE and still ONE. Separation is an illusion.
- There is no other place to go or be, so you are not and cannot get lost.
- Your target is so big, INFINITE, that you can't miss. And you are in the very center of IT now.
- You have all eternity to get there—which is but where you are now. So you will never run out of time.

So, there is no place to go and you have all eternity to get there, where you already are. There is no such thing as "getting to heaven"—you only have to real-ize that you are already there. Enlightenment is experiencing that there is nowhere to go, nothing you have to do, except BE Here Now perfectly—which requires you to be out of your mind.

All you have to do is realize and experience WHO You Are. This is a BE-FEELing, not a DOing and not a THINKing, much less a HAVEing. All you have to do is BE Here-Now and BE Who You Are

When you finally experience that you are an eternal, immortal BEing, you relax into the Now to suck the maximum juice of experience out of the present moment. You realize your NEVER cease to BE-FEEL, and your experience NEVER ceases, so you stop worrying about the future.

Your focus is the present to get the most out of it as you can, as you pass through the Here and Now. It is your mind that creates the illusion of Time, of past and future. Eternity is not a long time; eternity is the eternal present in which time does not exist at all.

In order to truly know God, you have to be out of your mind. (5-1-94)

Thus, the question is not, "Will you return?;" but "When, How, and After How Much Pain and Suffering?"

If you are not participating in and contributing to your process of Return; the UNIVERSE will "herd" you back. The problem with this—for you, not the UNIVERSE, is that IT will often do so using "negative" events: those that activate your NIR masses, which means UPS for you. Such negative events (loss of job, no money, "accidents," sickness, etc.) shock you loose from your comfort zone and your attachments, force you to question life, to seek answers, and so to re-evaluate your goals and priorities.

Think of life as living blindfolded in a dark jungle. People live not knowing who they are, where they come from, where they are, where they are going, or what life is about. Blindfolded, they move through life bouncing off the trees. Each tree represents a negative event, and the pain of the bounce is the UPS of their NIR masses. They think the tree = events are causing their pain, but really the only pain is their negative IDentities→Self-AntiLove.

But they do not even know that; they are spiritually ignorant. So they wander around the jungle, meandering in all directions, thinking there must be something important and happy-making in the jungle, if only they can find it (the External Quest). And they keep bumping into the trees. Ouch, again.

Eventually, bumping into the trees and the attendant pain causes them to begin to question and to seek to understand the jungle. This opens their minds to begin to receive the LIGHT of true knowledge

When you understand what is going on, the purpose of Life, the Existential Imperative of your Return to the ONE, there appears LIGHT in your jungle. Although dim and far away at first, you now have a target: the LIGHT. You can begin to move towards IT. You begin to see the trees and understand them instead of bumping into them. They no longer cause you suffering; only a very temporary pain, as you cut them down with discreation. Thus, you clear the jungle in which you have been living, letting evermore LIGHT in, and clear your path back to the LIGHT. Furthermore, after clearing out the jungle, you use creation and manifestation to plant flowers and fruit trees. You transform your previous dense, overgrown, dark jungle of unintended, negative creations (especially NIR masses); so that you now live in a SPacious, beautiful, and plentiful garden, where all that you need drops into your hand like fruit from a tree.

Are you going to consciously work on your Return, or are you going to let the UNIVERSE bounce you back, bounce you off your failed goals, resistances, aversions, prejudices etc., until you align with IT? You either get with the Program; or the Program gets behind you and pushes.

Here are some Tools for your Return

1. ACKNOWLEDGEMENT and ACCEPTANCE of Who You Are. WAKE UP within the Illusion of Created Reality, to BEing an immortal spirit, and ONE with IT ALL. Stop identifying yourself with Created Reality, with the illusion, with matter, with the holograms of the physical universe, and with your body and human identity. Then decide and determine to demonstrate Who You Are.
2. REMEMBRANCE of SELF, one of the meditative disciplines. Maintain a moment to moment remembrance and awareness of yourSELF, of WHO YOU ARE, and consciousness of your decision to express your Highest Ideal to become God = LOVE.
3. BE HERE NOW (with REMEMBRANCE of SELF). Control your mind to stay out of it, out of past and future, and into the HERE and NOW. Enjoy the show, the parade of events. Create everything you want, and enjoy whatever shows up without activation on not getting what you wanted.
4. Your DO: Act as God = LOVE would in each instant. Live in the question: What would God = LOVE DO now? If it is not very real for you that you are God, never has there been a better situation or higher call for: "Act as if." (3-18-312) Fake IT until you make IT! Pretend IT and practice IT and that will help make IT real.
5. Meditation: your cutting-open tool for stopping thought and penetrating inside your BEing. You cannot be totally awake while you are thinking. Thinking is a form of being in a dream state because what you are thinking about is the illusion. (4-9-200)
6. CDT (Creation and Discreation Technology). Discreation of your God Suppressor Mass, and Creation of Who You Want to BE, of PIRs for every event, and generally, all the time in your life. Every time you FEEL or ACT with AntiLove, you are looking at your AntiGod that you need to discreate.

7. The question is not: "To BE, or not to BE."

The challenge is:

To BE all the God that you can BE.

If you BE God, then you DO as God would DO.

Thus, live in the question:

What would God do now? – to then do it.

DOing is BEing in action.

As God is Love, this question can also be phrased:

What would Love do now?

What would God = LOVE DO now?

When you are God (BE), then you act (DO) as God would.

Reverse this: DO as God would to BEcome God.

Your DO then feedbacks into your BE, and thus strengthens your BE-FEEL and entire Causal Sequence as God.

The primary answer to this question is: Love and Create (express Power).

Both of these, Love and Power, require Wisdom.

All of these three disciplines, Meditation, CDT, and Self-Remembering work together and reinforce each other. Meditation gives you the ability to stay out of your mind and into BE-FEEL and so penetrate your "I," which will activate your God Suppressor Mass. If you are meditating well, negative energy will arise constantly.

CDT gives you the ability to discreate all the negative energy that will come up in meditation and at any time in your life. As you will have noticed, life is full of trigger events. You should apply CDT every time you are activated (in any negative emotion), immediately if you can, as soon as possible otherwise.

Both meditation and CDT strengthen your ability to maintain your Self-Remembering, to stay out of your mind and focused into your Here and Now experience. CDT allows you to discharge anything negative as it comes up.

CDT is important not only for the Return. Even if a person is not interested in mysticism (the science and art of Return to the ONE), CDT gives you tremendous control over your Causal Sequences, i.e. over your life at the human level.

The Journey HOME

The Journey through Life and to HOME
is not a search for God—
I am inside of HER, in the very center of the
INFINITE SPHERE of BEing,
in the Kingdom of Heaven
even now—I never left.

It is a question of Real-izing
Where I am and Who I am.

I am not searching for God,
I am experiencing HER.

The Journey HOME is an
endless EXPERIENCE of GOD,
place by place, part by part,
in which the Game of I<>Not-I
creates for me the opportunity
to define and experience

Who I AM in relation to Not-I = Other
until I transcend the illusion of
individuality and separation, and realize that
IT is ALL ONE, and I am IT ALL.

I only need to live in the affirmation of "I AM ONE,"
discreate all experience of BEing less than God,
and be fully Present in the Here and Now
to capture all of the Experience.

Chapter 23

The Ten Stages of Human Consciousness

As we have seen, because of Polarity, we cycle into Materiality and the minimum BEingness of being human. All humans obey the Existential Imperative to Return to the ONE from the time of their first incarnation as a human being until their Re-Integration to the ONE. The spiritual progression of a BEing from Materiality (human beingness in the physical universe) back to full and free Spirituality long journey from maximum unconsciousness to cosmic consciousness.

We can distinguish 10 stages of Consciousness on this journey. These stages are characterized by what consumes the TE (Time and Energy) of the person. TE includes attention and all THINK→DO→HAVE of the person: time, and interests, goals, desires, thoughts, planning, resources, money and resources, and efforts. The stages are, therefore, a progression of values and motivations in life.

The Ten Stages operate over dual time frames. The first time frame is the entire cycle of incarnations of a spirit from first entry into human materiality until final Illumination and departure from all incarnations on earth. For the average human being, this is a cycle of about 600 to 700 lifetimes. In each incarnation, the person advances a little bit on his "vertical" progress back to the ONE. At "death," each psycan returns to the ONE with the progress made in that lifetime in increased consciousness and any reduction of hir God Suppressor Mass (Essence Suppressor Mass).

In the first five stages, the "Dark Ages," progress is slow and mostly driven by suffering. We might say that the desires and attachments of the lower levels of consciousness must be burned out in the BEing by suffering through them until the BEing finally gives up and seeks other values, spiritual ones. In the later stages, Enlightenment; a person can contribute consciously to hir growth and so advances much more rapidly than in the Dark Stages. In the Commitment or Warrior Stage, the BEing's intent and effort are at a maximum and this stage can be completed in as little as three lifetimes.

The second time cycle is each lifetime. When you "die," you return to the ONE for a while. (See the *Conversations With God* series book *Home With God.*) You eventually come back to your unfinished Supreme Game in this realm, shoulder your "cross" again (your Essence Suppressor Mass), and re-incarnate to continue your Human-back-to-God Polarity Game. In each lifetime, you progress very rapidly through the levels already mastered in previous lifetimes to the point on your vertical progress where you "died" in your last lifetime. You then advance forward slowly from that point into new territory not covered in previous lifetimes.

The progression from one stage is neither sudden nor definite. The stages fade into one another and overlap so that there will be vestiges of the previous stages in the higher ones, and a lower stage motivation can activate and predominate temporarily in experience over a higher stage already obtained. For example, even in First Awakening; the person will still have Survival, Security, and Sensation motivations. The Dark Night will last well up into the Second Awakening and there can even be attacks of it in the earlier parts of the Warrior Stage. Here is a brief explanation of each stage:

The Dark Ages

In the Dark Ages or Stages, the human being lives in spiritual darkness (i.e. ignorance). S/He does not know what s/he is, where s/he is, where s/he came from, how s/he got here, the purpose of life, or how life works. Hir life revolves around the body and controlling matter with great desire, effort and struggle. S/He does not perceive hirself as a spirit, and may believe that s/he has evolved from matter itself. S/He perceives others as competitors for the scarce and hard to get goods of the material plane. Hir accounts with higher reality are usually satisfied by the authoritative, dogmatic beliefs systems called religions, which often forbid questioning and seeking any truth outside of themselves. The Dark Ages are characterized by the External Quest and search for pleasure (MOPs) and the avoidance of pain, efforts which are never more than momentarily successful.

Survival

In this first stage, the person is totally occupied in just staying alive. Life is a struggle to satisfy the basic needs of the body. This level has a hierarchy of needs: air, water, food, clothing, shelter. As each need is satisfied for the moment, the person's attention and effort will move to the next. The person has little TE left over from the struggle to stay alive to do much else. The dominant energy is frustration, desperation, fear, and sorrow. Perhaps 50% of the world's population is in this stage in the year 2007.

Security

In the second stage, the person has immediate Survival (the first stage) handled, and can put some TE to assuring survival into the future. Hir consciousness will now focus on securing that s/he (and then hir loved ones) can eat and have a place to live tomorrow and the next day and the next month. Many people experience this level as anxiety and fear about job security and paying the bills. People hoard money and material things trying to assure their future security.

Sensation, Pleasure

In the third stage, the person feels that s/he has survival and security under control for the moment. S/He will then turn hir TE to gratifying the physical senses, to seeking pleasure. In this level, life is about "having fun." The person seeks to wine and dine, and fete the senses with finer clothes, jewelry, perfumes, luxury items, music, parties, travel, vacations, sex, drugs, etc.; anything that provides sensual stimulation. The person equates happiness with physical well-being and sensual pleasure.

Dominion or Egoic Power

As the spirit grows, and sensation needs are satisfied but the person is not, s/he must seek bigger games in hir compulsive efforts to fulfill the Imperative to happiness. In the Dominion stage, the person moves into wanting **power** and **mass**. S/He wants to control people, places, things, events, and energy; and to **accumulate** material things or money. This part of the External Quest is the search for fame and fortune: recognition, prestige, fame, social position, money, and economic, political, business, or military power. It can take the form of striving to move as high as possible in a hierarchy, be it a corporation, the government, the military, or a church. However, it is egoic power: power used for the benefit and glory of self; as opposed to love power, where everything is administered for the good of all.

Dark Night of the Soul

As the person grows through the Dominion state, there will come a time when its targets and values no longer satisfy the spirit. **Life begins to be experienced as empty and meaningless.** The person looks up from hir beguilement with Matter and **asks the Philosopher's Questions**: Where am I? What am I? Who am I? What am I doing here? Where is here? How did I get here? Where am I going? What is the purpose of my life? What is the purpose of it all? **There has got to be something more!**

Complete transition into the depths of the Dark Night can take years, but eventually the BEing is in the experience of the dryness and emptiness of life most of the time. It is usually an extremely painful era, filled with frustration, desperation and depression. The painful urgency for solution sends the BEing into the next stage: The Search, which is the beginning of the Enlightenment Stages.

The Enlightenment Stages

Enlightenment is just that: the coming, the Dawn of the Light, of the Gnosis, of true knowledge of the nature of existence. It is the transformation of a person from the realities, values, and behaviors of the lower stages, of the External Quest, to those of the higher stages, the Internal Quest. It is an awakening of the spirit to itself. Spiritual values and efforts; study and personal growth; love and service to others, and Illumination, the re-Birth of the Spirit, begin to take the upper hand in the person's TE. (There is a list of the characteristics of Enlightenment at www.psycanics.org.) The Stages of Enlightenment are:

Search

The pain of the Dark Night of hir soul impels the BEing to begin a Search for Light, for relief from the suffering, for answers to the Philosopher's Questions, for real Knowledge. The person's religious beliefs are seen to be inadequate as answers to the Philosopher's Questions and to hold no real Light. The person begins to seek for Knowledge: to investigate other religions, but above all to seek outside of traditional religions: to read books, to attend courses, to investigate spiritual systems. The person must accumulate a mental mass of spiritual ideas and concepts.

The First Awakening

First Light, the **Dawn**, the real-ization of the **Possibility** that life is fundamentally spiritual In hir Search, eventually the person accumulates sufficient, true spiritual information that the possibility that life really is spiritual arises for the person. (This awakening must not be confused with religious beliefs or fervor. Religion is mental and consists of others's realities about God; not one's own experience and conclusions.) The person begins to see that hir suffering in the Dark Night is a spiritual problem. The Dark Night is still very much present, and the person is still in great confusion about the nature of spirituality. The Search for ever more Light, now whetted by the success of the First Awakening, continues and leads to:

The Second Awakening

Sunrise, Reality. The person continues to read, study, and attend schools; and the quantity and quality of true spiritual knowledge, the Light, increases, and the Darkness of the soul decreases. Eventually, the Light, the total mass of reality and conviction that life is fundamentally spiritual, passes the 50% mark. The Reality that life is spiritual is now **more real** than the ignorance that characterizes hir Dark Ages. This point, when the Light is 51% or more, when consciousness of spirit takes the upper hand in the person's awareness and values, is the Second Awakening. However, especially at the beginning, it is only 51% most of the time, and the person will still have periods of **great confusion** and attacks of the **doubts and despair of the Dark Night**.

Commitment (Warrior)

Eventually, the Light of Truth that the person has been nurturing within becomes so strong that s/he can no longer ignore its brilliance and its call. S/He now begins to obey the injunction of Jesus: Seek FIRST the Kingdom of Heaven.

Previous to this stage, no matter how much attention the person had on hir spirituality, it was still not **first** in hir priorities. S/He would still "lay up" hir "treasure" (TE) more towards worldly things that spiritual ones. Previous to Commitment, the person puts worldly considerations of family, work, pleasure, fame or fortune ahead of hir spirituality. The Commitment stage begins when s/he reverses hir priorities. Now, hir spirituality is more important to hir than hir worldly affairs. S/He intensifies disciplines like meditation.

This stage is also called **Warrior** (of the First Level), as the person now enters into full "battle" with hir lower self to eliminate all negative states and to discreate the Essence Suppressor Mass. Where the normal human being flees or attacks negative things, the Warrior welcomes everything, no matter how painful, that helps hir grow spiritually. As it is said in mysticism: "There is s/he who has conquered a thousand armies. There is s/he who has conquered hirself. Far greater is the latter."

Illumination

The journey from Darkness to EnLIGHTenment finally terminates in Illumination, the totality of the **LIGHT**.

This state has been called many things throughout mystical history: The Third Awakening; the Return, Re-Integration to the ONE, Cosmic Consciousness, Nirvana, Samadhi, the Beyond, the Kingdom of Heaven, Self-Realization, God-Realization, the Birth of the Spirit; to name just a few. It is the recovery of your true identity: the Infinite One God Being. The state of Illumination is far beyond any capacity of the human being to understand and nothing we say about it can really convey what it is. The psycan slips the surly bounds of Matter (of the Essence Suppressor Mass) and re-integrates hir spirit to the ONE. It is now experientially ONE with ALL THAT IS and literally God. It has total, instant power over the physical universe. This is the state of Buddha, Jesus, and Lao Tse. Only about 235 human beings have ever attained it since the beginning of humanity. This state seems to have two levels. In the first level, individuality remains. The BEing may remain an individual, and do so for all eternity; or return completely to BEing the ONE, as s/he pleases, by dropping all individuality. However, because of the Laws of Polarity, this last stage will eventually require another descension into limited individuality.

Illumination is the culmination of life on earth. However, it is but the beginning of true spiritual existence, as it is the re-entry point of a fully Self-Realized and free spirit back into the cosmos of all creation that consists of innumerable universes.

**Psycanics is a Path of Knowledge and Joy for Return to the ONE.
It is not the only the path. Only you can decide if it is
the best path—and that only for you.**

Illustration 23-1: The Ten Stages of Human Consciousness

(Full color version available from www.psycanics.org)

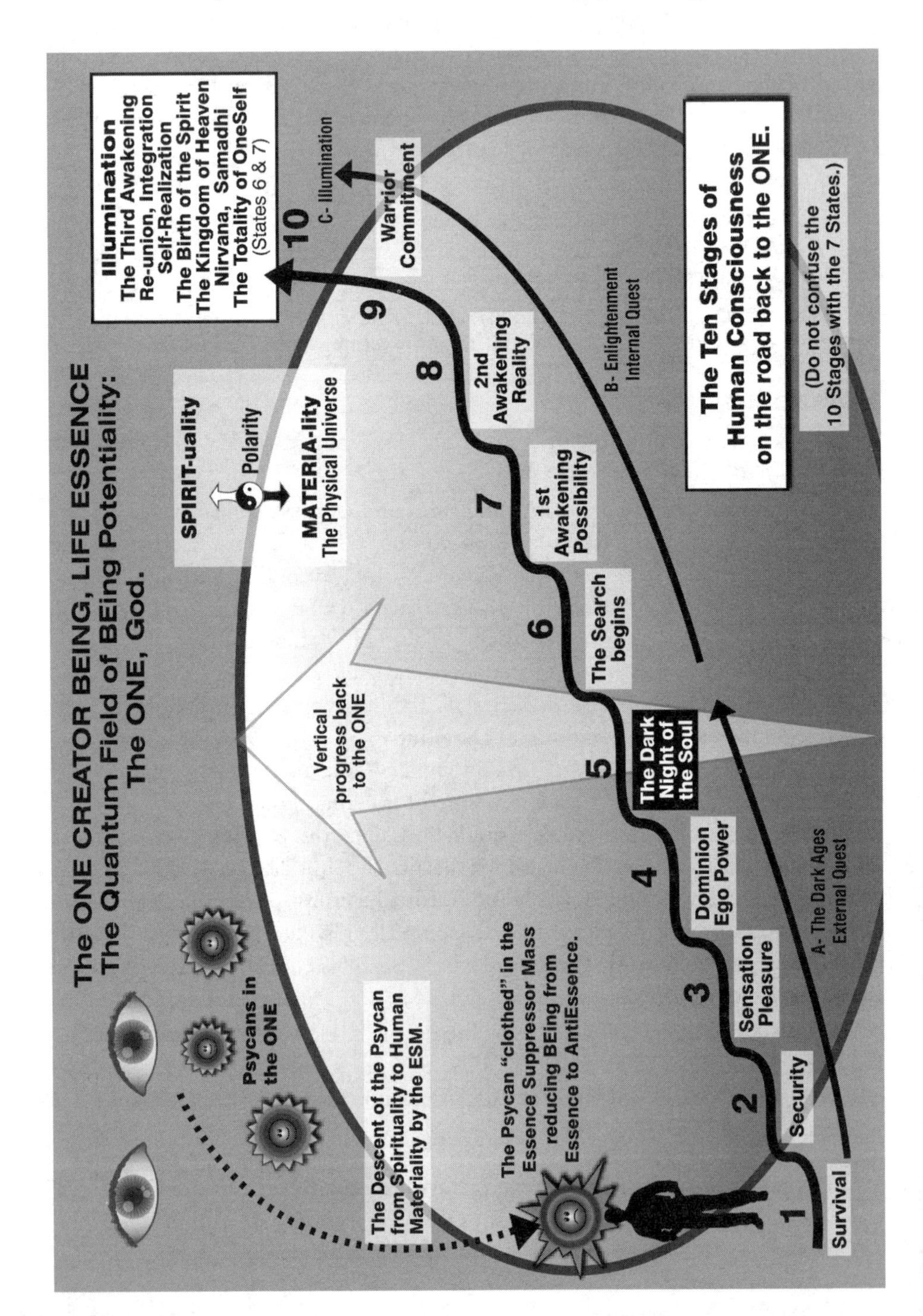

Chapter 24

Final Words

The *Conversations with God* books are, in my opinion, the most important documents on the planet. They are exactly what humanity needs to know to transcend the condition of No-Love and AntiLove that reigns on this planet.

There is only the ONE, and you are ALL of IT. This is not new news; Hinduism has taught this for 3,500 years. However, the confirmation of it in *CWG* should bring this all important datum at least theoretically alive for the Western World. At least it has for you, or you would not be reading this.

The ENERGY is infinitely powerful and IT operates according to laws. Everything that IT creates out of ITself is created according to laws of Cause-Effect, Energy, Mass, Realities, Creation, Polarity, and Resistance—to name a few. The physics of our physical universe are but a derivation of the General Laws of all Existence. The creation of your illusion of being human is not magic: it is science; it is physics. Knowledge is Power. To have Power, you must know and apply these laws. This book is but an introduction to them.

You may have difficulty learning CDT (Creation and Discreation Technology) from a book, and may need a Pilot until you get the "hang of it." In that case, you should contact the Psycanics Foundation to find out about one-on-one guidance sessions (by telephone or in person), as well as live seminars. This book presents CDT only very generally: each area of life such as couple relationships, money, raising children, finding and aligning with your Life Script, manifestation, personal freedom, and the mind; all have laws and special processes.

EVERY mental or emotional discomfort in your life is an opportunity to discreate a piece of your God Suppressor Mass. Take advantage of every opportunity that life presents you to permanently eliminate that discomfort and to increase your overall level of happiness. The purpose of life is to be the mirror in which you can see yourSelf, so that just as a mechanic works on fine machinery; you can form, adjust, and polish your BEing, and re-member Who You Are.

May you walk with and as God.

The point of life is not to get anywhere—it is to notice that you are, and have always been, already there. You are, always and forever, in the moment of pure creation. The point of life is therefore to create—who and what you are, and then to experience that.

Conversations with God

Appendix 1

The Secrets of Comprehension and Learning

Knowledge is Power. Knowledge indicates and guides correct action—from among the infinite possibilities of ineffective action—to produce the desired results.

Only Comprehension constitutes Knowledge. Memorization of data without understanding it is useless. And if you understand it, you don't need to memorize it: you know it.

Therefore: **Study is the process of achieving comprehension.** Without comprehension there is no knowledge, and without knowledge acquired, no study has taken place.

Ideas and Concepts

The main reason why any reading or study becomes confusing and difficult is MUCs: MisUnderstood Concepts.

Knowledge of any subject, including science, technology, and psycanics is taxonomic = hierarchical = ordered in gradient. The comprehension of advanced concepts depends upon the comprehension of the previous, more basic concepts. Just as you must assemble a machine in a certain order or it will not go together; you must learn a subject in a certain order, the order of "basic and simple" to "complex and advanced." It is impossible to understand the advanced concepts of any subject without having first understood the basic concepts.

To continue reading beyond not-understood, misunderstood, or partially understood ideas is guaranteed to impair or totally impossibilitate[56] the comprehension of some, and often most, of the subsequent ideas, and therefore of the science itself.

Definition: **MUD: MisUnderstood worD**.

Definition: **MUC: MisUnderstood Concept**.

The correct definition of all the words in an idea makes the idea clear and easily understandable. MUDs, **M**is**U**nderstood wor**D**s cause MUC, **M**is**U**nderstood **C**oncepts. Together they create failure in comprehension and therefore in learning.

---

56 Verb meaning to "make impossible."

Words

Just as ideas, concepts, principles and laws are the building blocks of science; words are the building blocks of the ideas, concepts, principles and laws. The basic concepts as well as the advanced ones are formed of words. When you do not understand a concept (have a MUC), the cause is one or more MUDs: **M**is**U**nderstood wor**D**s—almost always. Basically, there are no misunderstood concepts, only misunderstood words. Words are the critical components, the building blocks, of knowledge.

The failure to correctly understand just one word is sufficient to block the understanding of an entire sentence, paragraph or chapter in a text. The failure to understand correctly just one word or one idea is sufficient to ruin the comprehension of an entire area of knowledge, of a science.

Let me repeat that: It has been proven that the failure to understand just one word that then produces the failure to understand just one key concept is sufficient to sabotage the understanding of an entire area of knowledge.

MUDs cause MUCs. The cause of a MUC is almost always one or more MUDs in the expression of that idea. **It is not the ideas that are misunderstood, but rather words.** Ideas become clear when the words used in the expression of the idea are all correctly cleared as to their definition in that context.

MUDs→MUCs inevitably snowball. The first MUC in a subject will cause other MUCs because the failure to comprehend a basic idea will make impossible the comprehension of all subsequent ideas whose comprehension requires the comprehension of that basic one. MUDs and MUCs lead to ever more MUDs and MUCs. To try to study jumping over misunderstood words will quickly bury the student in a mucky mudslide of ever increasing incomprehension, difficulty in learning that lead to eventual failure in the subject.

Therefore, **never proceed beyond something you don't understand, be it a word, a sentence, an idea or a paragraph**. To do so is a guaranteed formula for failure in your learning.

Here is just one example of common MUDs: Spiritual versus Religious

> The word "spiritual" is often used in psycanics, and it is important to distinguish between it and "religious." "Spiritual" means related to spirit," to a non-physical, Life-energy entity. Spirit means "Life" or the "Aware-Will unit," or "Conscious-Cause entity." You are a spirit, a Life-Energy entity, temporarily focused in a physical body. "Spiritual" is a synonym for "psycanic," just as "psycan" is a synonym for "spirit."
>
> Spiritual must not be confused with "religious," meaning "related to a registered brand of dogmas, doctrines, and rituals about God." Something can be very religious and not at all spiritual (i.e. holy wars), and very spiritual but not at all religious (i.e. meditation).

Appendix 2

Conventions

These conventions are followed in all the psycanics materials.

Acronyms, Abbreviations, Symbols, Formulas and Equations

→ causes, produces, determines leads to. Examples: "THINK→DO" means THINK determines DO. "Rxx→Perxx" means Resistance Causes Persistence.

= equal to, similar to, included in, part of, very related to.

<> sign used between two poles indicating that they are a Polarity.

+/- sign used after a phenomenon indicating that it is a Polarity.

emo: emotions, emotional energy.

E: energy

ELH: Emotions, Love and Happiness

ELJ: EmoLoveJoy

EMR: physics term for ElectroMagnetic Radiation.

Exp: experience

Exp2: Experience experienced

ID: IDentity, IDs = IDentity; almost always the Essence IDentities.

IT: the ONE SUPREME CREATOR BEING: God.

MoAs: Moments of AntiLove due to NIR mass activation: same as MoDs.

MoDs: Moments of Dolor = Pain: NIR mass activations, same as MoAs.

MoPs: Moments of Pleasure, Moments of PIRs: fleeting activations of PIRs.

Neg, neg: negative

NIR: Negative IDentity Reality.

PIR: Positive IDentity Reality.

Perxx: Persistence

Pos: positive

R: reality

R→Exp: Realities Cause Experience.

R/Exp: Reality = Experience: they are 2 sides of the same coin.

Resp: Response-ability

RespExp: Response-ability for Experience.

Rxx: Resistance

Rxx→Perxx: Resistance Causes Persistence.

SP: SPace

UPS: Unhappiness, Pain and Suffering; pronounced "oops."

Polarities and the Symbol +/-

Many of the most important phenomena of existence, and therefore in psycanics, are polarities (as explained in the text). When the concept of polarity is important to the term being discussed, the symbols of +/- will be added before or after the word. A polarity can also be represented by the signs <> between the two poles: for example Hot<>Cold.

Examples of the use of the polarity symbol +/-.

- "Emotion+/-" This means "both positive emotions and negative emotions," or "any emotion whether positive or negative," or "the entire Emotion Polarity Scale from lowest negative to highest positive."
- "Love+/-" means both positive love and negative love. (The concept of negative love will be explained in the text.) Love+/- means the same as Love<>AntiLove.

The term "anti" may be used to express the negative polarity, for examples:

- The concept of Power+/- includes Power+ and AntiPower.
- The negative polarity of Love is AntiLove.
- Love<>AntiLove is the only Happiness<>Pain that exist.

Gender

Where a sentence includes both or either gender, I use these dual gender forms: **s/he** for she or he; **hir** for him or her; **hirs** for his or hers; **hirself** for himself or herself. Example: S/He is very intelligent, but s/he left behind hir computer.

Word Equations and Formulas

You will often see two or more words with an equal sign between them, and all the words underlined to group them into that thusly-created word equation. The equal sign between the words means that the underlined words share the same concept; or one thing is included in the other, or they are in some way highly related as to meaning. The underline is NOT used for emphasis; it is used for grouping symbols in equations and formulas.

Underlined word equations connect or unite different words that refer to the same phenomenon. This is extremely important to full conceptual comprehension.

Three examples of word equations:

1. <u>Negative Emotions = MoDs = Activations = Resistance = AntiLove = UPS</u>
2. <u>Consciousness = Perception = Feeling = Experience = Knowing</u>
3. <u>Emotions+/- = Love+/- = Happiness+/-</u>

In each example, **these words appear to be different phenomena, but they are really all the same thing**. It is unfortunate that we have different words for the same thing as this has prevented real understanding of the phenomenon.

For example; we show that Emotions+/- = Love+/- = Happiness+/- are all the same thing. Until you understand this, you do not really understand any of them and are lacking critical data about how your life works.

When studying, until you understand why and how the equation-linked phenomena are all the same, you have not understood any of them fully. Any time you do not understand why the equal sign is there, why and how the terms are intimately related, you do not have full conceptual understanding in the area.

Make sure that you understand the sentence with each of the words individually and with all the words together. At first, word equations may feel a little awkward, but you will soon get used to it and eventually appreciate how they add to your understanding.

Words in All Caps

All words referring to that indefinable FIRST CAUSE beyond human comprehension (aka God) are written in all caps; and there are many. Examples include: INFINITE, CONSCIOUSNESS, INTELLIGENCE, LOVE; WISDOM, CREATOR, CAUSE, WILL, POWER, ENERGY, ESSENCE, SPACE, the ONE, the ALL THAT IS, IT, the EVERYTHING-NOTHING, TAO, SOURCE; ESSENCE, etc. Pronouns referring to IT are also capitalized and will usually be dual gender: S/HE, HIR, ITSELF, etc.

The elements of the Causal Sequence, BE→FEEL→THINK→RELATE/DO →HAVE, are always written in all caps to make sure that the reader recognizes that we are referring to elements of the Causal Sequence. This rule includes their derivatives such as BEing, FEELing, FELT, RELATEing, RELATIONs, DOing, DID, HAVEing, HAD, etc. When you see any of these words with capital letters, remember to add in the entire concept of the Causal Sequence, and of that element of the Causal Sequence in particular.

Your BEing consists of all your IDentities. IDentities are often written in capital letters: for example: I AM ABLE; I AM INTELLIGENT; I CAN DO IT. The purpose is to insure that the reader recognizes that these are IDentities and that all the laws of IDentities apply. Like BAD and the Causal Sequence, IDentity is acrucial concept in psycanics.

BAD and, when important: TRUTH are written in all caps to remind the reader of their total concept and the extreme importance of those concepts to human existence. As an example of such importance: BAD is the only entry point to AntiLove; it is the ONLY cause of all pain and suffering.

The first time a technical term of the psycanics terminology is introduced in the text, it may be written in capital letters for emphasis: e.g. ACTIVATION. It will also be defined at that point.

Capital First Letter Only

Words with a capital first letter refer to the entire psycanics concept of that phenomenon. The major psycanics concepts are usually so complex and extensive that they require multiple chapters, even entire books to explain. Examples of such major concepts include: Love, Power, Cause, SPace, Polarity, Response-ability, Fatal Paradigm, and Victim. IDentity and SPace are often written with the first two letters capitalized that are also their abbreviations: ID and SP. Each of these concepts is a major and important concept in psycanics and the first letter is capitalized to help the reader remember this when s/he sees the term.

Repetition of Data

In the first level of books on psycanics, I try to make each book a conceptually complete unit, so that each can be understood without needing to have read previous books. To do this, I must repeat certain fundamental concepts in each book. For example: no serious philosophical discussion of life can be complete without Polarity and the Causal Sequence. Therefore, I must include these in all books that are intended to be read separately rather than as a series.

In the advanced books, I presume that the reader already understands the fundamental concepts, and so make a minimum mention of these so that we can proceed to advanced concepts.

Appendix 3

Glossary of Psycanics Terminology

A

Activation: The movement into consciousness = experience = FEEL of a NIR Mass. An activation is primarily experienced as negative emotional charge = MoA = MOD = UPS. However, NIRs and BAD are always present. The event that sets off the activation is a TRIGGER.

Anger: Present time AntiPower AntiLove. The negative emotion that motivates attack to stop, change, damage, or destroy.

AntiEssence: The opposite polarity of ESSENCE which is Wisdom, Power, Value, and LoveJoy (WPVLJ). AntiEssence is any IDentity that denies or suppresses Wisdom, Power, or Value, and therefore triggers Self-AntiLove = negative ELJ. AntiEssence (AntiWisdom, AntiPower, AntiValue and AntiLove) is the ONLY source of all UPS.

AntiLove: The polar opposite of positive Love. Negative EmoLoveJoy. All the negative emotions. It is the lower half of the Love<>AntiLove energy polarity spectrum. AntiLove is any form of negative energy: AntiLove is both FEELing = emotion and DOing = action. 1- As emotion, AntiLove is negative, unpleasant, painful emotions; the lower half of the emotion spectrum that is hostility to anger to fear to hate to grief to depression to apathy. 2- As action, AntiLove is any action to punish, damage, or destroy. The point of entry for all generation of AntiLove is always the opinion of BAD.

AntiPower: The opposite polarity of Power, which is one of the four factors of ESSENCE. AntiPower is any IDentity (belief about self) that denies Cause: knowledge, power, ability, capacity, Response-ability, strength, etc. These are expressed in the AntiPower NIRs, including: I am unable, I am incapable, I can't, I am weak, I am powerless, I am a failure, I am not response-able, I don't know, I am stupid, I am the victim.

AntiWisdom: The opposite polarity of Wisdom as the first of the ESSENCE energies. The concept of Wisdom includes Awareness, Consciousness, Intelligence, Knowing, Experience, Knowledge, Memory, Creativity, Intuition, etc. AntiWisdom is any IDentity that denies or suppress Wisdom or Consciousness. Example: I can't learn, I don't know, I am stupid/dumb, It is hard for me to learn, I am less intelligent than others, I can't think, I can't feel, etc.

Attachment: The emotionally-backed (neurotic) compulsion to possess or hold on to any person or thing to avoid NIR activation. Attachment has the same mechanism as Addiction.

B

BAD: When spelled with all capitals, BAD is the abbreviation for the Creation = determination = decision = evaluation = opinion of BAD. BAD is that which should not BE as it is or at all, thereby appearing to justify the use of negative energy = AntiLove to change, stop, damage or destroy the BAD thing. BAD is always a judgment, an opinion, a mental creation of the psycan: it has no existence outside of the human mind. Thus it is always an illusion, a delusion, a hallucination, a lie, and a distortion of reality. "Nothing is Good or BAD, but thinking makes it so," to quote Shakespeare. BAD is the most nefarious of all human creations. It is the entry point to all Rxx→Perxx and to all pain and suffering: it is impossible to be unhappy or to suffer without having first created BAD. The most critical of all BADs is the BAD to self for BEing a NIR. The only pain that exists is the self-AntiLove = negative emotion triggered by the creation of BAD. As the psycan is always the only creator of BAD in hir universes, s/he is always the only creator of hir own suffering.

BE: 1- The first and most important factor in the Causal Sequence = The Formula of Life: BE→FEEL→THINK→RELATE/DO→HAVE. 2- The state of existing; to exist; that which is as it is. 3- The set of unique characteristics that give any reality its identity and make it what it is, distinguishing it from all other things.

verb. To be: to BEcome and remain any thing; the taking on, the assumption, of an identity. Complete integration with anything is to BE that thing which is to fully experience that thing.

BE-FEEL: BE-FEEL is the first two elements of the main Causal Sequence written together to indicate that they are inseparable and part of the same thing: ESSENCE of BEing. The psycan is formed of the LIFE ESSENCE ENERGY that consists of four kinds of energy: Wisdom, Power, Value and EmoLoveJoy. BE we consider as the Essence IDentities+/- of Wisdom, Power and Value. We consider the 4th energy, LoveJoy as FEEL, although it is really one thing, the LIFE ESSENCE ENERGY. Thus the psycan is BE-FEEL in the Causal Sequence. These two elements, BE and FEEL = Identities and Emotions are so closely connected that it is impossible to separate them, to have one without the other.

BEing: *noun.* BE is capitalized as referring to the first element of the Causal Sequence. The sum total of the identities, qualities and characteristics of any thing that make it that particular thing. As regards life entities (spirits) including the human being, the BEing is the psycan as modified by all hir IDentities; the BEing is the psycan plus all hir identities; Essence modulated by Identities. The BEing is everything that a psycan is being, also defined by everything s/he is not being. Your **BE**ing consists of all the creations you have had made about yourself, called **identities**. "BEing" is also used as a stative verb.

Being, human; the human being: A psycan who has counter-created hir ESSENCE with NIRs sufficiently to lower hir down to the human level and who then incorporates in a human body.

C

Causal Sequence: Any sequence of events in which the previous ones cause or determine the latter ones. There are a number of Causal Sequences in psycanics, the principle ones being:

1- Causal Sequence of Life:
BE→FEEL→THINK→RELATE/DO→HAVE.

2- Causal Sequence of BEing or Essence:
Wisdom→Power→Value→LoveJoy.

3- Causal Sequence of BAD: Should Not Be→BAD→Neg E = Rxx and UPS→Perxx→more Rxx and UPS.

4- Causal Sequence of Fatal ID→Fatal Paradigm→Programs→External Quest (one form of the Causal Sequence of Life).

Each element of a Causal Sequence determines the next element. Your life emanates from Who You Are, from your BEing. BEing = IDentities determine FEEL = emotion; that then determine THINKing. Your form of THINKing (ideas, knowledge, programs, etc.) then decides what you DO = how you ACT, including how you RELATE (communicate and treat others). Your DO = actions determine your HAVE = results in your life. The importance of the Causal Sequence is that by controlling just your BEing, you easily control everything else in your life.

Cause: *noun.* Any agent of will, power, force or action that creates, forms, initiates, decides, acts, moves, controls, changes, affects, or otherwise produces effects = results. The "northern" pole of the Cause-Effect Polarity Spectrum. RESPONSE-ABILITY is the point of transition between Cause and Effect.

Cause, *verb. tr.* The action of originating, starting, creating, controlling, changing, moving, affecting, or effecting something. The action of producing an EFFECT. *Synonyms:* to create, to produce, to effect. Notice that *to effect*, to carry out an action, is a synonym of the verb CAUSE.

CDT: Creation and Discreation Technology. This technology includes the Laws of Realities, and of Creation and Discreation of realities, all the data on the structure of NIR Masses, the advanced Communication Courses, and the CDT Trainer data, among other things. It also includes hundreds of procedures and processes of all kinds and for all purposes. CDT is any of many styles of creation and discreation of psycanic realities and of manifestation of physical ones. Creation involves energizing a reality until it has sufficient energy to be real, dense and permanent in experience. Discreation involves de-energizing a reality until it no longer exists and therefore is no longer real = experience-able. In CDT, the explorer enters into psycanic (interior) focus and works with hir mental and emotional realities to change them to the desired form. The explorer may or may not be guided by a CDT Trainer or Pilot, a person trained in psycanics and guiding CDT

Charge: Charge is emotional energy available to flow through consciousness thereby causing the experience of its flavor of emotion; thus it is negative emotional experience

Consciousness: A super high frequency ENERGY that serves as the field that detects and senses = experiences the modulation of all other forms of energy. Consciousness is the basic energy from which all other realities are formed and that which then perceives = experiences them. It, along with Will, is the basic energy of ESSENCE, of all BEing, of the psycan. It is the capacity of the psycan to perceive energies and realities.

Cosmos: The entire creation; all of Created Reality (as opposed to ULTIMATE REALITY). The cosmos consists of countless universes populated by innumerable BEings. The physical universe we humans know is but one among billions.

Counter-Create/Counter-Creation: to create an reality that creates a block or counter the experience of a previous reality. " I AM WEAK" is a counter-creation to "I AM STRONG." The Essence Suppressor Mass is a counter-creation to our being the ONE.

Create: To cause to exist that which did not exist previously (as distinguished from MANIFESTATION, which is to attract into your life = experience something already created, often by others). The use of Will to form new realities out of energy.

Created Reality: Created Reality is the cosmos: all creation, all BEings and all things, as opposed to the underlying field of ULTIMATE REALITY, that is the Creator—as well as all Created Reality, for IT can only create out of ITSELF. All created realities appear "real," and appear to be individual and separate entities.

Creation: Anything that exists other than the CREATOR HIRSELF. All realities (things and energies) are creations: every thing had to be created at the beginning of its existence.

Creator: Any agent of cause that brings into being something that did not exist previously. The psycan in relation to all hir realities. When in all caps, CREATOR it refers to FIRST CAUSE OF IT ALL, aka God.

D

Density: Technically, the amount of energy = mass in a reality divided by the amount of space occupied. More generally, the mass or amount of energy in a reality.

Determination: A creation of a reality (belief) about life—as opposed to Identities which are realities about Self. For example: "You have to work hard to get money," is a determination. During CDT, after discreating the NIRs, you then discreate your negative (limiting) determinations, and create positive ones according to what you wish to experience in the future. For example: "Money comes to me easily and naturally."

Dichotomy: Two poles of a polarity that have no spectrum between them.

Discreate/Discreation: To cause something to no longer exist. To take any creation = reality and terminate its existence by liberating the modulations in its energy. As it no longer exists, it is no longer real and therefore no longer causes experience. Discreation contrasts with trying to make something not-real, not experience-able, by resisting, denying, blocking or suppressing its experience. Creation and Discreation are the purposes of CDT.

DO: The fourth factor in the Causal Sequence. It includes all behaviors, efforts and actions of a person, including habits, addictions, attachments, work, play, and hir manners of relating with (communicating and treating) others. A person's BE→FEEL→THINK determines hir DO. DO then determines HAVE = results. DO can be divided into three elements: 1- DO with and to Self; 2- DO with people = RELATE; and 3- DO with things. DO includes RELATE when RELATE is not specified separately.

Drama: Intense experience produced by exploring the limits of polarities, especially the Power polarity (I CAN–I CAN'T). Maximum uncertainty over the outcome of important efforts, thereby creating suspenseful and highly emotional experience. "Juicy" experience derived from the pushing the limits of BEing, FEELing and DOing.

E

Effect: The "southern" pole in the Cause–Effect polarity; the opposite of CAUSE. That which is created, acted upon, moved, or produced by a Cause. The result of the action of a Cause; the change or result produced by a

Cause. *Synonym:* result, impact. To believe oneself in negative Effect without Power to change it is the condition of VICTIM.

Ego: Any effort to exalt oneself by diminishing others. Ego is any attempt to increase one's BEing (Power or Value), not by actually working on oneSelf to increase these, but by invalidating, lowering, or "stepping on" others so that they appear smaller and oneSelf larger. Ego is all AntiLove behaviors that attack others to exalt Self; it is always AntiLove for others. The specific forms and behaviors of ego are almost infinite.

EmoLoveJoy: A word created from three words: emotions, love, and joy; joy representing happiness. All of these are polarities and they are all the same polarity. FEEL in the Causal Sequence. The word "EmoLoveJoy" signals the reader the supremely important fact that these three things, these three polarities: Emotions+/-; Love+/-, and Happiness+/- are all one and the same thing. EmoLoveJoy+/- is the fourth energy of ESSENCE, the LJ in WPVLJ. Many people think that love is just one emotion of many. This is not true. Love is the entire emotional polarity scale from ecstasy down through joy to indifference to anger to fear to apathy and depression. <u>Emotions = Love</u>; and <u>Love = Happiness</u>. Thus, emotions are also the polarity scale of happiness. The emotions are the ONLY happiness or UPS (Unhappiness, Pain and Suffering) there is. The positive emotions are degrees of happiness; the negative emotions are degrees of UPS.

Emotion: The emotions are the psycanic experience of the Love Energy Polarity Spectrum. EmoLoveJoy+/-. <u>Emotions+/- = Love+/- = Happiness+/-</u>. The emotions+/- are the fourth energy, (Emo)LoveJoy, of the four main Essence of Life Energies. The emotions are the polarity spectrum of Love: the positive emotions are love and the negative emotions are AntiLove. FEEL in the Causal Sequence. The emotions are the internal experience of Love+/- and the impulse and motivation energy for the external DOings of Love+/-. The emotions are a psycanic energy polarity spectrum that runs from apathy to ecstasy. The cause of your emotions is your Essence IDentities. Your emotions are your love or AntiLove for yourself according to the IDentity+/- you have activated at the moment.

ENERGY: The ENERGY, in all capital letters is another name for God. All that exists is formed by and out of the ONE CONSCIOUS INTELLIGENT CREATOR ENERGY. IT is both CREATOR and CREATED, forming all that exist out of ITS own substance. The universe is made by God, of God. The universe is God exploring, experiencing and play with HIRSELF in all HIR infinite possibilities of BE, FEEL, DO and HAVE.

Energy: The basic substance from which everything else is formed and the force that moves all things. All <u>creations = realities</u>, physical and psycanic, are made of energy.

Energy as Mass or Matter: Any object; any reality, physical or psycanic, is formed of energy. All matter, whether physical, mental or emotional is a conglomeration of energy. Matter is any mass = conglomeration of energy which persists = maintains its form over time. Mass is the quantity of energy in an object (as measured in physic by resistance to acceleration).

ESSENCE: ESSENCE is the basic ENERGY and NATURE of LIFE = BEING = IT = GOD. ESSENCE means the ESSENCE of LIFE, or ESSENCE of BEING. The ESSENCE energies are abbreviated to Wisdom, Power, Value and LoveJoy; and then to WPVLJ. ESSENCE and each element of ESSENCE is a polarity and all the laws of polarity apply.

- Wisdom IDentity Polarity: I am smart–I am dumb; I know–I don't know; I am smart–I am stupid.
- Power IDentity Polarity: I can–I can't; I am able–I am unable; I am strong–I am weak; I am creative–I am not creative.
- Value IDentity Polarity: I am good–I-am bad; I am worthy–I am unworthy; I am deserving–I am undeserving.
- Love: The emotions are the Love and Happiness Polarity: EmoLoveJoy+/-.

Essence Suppressor Mass (ESM): The Essence Suppressor Mass is the sum total of all the NIR Masses. The Essence Suppressor Mass is a mass of NIRs and Self-AntiLove that lowers BEing from that of God to Humanity. The ESM is a thick shell of energy = mass = reality around the human psycan, a shell in which the human psycan is encased. The human psycan is at the effect of this mass which shapes hir experience, hir BE-FEEL to AntiEssence. Synonyms for the Essence Suppressor Mass include God Suppressor Mass, AntiEssence Mass.

Event: An event is any change that a person perceives. It can be change, movement, arrival or departure of any thing including people, words, actions, places, situations, things, thoughts and emotions. One of the importance of events in psycanics is that they may trigger a NIR Mass activation. See also **Trigger event** and **Externals**.

Experience: Consciousness at work. The perception, sensing and feeling of any energy. The effect of energy = realities on consciousness. The sensing of the modulation of any energy form. That which you perceive, feel or know. Synonyms include: perceive, sense, feel, be, live. Experience is life. The highest experience is ESSENCE = WPVLJ = GOD. Experience is the purpose of existence and the ESSENCE experience is ultimate motivation of all human behavior: the Existential Imperative.

Externals: Abbreviation of "external realities" or "external events" or "external agents." Any reality or event external to the psycan.. Refers to events or things in the outside world such as other people, things, situations, circumstances, and events—as opposed to the internal world (psycanic universe). All your externals make up your personal world or universe. An EVENT is any change in external realities.

External Quest: All THINK→DO→HAVE to control experience = BE-FEEL = find ESSENCE with externals. The three main routes of it are: 1- Attack externals to stop, change, punish, or destroy them as apparent cause of UPS. 2- Avoid activation or, or suppress UPS with things, substances, chemicals, or activities (the mechanism of attachments and addictions). 3- Amass material things, power, wealth, fame, etc., to be happy.

Existential Imperative: The basic driving force of all human behavior is the compulsion, the imperative, to control one's experience, to avoid pain and to seek ever higher levels of positive experience (pleasure and happiness). In the physical realm, this is the pleasure-pain principle of psychology. In the psycanic universe, it is felt as the imperative to control one's emotions = FEEL = Happiness/UPS, which, of course, comes from one's BE = the Essence IDentities; so that it is the imperative to control BE-FEEL. The quest for ever higher BE-FEEL of ESSENCE only ends when you return to the Ultimate Experience: ESSENCE = WPVLJ = GOD. This force within, this imperative to reach ESSENCE is the Existential Imperative. Improperly understood, the Imperative devolves into the External Quest, which is the effort to work the Causal Sequence of life backwards; to control psycanic experience by controlling external events. Also called the Experiential Existential Imperative.

F

Fatal Identity: All the identities = determinations of self that deny Cause. Examples include: I AM NOT CAUSE; I AM NOT CREATOR; I AM NOT RESPONSE-ABLE; I AM THE VICTIM, etc.

Fatal Paradigm: A large network of interconnected beliefs (THINKs) that assign Cause and Response-ability for experience to externals. The basis of the Fatal Paradigm is the belief that: Given that I AM NOT CAUSE (the Fatal Identity), externals must be. Ergo: "X" causes my experience or controls me or my life. Ergo, I AM AT THE EFFECT, I AM THE VICTIM, of "X." The Fatal Paradigm is a THINK that then generates the enormous range of behaviors (DOs) known as the External Quest: the vain attempt to control experience by controlling externals.

Fear: The neg EmoLoveJoy associated with Future AntiPower ID.

FEEL (in capital letters): Refers to the second element of the Causal Sequence of BE→FEEL→THINK→RELATE/DO→HAVE. Your FEEL is your Love or AntiLove for Self according the IDs+/- you activate. The primary

FEEL is EmoLoveJoy+/-. See also **BE-FEEL**.

FIRST CAUSE: That which existed before anything existed and caused = brought all that exists into existence; aka the CREATOR, the SUPREME BEING, God. See *Cosmology*. An interesting philosophical question is "What Caused First Cause?" or "Where did God come from?"

G

Game: The effort to overcome an obstacle and reach a goal.

God: The SUPREME BEING, the ESSENCE ENERGY of BEing, the INFINITE LIFE FORCE. The original ONE and ONLY, CONSCIOUS ENERGY, AWARENESS, INTELLIGENCE, FIRST CAUSE-CREATOR-WILL-POWER, SPACE, LOVE, JOY, BLISS entity beyond human comprehension. The Quantum Field of Potentiality of BEing. IT is the INFINITE, TIMELESS, ETERNAL-NOW "I AM." IT is THAT WHICH IS BEFORE ANYTHING WAS. The UNMOVED MOVER, The NOTHING-WITH-THE-POTENTIAL-TO-BE ANYTHING THAT IS EVERYTHING, THE CREATOR AND THE CREATED, Everywhere, Always. The TAO.

God Suppressor Mass: Synonym for Essence Suppressor Mass, the totality of the NIR Masses that counter-creates Godness and creates the psycan as a human being.

H

Happiness: A state of positive BE-FEEL all the time, no matter the external circumstances. It requires imperviousness to triggers and freedom of the quest of MoPs. Happiness is a FEEL condition of positive emotion (i.e. contentment, enthusiasm and joy) all the time. Happiness is emotional; it is how you FEEL and only how your FEEL. Your happiness is never the events, but rather how you BE-FEEL during the events. The only true happiness is self-love. Thus the only real happiness is in BEing who you love. Happiness is the experience of self-love.

The ultimate Happiness is the ecstasy of the reunion with the ONE SUPREME LIFE ESSENCE WPVLJ BEING = GOD from whence you come. This is the return to the Kingdom of Heaven. The Existential Experiential Imperative is the compulsive driving force within each BEing to seek this Happiness.

HAVE: Last element of the Causal Sequence: DO→HAVE. The results of action or inaction. The results of creation and manifestation. Your HAVE is everything that shows up in your life, whether you take Response-ability for putting it there or not. HAVE also includes your negative HAVE: the things you have that you don't want (e.g. sickness, accidents, lack of money. etc). It includes your NOT-HAVE: all that you do want (e.g. a better job, more money), but have not been able to manifest.

Humbe: short for human being.

I

IDentity: When spelled with capitalized first two letters, it means an ESSENCE IDentity, WPV, as opposed to other levels and kinds of identities.

Identity: Generally: What something is. The unique characteristics and qualities of a reality (mass of energy) that makes it an individual and distinguishes it from all other forms of energy. A table is an identity; a house is an identity. However, in psycanics, we are interested in the identities of the psycan, creations of Self usually in the form of I AM and I AM NOT some characteristic of BEing. Your BEing is your psycan modified by your identities.

Ignorance: Usually refers to ignorance of psycanics, of the physics and mechanics of your BEing and its functioning. The price of ignorance is suffering = AntiLove and Antipower. In mysticism: The ignorance of Who You Are, of your divine origin and nature, of your ONEness with all that is. Hinduism: Advidya. As Buddha said, "Ignorance is the root of all evil."

Ignorant (person): This always means a person who is ignorant of psycanics. The person may be a scholar or expert in other areas of knowledge. However, on not knowing how hir own BEing functions, s/he is ignorant of the most important thing in hir existence: hirself. See **Ignorance**.

Internal: in psycanics, internal means internal to the psycan, out of the external, physical universe and "inside" the consciousness, mind or emotions of the BEing.

Internal Quest: the search "internally," within oneself, for ESSENCE and Happiness by working on one's BEing and therefore FEELing. It is the correct way to spiritual development and happiness as opposed to the External Quest. "The Kingdom of Heaven is Within."

IT: When in capital letters refers to God, the TAO, the original, incomprehensible INTELLIGENT ENERGY CONSCIOUSNESS CREATOR.

J

K

Kingdom of Heaven: The residence of God. The place/state of INFINITE ESSENCE and therefore of bliss and ecstasy. It is within you: you are IT. The ultimate goal in the game of existence is to return to the Kingdom of

Heaven—from whence you came. This return is an expansion—or realization—of your identity to BE everything = God again; that you are ESSENCE.

L

LOVE: in all capitals: God. The fourth energy of ESSENCE: EmoLoveJoy. One of the natures of God is LOVE. FEEL and DO in the Causal Sequence.

Love: Will, SPace and Energy. Love is the act of **will**, expressed in the **action** to give **SPace** to yourself and to others to be as they are and to be as they are not; and to **care for, teach and grow the energies** around you. To this can be added the *Warrior's Oath*: At all times, under all circumstances, to the 100% of my ability, no matter what.

Love begins at SPace on the Love-AntiLove Polarity Spectrum.

Love is all forms of positive energy. There are two major divisions of energy: 1- internal = psycanic; and 2- external = physical.

1- **"Internal" Love = FEEL:** Psycanically, love is experiential; the emotions are the primary love energy and experience. The positive emotions are love and the negative emotions are AntiLove. As you live your emotions moment to moment in your life, you are living your love or your AntiLove.

2- **"External" Love = DO:** A- Love as a Verb: Love is action. To love is to act (energy in motion and at work) to care for, support and grow that which is loved. B- Love as a noun, as HAVE: love is also any form of positive energy; food, and money, for examples.

M

Manifest/Manifestation: To cause to exist in your experience something already created, usually by others. You create a painting; however, you manifest a car; it is created by the factory. See also **Creation**.

Mass: 1- The amount of energy in a reality. 2- Another name for a reality, for a conglomeration of energy, especially when the exact nature of the reality is not identified. In CDT, a reality may be experienced as a mass pressing on consciousness or some part of the body without the Explorer being able to feel the exact nature of the reality. See **Energy as Mass**.

Mind: The most useful point of view in psycanics is that there is no such thing as a mind. There are only mental frequency realities and the ability to manipulate, compare, analyze and store those realities. The mind, then, in psycanics is the interplay of will, consciousness and thought realities. "Mind" must not be confused with "brain" which is a physical organ that controls the body and transduces physical energy to psycanic energy for perception by the psycan.

Mind as opposed to Experience: Mind is the process of the psycan "looking" at hir mental realities, analyzing and trying to understand them. As such, it diverts attention (consciousness) from experiencing→discreating. Humans run to mind, to thinking about or analyzing matters to avoid experience, to avoid feeling. Thus mind is often one of the forms of resistance to experience. However, life—and discreation—occur in experience, not in mind. A CDT Trainer must always be on the look out for hir explorer running to mind and bring him back to experience.

MoD: Moment of Dolor (dolor is Latin for pain). Any activation of a NIR Mass bringing into consciousness = experience the AntiLove = negative emotions = negative FEEL = UPS associated with that NIR. *Synonyms:* MoA and UPS.

MoP: Moment of Pleasure or Moment of PIR: The fleeting moment of positive emotions = +FEEL= self love = happiness that results from the activation of a PIR. This occurs when some "good" trigger event shows up in the person's world. MoPs are a mirage of happiness that feeds the External Quest. By chasing externals as triggers for MoPs (as opposed to the internal handling of IDs), the human being maintains hirself on the emotional roller coaster of hir uncontrolled identities and emotions.

Mysticism: The study of, and especially the personal experience of, levels of consciousness = BEing beyond normal human perception, and especially the perception of the Deity. The body of knowledge and disciplines designed to enable a human being to return to those levels of BEing, to the ONE INFINITE ESSENCE.

N

Negative IDentity Realities = NIRs: The AntiEssence IDentities. Any of the IDentities = BE that suppress or deny ESSENCE = Wisdom, Power, and Value. Examples of NIRs include: I AM STUPID, I CAN'T, I AM UNABLE, I AM WEAK, I AM A FAILURE, I AM UNWORTHY, I AM NOT GOOD ENOUGH, I AM STUPID, I AM BAD. As a result of these IDs and hir creation of BAD to BE such IDs, the psycan generates AntiLove for Self, experienced as the negative emotions. The rest of the Causal Sequence—THINK→DO→HAVE—also turn negative as the psycan tries to change hir IDs back to positive by manipulating externals (the External Quest).

NIR: see **Negative IDentity Realities**.

NIR Mass: A NIR Mass is the conglomerate of negative psycanic energy (thought and emotion) created around a NIR and catalyzed by the creation of BAD about that NIR. NIR+BAD triggers negative EmoLoveJoy that is the only UPS that exists. A NIR Mass usually contains other BADs, including to the trigger event, other negative thoughts, determinations; and often contains a chain of NIRs and multiple negative emotions, and may network with other NIR Masses. The mass is all the negative energy of resistance and counter-creation generated in an attempt to deny, suppress or otherwise make not-real the NIR IDentity. NIR Masses are the ONLY source of all UPS. The totality of the NIR Masses make up the Essence Suppressor Mass. NIR Masses discreate when you discreate the root NIR.

NOT-HAVE: Anything you want but have not been able to manifest.

NOT-DO: Anything you want to DO, or know that is best for you to DO, but don't DO. The most common reasons for not acting are to avoid NIR activations (fear, sadness, loneliness, etc); or because the person is selling out to others to buy their acceptation, approval or "love."

O

Opinion: One of the many forms of thoughts. It is the creation of a reality about another reality. The most deadly of all opinions is BAD. The word "opinion" in psycanics usually refers to the opinion of BAD. An opinion is a mental creation and it is a psycanic reality. *Synonyms:* judgment, evaluation.

P

Pain: Negative, undesired, unpleasant experience. In psycanics, "pain" and "suffering" always refer to mental and emotional pain, especially to the negative emotions, to negative EmoLoveJoy, except when specified as "physical pain."

Pilot: a CDT Trainer: a person well-versed in psycanic theory and able to guide CDT processes while teaching others to be able to apply CDT to themselves.

PIR: See **Positive IDentity Realities**.

Polarity (Polarities): A singularity pulled apart and stretched in opposite directions towards opposing terminals or poles, thereby creating a spectrum of gradients of experience between the two poles. E.g. hot-warm-cold; smart-average-stupid, big-medium-little. Life and many forms of experience within life are polarities.

Poles: See **Polarity**.

Positive Identity Realities = PIRs: All the IDentities that affirm ESSENCE: Wisdom, Power, Ability, and Value, and therefore trigger self-love→happiness. They thereby produce a positive BE→FEEL→THINK→DO→HAVE sequence. Examples of PIRs: I CAN, I AM ABLE, I AM WORTHY, I AM GOOD ENOUGH, I AM INTELLIGENT, I AM STRONG.

PosLove: The word "Love" spelled refers to the entire love polarity spectrum. This polarity includes both positive love, the positive emotions; and AntiLove, the negative emotions. When it is necessary to refer specifically to the positive half of the polarity, the word PosLove can be used. Thus the Love polarity consists of PosLove and AntiLove.

Power: 1- Actively, Power is the ability to produce the desired result. 2- Passively, Power is the ability to hold a position despite all counter effort and attack.

Point of View or Viewpoint: 1- Any position in physical or psycanic space from which something is observed. 2- Any mental creation (thought, belief, opinion, judgment) about another reality. The psycan is a viewpoint onto the universe (outgoing), and also an experience point (incoming). God is all viewpoints in the cosmos and all experience points. The "opposite" of a Viewpoint is an aspect: that part of something that is viewed. *Abbreviations*: PV, PoV.

Process: *noun.* In psycanics, any of wide range of techniques and procedures to handle psycanic energies, which energies include identities, realities, emotions, consciousness, perceptions, etc. The two basic flows of processing are CREATION and DISCREATION.

Program: A mental model, a psycanic "virtual reality," of how things should or should not be; therefore of what is Good<>BAD. Programs are one kind of THINK, of mental realities. A program is a mental model of how the world should be = the HAVE desired so that a person activates a positive BE-FEEL.

Psycan: A point or unit of Aware-Will. The non-physical = spirit-ual energy entity consisting of Will, Consciousness, Intelligence and Love, of the ESSENCE Energies. A localized concentration of God, the CREATOR BEING, at a particular point in the cosmos.

Psycanics: A scientific model of non-physical existence. It presents a unified field theory that brings together the fields of philosophy, psychology, spirituality, and mysticism. The laws and principles of non-physical existence.

Psycanic Universe: Just as the physical universe is the totality of all the realities in the physical universe, the psycanic universe of each person is the totality of a person's non-physical realities. These include all thoughts, memories, knowledge, values, desires, goals, beliefs, programs, paradigms, identities, and all emotions, conscious or subconscious. The psycanic universe of each psycan is that space of consciousness and subconsciousness in which hir mental and emotional realities exist, and come forth to cause hir experience. *Abbreviation:* PsyU.

Q

Quantum Field or Quantum Matrix: The word used in physics for the ONE SUPREME ESSENCE. The underlying, interconnected (entangled) field of non-local no-thingness that is the potential to be anything. It underlies all Created Reality. All BEingess springs from IT by processes described in quantum mechanics mathematics.

Quest: see **External Quest** and **Internal Quest**.

R

Reactivity: The facility and degree to which a person's NIR Masses activate. Reactivity is the result of the size, availability and the sensitivity of the psycan to hir NIR Masses and hir degree of Response-ability and Cause over hir masses. Some people are highly reactive; others much less so.

Real: *adjective.* The condition of a reality when and while it is being perceived = experienced. Something is REAL only while it is being experienced. Do not confuse the term "real" with "reality" or with "exists." When not in experience, something is a reality and continues to exist, but it is not real. The objective of discreation is to make realities not real by discreating them, as opposed to the futile efforts to make them not real by resisting them or suppressing them.

Reality: Any thing or form of energy, physical or psycanic. Everything that exists is formed of energy. A reality is any form of energy; it is energy with an identity. A reality is any energy-form-mass modulated to cause a particular flavor of experience. Realities may be mental, emotional, physical, psychic, mystic, etc. All creations are realities; all realities are creations: they were created at one time or another by someone. All identities are realities; not all realities are identities. The word "creation" may used for "reality" when you wish to emphasize that aspect of a reality.

A reality may be subjective: perceptible to only one person, as are one's thoughts and emotions; or they may be objective: perceptible and therefore verifiable by others. Objective reality is also called What Is As It Is.

Do not confuse the concept of "real" with "reality." A reality may or may not be real at any given moment. Do not confuse reality with Truth (or Knowledge). A reality may or may not be true: something can be real and not True, or True but not real (explained in *Cosmology*). Realities may be beliefs and therefore NOT TRUE, or they may be TRUE and therefore Knowledge. Truth requires correspondence between a reality and the statement about that reality. See **Truth**.

RELATE: RELATE is part of DO in the Causal Sequence. The concept of DO includes actions involving things (e.g. work) and people. RELATE is that part of DO that impacts others. It includes one's communications, treatment of, dealings with, responses and reactions to others. What one receives from others, how they treat one, is the HAVE in the area of relationships. See **DO**.

Relativity: 1- All is ONE; all things are interconnected related to everything else. 2- In polarity; any position on a spectrum can only be defined relative to another position. For example, whether something is big or little can only be determined by comparing = relating it to something else. If a person is strong, then s/he is not weak. If s/he is kind, then s/he is not mean. It is all relative.

Religious: related to a registered brand of dogmas, doctrines, and rituals about God. Religions are mostly belief systems, and beliefs are Not-True as they have no objective proof of their statements.

Response-ability/Responsability: Spelled with an "a" in psycanics. The ability to respond, to act. 1- Consciousness of Cause. 2- Any possibility of taking action. Any time there exists a possibility of action, Response-ability exists—it is not necessary to be the initial Cause. Thus a person may be in a negative situation caused by another, but if s/he has a possibility of action to stop, change or escape that situation, s/he is responsable. 3- The capacity to respond, to act, from controlled CAUSE and hopefully Wisdom and Love+; as opposed to impulsive negative reaction at the effect of NIRs and AntiLove.

Resistance: There are two levels: 1- negation to approach, to experience. 2- negative energization to stop, change or destroy. Resistance is any form of negative energy, mental or emotional, directed towards a reality of any type. Any kind of denial, block, suppression, or counter-creation. All negative emotions are forms of resistance. Also many negative thoughts. Thus, resistance is the parent of UPS. All resistance starts with the opinion of BAD. The purpose of resistance is to avoid experiencing something BAD, to make it not-real in some manner. However, resistance is energy and all energy, regardless of polarity, energizes. Thus Resistance Causes Persistence and UPS. (Rxx→Perxx and UPS). Realities should be made not-real by discreating them, not by resisting them.

Role, roles: The human identities as opposed to spirit-ual = ESSENCE IDentities. Human roles include such identities as father, mother, brother, carpenter, musician, doctor, etc.

S

Sadness: A form ("flavor") of AntiLove.

Self: One's BEing (psycan plus identities). All that one is. *Synonyms:* BEing.

Self-Esteem: Your "esteem-ation" of yourself, of who you are. Your "e-Value-ation" of Self where Value is the 3rd element of Essence (WPV). Self-Esteem depends entirely on the Essence IDentities: Wisdom/Know, Power and Value, which are a Causal Sequence. When you FEEL able and competent (Power) to handle life, then you assign yourself a positive Value as a person and this activates self-love. That is self-esteem.

Self-Image: Your conception and experience of self, determined primarily by your Essence IDentities. Self-Image is very related to Self-Esteem. See **Self-Esteem** above.

Should Be<>Should Not Be: The polarity of mind creations common to all Programs, and the precursor of the creation of BAD.

Sorrow: An emotion of the Grief group triggered by the Past Time AntiPower NIRs such as: "I couldn't prevent it."

Space: Usually spelled with capital S and P: SPace. Nothingness. The absence of energy and matter, especially of negative energy. Pure consciousness with no realities present and especially with no activations. The neutral spot between positive and negative energy. Mentally, Space is the absence of thoughts, but especially of the opinion of BAD and therefore of Resistance. Emotionally, it is the absence of activations. It is the end of resistance and therefore the beginning of Love. SPace is the midpoint on the Love-Energy Spectrum. It is the "north" pole on the Density Spectrum. Space is the end point of negative energy discharge in processing ideally reached before commencing positive creation. (Space is a big concept with 21 definitions that are beyond the parameters of this glossary.)

Spectrum: The entire scale of possibilities or gradients of energy or experiences between two opposing poles. See **Polarity**.

Spirit: Non-physical Life-Energy entities. Individualized portions of the ONE LIFE FORCE, made of ESSENCE. The basic unit of BEing. Those that are endowed with Creator-Will-Power are called psycans.

Spirit-ual: *adjective.* related to spirit, to non-physical BEing, to the psycan. The hyphen is sometimes used to assure that "spiritual" is not confused with "religious." Spiritual means "related to spirit," to a non-physical, Life-energy entity. Spirit means "Life" or the "Animating Factor" in the universe. Its prime characteristics are Awareness, Will and Essence. There is only ONE SPIRIT or LIFE ESSENCE BEING (aka God) that in different levels and amounts, imbues ITSELF into forms, creating the appearance of many separated, individual BEings.

Subconscious: The psycanic space around the psycan where "old" psycanic creations (thoughts forms and emotions and NIR Masses) continue to exist and "hang out." The subconscious is the "warehouse" of old thought energy forms outside of consciousness. All thoughts and emotions are "realities" and can move into or out of consciousness = perception = experience and thus are perceived or not perceived in a given moment.

Suffering: Suffering is resistance to pain, which is pain about pain. It is resistance to negative experience, to negative emotions, that is therefore even more pain and also causes the persistence of the original pain. The application of psycanics ends suffering.

Supreme Game: The Game (the effort to overcome an obstacle and reach a goal) of descending out of the ONE SUPREME ESSENCE BEING into individuality and AntiEssence for the challenge (game) and adventure of ascending again to BE the SUPREME BEING, which is the purpose and goal of the Existential Experiential Imperative.

Suppress: 1- To reduce or block consciousness to avoid FEELing. There are many ways to suppress experience: tense the body, distract oneself, use drugs, eat, smoke, etc. The impulse to suppress and avoid negative experience is the compulsive force behind all addictions. 2- In Relationships: To counter-act and reduce the Self-Determination of another person; to try to control another's Causal Sequences (BE→DO→HAVE).

T

TAO: from the Chinese philosophy and book *The Tao Te Ching*. The ONE, the incomprehensible INTELLIGENT ENERGY CONSCIOUSNESS that is both CREATOR and the CREATED, and that is behind and present in all things. God.

THINK: The third element in the Causal Sequence. 1- All mental activity: creation of thoughts, analysis, comparison, remembering, memorizing, planning, creativity, design, etc. 2- All content of the mind, all mental = thought-frequency energy realities: thoughts, ideas, memories, dreams, visions, images, programs, paradigms and Should Not BE→BADS. It includes the subconscious which is warehouse of mental creations outside of present time perception.

Thoughts: Mental realities. Thought-frequency energy realities. Realities formed of mental frequency energy modulated with images or data, that then impress consciousness with that modulation and are thus perceived by the psycan as mental images or data.

Time: Change (includes change of position = movement in space). From the human viewpoint: time is created and measured by change and movement. If there were no change, there would be no Time.

Trigger: short for Trigger Event: To understand Trigger Event, you must first understand Event as a technical word in psycanics. A Trigger is any event that sets off the activation of a NIR Mass, which are experienced mainly as emotional charge.

Truth: The degree of correspondence between a reality and a statement about that reality. TRUTH exists only when there is a demonstrated, verifiable-by-others correspondence between a reality and statement about or description of that reality. Therefore, when a reality is not-real (not available) so that the correspondence can be verified by all those concerned, the conditions for label, the certification, of "TRUTH" are not fulfilled, and the condition/certification of TRUTH may not be applied.

To declare that something is TRUE when there is no proof of its TRUTH is to create a belief, and "belief" is a dirty word in psycanics and all science. As a belief believes itself to be true, all beliefs are founded on a lie. One of the purposes of science is to eliminate beliefs, eliminate all personal opinions and points of view, and find the TRUTH of how things work. Therefore, in the absence of verifiable evidence such that rational people must agree that something is so, TRUTH does not exist, and that statement must be labeled Not-True or Not-Truth.

The fact that something is Not-Truth does not necessarily mean that it is False. To declare something False, we need the same condition of evidence proving that it is false. Thus, we have three conditions for statements: True, Mu (Truth or Falsity not established, therefore Not-True), and False. The vast, vast majority of ideas and information that you will be bombarded with on this planet are Not-True (Mu).

U

ULTIMATE REALITY: IT = God = The TAO = The ENERGY, before and beyond Created Reality. The Ultimate Truth of What Is: the ONE, the uncaused FIRST CAUSE, as opposed to the illusion (Maya) of Created Reality = the cosmos. See **Created Reality**.

Universe: A unique space of existence operating under the same set of laws and principles of SET (Space, Energy and Time). There are innumerable universes within the cosmos, many are non-physical. The cosmos consists of all universes, of all created realities. The physical universe we humans know is but one of many.

UPS: pronounced "oops." Abbreviation for Unhappiness, Pain and Suffering. Any form of unpleasant psycanic experience, especially the negative emotions. UPS always refers to negative psycanic experience, not to physical pain. The ONLY the source of UPS is negative EmoLoveJoy = self-AntiLove generated around an NIR. Synonyms or highly related concepts include: NIR Mass, Activations, neg emo, neg EmoLoveJoy, self AntiLove, MoAs, MoDs, and BAD→Rxx→UPS.

V

Value: One of the Major Polarities, and part of ESSENCE. The estimation or assignation of worth or deservingness, especially to oneself through IDentities. Value is a position on the Positive–Negative Spectrum or Worth Spectrum. Value is essential to movement and to Games. Humans usually distort the Value Polarity to create the Good–Bad Polarity and so create UPS. BAD is the arbitrary assignation of negative value with the authorization to attack with negative energy to change or destroy. Value to self is self-esteem.

Victim: A person who denies Response-ability for negative events and for hir experience, and therefore perceives and believes that s/he is at the EFFECT of the BAD CAUSE of others or the universe. S/He believes that BAD EVENTS happen to hir without hir participation, contribution, or any other form of hir Cause. The unmistakable characteristic of a Victim is negation of Response-ability. A Victim will complain to attract sympathy and support, and will try to manipulate others with duty, blame or guilt to get them to use their CAUSE to eliminate hir problems and suffering. Victim is a lie: the Victim is always responsable, including for creating hirself as a Victim.

Viewpoint or Point of View: 1- Any position in physical or psycanic space from which something is observed. 2- Any mental reality (thought, opinion, judgment) created about another reality. The psycan is a viewpoint and an experience point in the universe. God is all viewpoints on the cosmos and all experience points. An aspect is the part of anything seen from a particular viewpoint. See **Point of View**.

W

Will: The force that moves energy. It is the highest known frequency of energy, so high that it is not certain that it is energy, but SPace; that which is beyond and creates energy. IT is the highest known essence of God and Humanity, the ultimate nature of existence. To experience Will, do something that hurts and continue to do it while it hurts; experience the force of your Will against the force of the physical pain.

WISDOM: Capitalized, is another name for God who knows all things and can predict all results of action.

Wisdom: 1- One of the elements of ESSENCE consisting of Consciousness, knowing and knowledge, intelligence, memory, imagination, intuition, and creativity. The first element of BEing in the Causal Sequence of BEing: Wisdom, Power, Value and LoveJoy. 2- Effective THINK in the Causal Sequence of THINK→DO→HAVE. That combination of knowledge, past experience, intuition, imagination, and creativity (THINK) that guides action

(DO) to produce the desired result consistently (HAVE) and with a minimum of TE (time and energy). 3- Therefore: the ability to foresee the consequences (HAVE) of action (DO). Wisdom is thus a pre-requisite for Power, and for Love. Without Wisdom, both Power and Love destroy, as these lack effective guidance.

WPVLJ: abbreviation for Wisdom, Power, Value, LoveJoy: The ESSENCE of LIFE; ESSENCE of BEING properties. The basic qualities of LIFE = BEING = GOD; However, in humans, ESSENCE is counter-created and suppressed by all the NIR Masses that make up the Essence Suppressor Mass, that are AntiEssence.

XYZ

Index

R

S

T

U

V

W

X

Y

Z

About The Author

Thomas Michael Powell is a Mystic, Philosopher, Author and Teacher of original and cutting-edge work in the area of Ontology and the universal scientific laws of the non-physical, spiritual aspects of how life works. From the discovery and codification of these laws comes the new science of Psycanics.

Thomas is the founder of the Psycanics Foundation, whose mission is to preserve, disseminate and teach the scientific, spiritual knowledge that will catalyze a Transformation of Consciousness. This Transformation of Consciousness is an evolutionary and revolutionary change from the current state of division, conflict, ignorance, inequality, poverty and suffering to the recognition that all is ONE. This new paradigm will create a world of Love, Harmony, Community, Cooperation, Abundance and Happiness for all humanity.

Companion book:

You Are The Creator of Your Life

An Operating Manual for the Human Being

You are the ultimate Cause of everything that exists and occurs in your experience, in your life. You are Cause of all that you think and feel, the quality of your relationships, and the conditions and events of your life.

Many people walk around thinking that life just happens, and they are basically at the mercy of random events and circumstances. Nothing could be farther from the truth. You innately have the Power—it is the Knowledge of how it works that you are lacking. It is your ignorance of the fact that you are Creator and of the process by which you create that blocks your ability to live the life that you desire.

While you may have been told that you are the creator of your life, what this book offers new and POWERFUL is exactly HOW you are creating your experience. This book presents cutting-edge knowledge of the mechanisms and processes by which you create your personal world. It spells out the universal laws of the operation of your spirit, mind, emotions, love and happiness. It shows you the precise mechanisms by which you create your experience. With this knowledge, you can take a quantum leap forward in understanding yourself, others, and life; and will be able to begin to create the life you desire.

Available at www.psycanics.org